Narrating the Mesh

Under the Sign of Nature: Explorations in Ecocriticism
Serenella Iovino, Anthony Lioi, and Kate Rigby, Editors
Michael P. Branch, SueEllen Campbell, and John Tallmadge, Senior Advisory Editors

Narrating the Mesh

FORM AND STORY IN THE ANTHROPOCENE

Marco Caracciolo

UNIVERSITY OF VIRGINIA PRESS
CHARLOTTESVILLE AND LONDON

University of Virginia Press
© 2021 by the Rector and Visitors of the University of Virginia
All rights reserved
Printed in the United States of America on acid-free paper

First published 2021

9 8 7 6 5 4 3 2 1

Library of Congress Cataloging-in-Publication Data

Names: Caracciolo, Marco, author.
Title: Narrating the mesh : form and story in the anthropocene / Marco Caracciolo.
Description: Charlottesville : University of Virginia Press, 2021. | Series: Under the sign of nature: explorations in ecocriticism | Includes bibliographical references and index.
Identifiers: LCCN 2020038854 (print) | LCCN 2020038855 (ebook) | ISBN 9780813945828 (hardcover) | ISBN 9780813945835 (paperback) | ISBN 9780813945842 (ebook)
Subjects: LCSH: Ecocriticism. | Narration (Rhetoric) | Fiction—History and criticism. | Climatic changes in literature. | Human ecology.
Classification: LCC PN98.E36 C37 2021 (print) | LCC PN98.E36 (ebook) | DDC 808.3/923—dc23
LC record available at https://lccn.loc.gov/2020038854
LC ebook record available at https://lccn.loc.gov/2020038855

Cover art: Alcuin/iStock

Contents

Acknowledgments vii

Introduction: Narrative and Interlocking Forms 1

1. Complex Narrative in the Anthropocene 27

Part I. Nonlinearity

2. The Form of the Butterfly 51
3. Negative Strategies and Nonlinear Temporality in Postapocalyptic Fiction 77

Part II. Interdependency

4. Five Ways of Looking at Nonhuman Actants 97
5. Minding the Anthropocene 115

Part III. Multiscalarity

6. Metaphorical Patterns in Anthropocene Fiction 139
   With Andrei Ionescu and Ruben Fransoo
7. Metaphor, Scale, and the Value of Conceptual Trouble 159

Coda: Thinking beyond Literary Form 179

Notes 187

Works Cited 201

Index 219

Acknowledgments

If this book exists, it is largely thanks to the European Research Council, which sponsored the NARMESH project under the European Union's Horizon 2020 research and innovation program (grant agreement no. 714166). Conceived when I was an Italian working at the University of Freiburg in Germany and hosted by Ghent University after I moved to Belgium, NARMESH is very much a product of European integration. As I write these lines in March 2020, the Covid-19 pandemic is shaking that European project at its core—the free circulation of people. Borders are closed, air traffic and train services are almost at a standstill, people across the continent are sheltering in place. While I am confident that Covid-19 is not here to stay, I hope the outbreak will prove once and for all that Europe's only desirable future involves a strong commitment to a society based on solidarity and resilience in the face of a radically unstable nonhuman world.

Just as the NARMESH project aims to bring into focus narrative's engagement with the "mesh" of human communities and nonhuman phenomena (to use Timothy Morton's terminology), this book benefited enormously from a vast human mesh. My partner, Wibke Schniedermann, made this fabric of connection so much more secure and vibrant. The core members of the NARMESH team, Susannah Crockford, Shannon Lambert, and Gry Ulstein, offered tremendously helpful input throughout the writing process. I feel immensely privileged to have worked day after day for more than three years alongside such inspired, knowledgeable, and fun human beings. I am also indebted to our many international guests and affiliated scholars and students—Santi Luca Famà, Ruben Fransoo, Kaori Inuma, Andrei Ionescu, Kaisa Kortekallio, Delzi Laranjeira, Sue Lovell, Melissa Luypaers, Reuben Martens, David Rodriguez, and Jonas Vanhove—for their rich contributions to the NARMESH project. Several colleagues visited us in Ghent and delivered highly stimulating guest lectures, which have left a deep mark on my ideas as they are articulated in this book; special thanks go to Ridvan Askin, Jon Hegglund, Erin James, Merja Polvinen, and Alexa Weik von Mossner for engaging in an extended conversation with me and my colleagues.

Ghent University offered a fantastic environment to develop my thinking on narrative form and the nonhuman. I discussed this project with Lars Bernaerts, Stef Craps, Mahlu Mertens, and River Ramuglia, all of whom provided thoughtful feedback and inspiration. I would also like to thank Boyd Zenner, my editor at the University of Virginia Press, for her continued support and astute advice. The editors of the Under the Sign of Nature series and three anonymous readers offered insightful commentary on various versions of this book.

Three chapters contain published material: chapter 3 draws on my "Negative Strategies and World Disruption in Postapocalyptic Fiction," *Style* 52, no. 3 (2018): 222–41, used by permission of Penn State University Press; chapter 4 on "Notes for an Econarratological Theory of Character," *Frontiers of Narrative Studies* 4, no. 1 (2018): 172–89, used by permission of Walter de Gruyter; chapter 6 on "Metaphorical Patterns in Anthropocene Fiction," coauthored with Andrei Ionescu and Ruben Fransoo, *Language and Literature* 28, no. 3 (2019): 221–40, used by permission of SAGE Publications, all rights reserved. I am grateful to these journals and my coauthors for granting me permission to reuse and adapt these articles.

The panels from Richard McGuire's *Here* in chapter 1 were originally published in *Raw* 2, no. 1, 1989, copyright © 1989 Richard McGuire, used by permission of the Wylie Agency (UK).

Narrating the Mesh

Introduction
Narrative and Interlocking Forms

Already from the title, Lauren Groff's short story "At the Round Earth's Imagined Corners" (2018), in the collection *Florida,* applies a geometric filter to physical space: paradoxically, the Earth is seen as both a round and an angular shape. This preference for geometric patterns characterizes the imagination of the story's protagonist, a child named Jude. Born in Florida, "at the edge of a swamp that boiled with unnamed species of reptiles" (Groff 2018, 15), Jude's mind is intensely attuned to the patterns of the natural world. When his family moves to a new house on the coast, he discovers "a new world, full of dolphins that slid up the coastline in shining arcs. Jude loved the wedges of pelicans ghosting overhead, the mad dig after periwinkles that disappeared deeper into the wet sand" (2018, 17). Like motion lines in a comic book, Groff's metaphors highlight Jude's ability to perceive the formal choreography of the dolphins' "shining arcs," or of the pelicans' "wedges." These patterns, the protagonist soon learns, are not limited to nonhuman animals—they underlie his subjectivity and the human world surrounding him: "He began to sense that the world worked in ways beyond him, that he was only grasping at threads of a greater fabric" (2018, 17). "Threads of a greater fabric" is a metaphorical expression capturing the interconnectedness of things, the way in which, through the mediation of abstract form, human and nonhuman realities converge. Later, Jude is given two books: "One was a collection of Frost's poems. The other was a book of geometry, the world whittled down until it became a series of lines and angles" (2018, 24). Thematically as well as stylistically, abstract form and literary language—geometry and Robert Frost's poetry—are coupled. The value of literature (certainly, literature as Groff practices it) consists in revealing the geometry of human characters' embedding in a more-than-human world. This embedding, in "At the Round Earth's Imagined Corner" and throughout Groff's oeuvre, is an expression of fragile ecological relations whose instability threatens nonhuman animals as well as the future of our own species.

Groff's short stories keep returning to a sense of expectant dread, as if danger was always lurking around the corner—from the unique local hazards of Florida's wilds to the global threat of rising sea levels, which is already reshaping Florida's coastline. This formal vision, which many of Groff's characters share, affords a unique perspective on the ecological crisis. Form provides aesthetic distance from humankind's predicament: through metaphor and imagery, the abstraction of literary form appeases, temporarily, the anxiety of living in times marked by radical, human-induced changes to ecosystems. At the same time, form brings out the vast "fabric" of interconnection in which both humans and nonhumans are intrinsically caught up. Cultivating the imagination of form puts us in a position to apprehend, like Jude, the complexity of humanity's implication in systems—of the climate, of the Earth's oceans and geological history—that culture has taught us to see as external and impervious to human activity.

This vision resonates with ecological philosopher David Abram's discussion in *The Spell of the Sensuous* of form and pattern as a privileged focus of our encounters with nature: "In contact with the native forms of the earth, one's senses are slowly energized and awakened, combining and recombining in ever-shifting patterns" (1997, 63).[1] Our connection to nature, Abram argues, is nourished by the imagination of "repetitive figures" (1997, 64)—geometric patterns—that bounce back and forth between human subjectivity and the natural environment. Because of the centrality of vision in human cognition, we tend to think about *form* in visual terms, as pictorial shape. However, we encounter formal regularities in other sensory modalities as well: sounds have a temporal contour (the undulating rhythm of cicadas singing), touch has texture (from silky to rough), and even taste has a distinctive shape, closely related to our somatic reactions to the taste of food (the sourness of lemon). For Abram, thinking with these various sensory forms is uniquely capable of breaking down the dualistic barriers that divide, in the Western world, human societies from nature. As Abram suggests, form and pattern are an essential step toward overcoming the ideology of frantic exploitation of nature that, in the wake of the industrial revolution, has brought our planet closer and closer to ecological catastrophe. Paying full attention to natural forms reveals human societies' deep entanglement with them—that we are never external observers of nature, but always part of a pattern that reaches far into our embodied minds and evolutionary history. Developing appreciation for pattern means letting go of human exceptionality and fostering a sense of our vital interdependency with the nonhuman world.

The tension between sensible patterns, the abstract geometry of human-nonhuman relations, and the aesthetic distance provided by literary form is central to Groff's work, including "At the Round Earth's Imagined Corners." Groff probes this tension through the form of narrative itself, as the short story encapsulates Jude's evolving understanding of his place in a world that is both strange and marvelous. Narrative captures and stages forms at multiple levels: the geometric imagery evoked by Groff's language, the stylistic patterning of rhetorical figures, the larger contour of Jude's life as Groff narrates it. This book argues that, as a flexible macroform, narrative has an important role to play as humanity comes to terms with the devastating impact of large-scale industrialization on the planet. In fiction—and particularly in contemporary fiction that, like Groff's, engages with the ecological crisis—form and pattern are employed to undermine dualistic thinking and bring the human back into the fold of the nonhuman world. These narratives can probe, through formal means, what Timothy Morton (2010) describes as the "enmeshment" of humanity in climatological, geological, or biological phenomena that have long been seen as operating independently of human societies and cultures. By examining a set of late twentieth-century and twenty-first-century novels and short stories, the following chapters explore the formal configurations through which the quintessentially human practice of narrative can channel our capture in nonhuman processes. The abstraction of the narrative forms we will examine re-creates, through the mediation of language and concepts, the sensory geometry experienced by Jude, with its potential for bridging the human and the nonhuman worlds.

The task of this introduction is to put the reader in a position to appreciate the value of narrative form vis-à-vis the climate crisis and the Anthropocene—the proposed name for the current geological epoch, which is defined by the dramatic impact of industrial societies and global capitalism on the planet. Developing this argument requires opening a conversation between three different fields of scholarly inquiry, which will be outlined in the following sections: first, current work in narrative theory, particularly (but not exclusively) in an "econarratological" vein; second, insights into the Anthropocene and the nonhuman within the environmental humanities; and, third, discussions on the significance of form in the scientific and cultural understanding of human-nonhuman relations. By weaving together these discourses, this study seeks to shed light on the power of narrative form to chart the ecological crisis and its ethical and epistemological ramifications.

IN SEARCH OF NARRATIVE FORM

What does it mean to say that narrative has a form? The question is anything but trivial. In sensory experience patterns are palpable and easily recognizable; Abram's account rests precisely on their phenomenological immediacy. In the more rarefied domain of narrative we may lose track of form completely. An option would be to equate form and the "structures" that early theorists of narrative have concentrated on in the wake of Ferdinand de Saussure's linguistics and Claude Lévi-Strauss's anthropology. Writing in the 1960s and building on Vladimir Propp's formalist study of the folktale (1968), Algirdas Julien Greimas (1966) and Roland Barthes (1975) sought to explain the constraints that act on the potentially infinite variety of narratives. If we took all the stories in the world and boiled them down to their most fundamental constituents, what would we be left with? In a word, we would have revealed their structures. Thus, Greimas looked into the skeletal structure of narrative—the system of semantic oppositions that make story possible. For his part, Barthes explored the sequencing of narrative, the way stories string together actions and events following a distinctive temporal and causal logic. Despite these and many other insights, the structuralist experiment didn't last long: it came to an abrupt end in the 1970s, splintering into the galaxy of so-called structuralism. Literary studies moved on, and even the field of narrative theory or narratology—which had been inaugurated by structuralism—entered its "postclassical" phase, with scholars starting to look for inspiration beyond structural linguistics.[2]

Identifying form with structure doesn't hold much promise for this book, either. Structures, as structuralist theorists saw them, are too stable and inflexible to be assimilated to the "ever-shifting" patterns of nature that Abram discusses. To capture narrative's engagement with these patterns, we need another conception of form—a more dynamic and open-ended one. A philosopher, David Velleman, offers a useful point of departure:

> A story . . . enables its audience to assimilate events, not to familiar patterns of *how things happen,* but rather to familiar patterns of *how things feel.* These

patterns are not themselves stored in discursive form, as scenarios or stories: they are stored rather in experiential, proprioceptive, and kinesthetic memory—as we might say, in the muscle-memory of the heart. Although the audience may have no discursive memory of events such as those of the story, it nevertheless has an experience of *déja senti*, because its emotional sensibility naturally follows the ups and downs of the story, just as a muscle naturally follows the cycle of tension and release. (2003, 19; italics in the original)

For Velleman, the form of narrative is fundamentally embodied and affective: it consists in variations on a basic somatic pattern of expectation and release. There are various possibilities for conceptualizing this somatic pattern; Ellen Dissanayake (2011) discusses its origin in psychological development, arguing that storytelling has its roots in infants' interactions with their caregivers, and more specifically in the regularities and surprising variations that underpin games such as peekaboo. In these playful activities, expectations are generated through the repetition of gestural patterns (in peekaboo, hiding one's face) or vocalizations (in baby talk): emotions arise whenever the caregiver decides to deviate from the expectations created by previous interactions (by delaying the peekaboo moment).[3] As infants grow up and acquire linguistic skills, narrative latches onto this emotional structure and displaces it to the level of verbal interactions. Thus, storytelling arouses interest by creating expectations—for instance, about the resolution of a conflict or a character's response to a situation—and by guiding the audience, typically through a number of complications, to an outcome. The "ups and downs" of story are therefore a more sophisticated iteration of the affective patterns laid down in development: the emotional rhythm of baby talk is replaced by an equally emotional (but word-involving) progression of characters and situations. Hence the link between narrative form and affect: *the form of narrative is the configuration of emotionally charged circumstances created by the telling.*

If this sounds too abstract, consider the way in which we categorize narratives on the basis of genre: Patrick Colm Hogan's "affective narratology" offers compelling cross-cultural evidence that literary genres, far from being purely arbitrary constructs, reflect prototypes of emotional experience.[4] For instance, Hogan discusses how the revenge tragedy builds on the patterning of revengeful feelings, with their temporally organized sequence of received hurt and desire for retribution.[5] In the field of digital humanities, a study by Andrew Reagan, Lewis Mitchell, Dilan Kiley, Christopher Danforth, and Peter Sheridan Dodds (2016) comes to similar conclusions about the correlation of narrative and the patterning of emotional experience. Adopting a "big data" approach, Reagan and his collaborators fed over 1,700 book-length narratives into a computer algorithm capable of "sentiment analysis"—that is, of identifying emotional language in the text and distinguishing between positive and negative emotions. The algorithm then tracked the development of affective language in the story: whether positive emotions increase or decrease, and in what sequence. The results highlight that the narratives fall into six basic emotional templates, which correspond to generic prototypes such as tragedy (a constant fall in positive emotions), rags to riches (a constant rise in positive emotions), and four combinations thereof (such as "Cinderella"-type stories, which cycle between rise, fall, and rise in positive emotions). While there are obvious limitations to Reagan and his team's statistical approach, their findings—particularly when read alongside Velleman's and Hogan's more theoretical and interpretive arguments—are highly suggestive. The form of story is its emotional patterning, which is grounded in psychological development and then performed, linguistically, through the dynamics of characters and situations. A textual strategy is "formal" when it is able to modulate this patterning.

This use of the concept of form resonates with a broader movement in literary studies known as "new formalism" (see Levinson 2007). With the end of structuralism and the rise of cultural studies, literary scholars have tended to sideline form in favor of approaches that emphasize the interaction of texts and their historical context. The widespread perception was that a narrow focus on form—taken usually in the sense of style, genre, or narrative levels and strategies—failed to do justice to the ways in which texts mirror and respond to broader sociocultural trends.[6] The ideological dimension of literature took center stage in literary studies and was analyzed in increasingly sophisticated ways by scholars working in critical theory and poststructuralist philosophy. Over the last two decades, form has been making a comeback, however. To a large extent, this shift is due to an expanded understanding of form that encompasses texts as well as their contexts. An important statement of this position can be found in Caroline Levine's *Forms*, where she describes her understanding of form as "all shapes and configurations, all ordering principles, all patterns of repetition and difference" (2015, 3). For Levine, such patterns exist in texts *and* in the sociopolitical world—for instance, through the rhythms of organized social life: her core claim is that "paying attention to subtle and complex formal patterns allows us to rethink the historical workings of political power and the relations between politics and aesthetics" (2015, xiii). Consider Levine's reading of a poem by Elizabeth Barrett Browning on Queen Victoria's accession to the British throne in 1837 (2015, 74–81): Levine argues that Barrett Browning's formal choices in terms of meter and prosody evoke, and yet at the same time resist, the official temporality of monarchic power. The forms of poetic time thus position themselves vis-à-vis the institutionalized forms of public life. Nor is Levine's interest restricted to poetry; on the contrary, she assigns a central role to narrative, which she sees as uniquely able to stage encounters and tensions between linguistic and ideological forms.[7]

The ideas laid out so far extend and deepen Levine's account of the significance of narrative form. The basic patterning of story is affective, and it is organized around generic expectations that tap into the forms of emotional experience.[8] This affective structure serves as a magnet, attracting a multitude of other patterns (textual as well as social and ideological) and staging the ways in which they reinforce or undermine one another. Put otherwise, narrative is an extremely capacious and flexible *macroform*. While new formalist arguments are typically positioned at the intersection of aesthetic and sociopolitical form, this book foregrounds narrative's engagement with the forms of the natural world—those identified by Abram and revealed by Groff's short story through the geometric imagination of the protagonist. This does *not* mean shutting the door on the sociopolitical implications of the narrative figuration of natural patterns. But it does mean placing those implications in a broader context, one that goes beyond a narrowly anthropocentric worldview. That discussion also prompts a reconsideration of words such as "nature" and "natural," with their cultural legacy (in a Western context) of dualistic separation between the human and the nonhuman. Our times make this language highly problematic. But form still holds value, as we'll see.

INTRODUCING THE HUMAN-NONHUMAN MESH

The framework of Abram's discussion of form in *The Spell of the Sensuous* is phenomenological: he sees "an abstract and objectifying science" (1997, 65) as deeply complicit with notions of human mastery over the nonhuman word. Instead, drawing on Maurice Merleau-Ponty's philosophy of the body, Abram argues that phenomenological exploration, when directed at the experience of natural forms, can reconcile Western subjects with the nonhuman world from which they have become alienated.[9] But it is worth keeping in mind that, just as there are limitations and dualistic biases in scientific knowledge, there are important limitations to what we can experience in a sensory way. Abram's examples of natural forms—the rippling streams, tree bark, and weed clusters that punctuate his discussion—are grounded in personal encounters with human-scale realities. Through that emphasis on the human scale, Abram's phenomenological method goes hand in hand with the "return to the local and . . . celebration of a 'sense of place'" that have, according to Ursula Heise (2008, 8), defined the environmentalist movement in the United States since the 1960s.

Abram was, after all, writing in the 1990s, when the planetary scale and ramifications of anthropogenic climate change were still on the margins of public debates and eluded even well-informed commentators like Abram. The scientific certainty of climate change, which is by now inescapable, introduces radically new challenges. In philosopher Dale Jamieson's words, "Climate change poses threats that are probabilistic, multiple, indirect, often invisible, and unbounded in space and time. Fully grasping these threats requires scientific understanding and technical skills that are often in short supply" (2014, 67). The problem with climate change is that its effects can be detected on a local level, sometimes dramatically, through catastrophic weather events such as deadly hurricanes and heat waves, but climate change per se is a scientific abstraction that works on a scalar level not directly commensurable with everyday experience. Conceptually, we may know (*if* we trust scientific models) that catastrophic events are made much more likely by the burning of fossil fuels that is reshaping the Earth system at a speed unknown before the industrial era. Yet the causal connections between industrial activity, meteorological patterns, and a particular heat wave escape sensory experience entirely. We perceive the heat wave; we don't perceive the complex causality behind it. Climate change is the most egregious example of what Timothy Morton calls "hyperobjects," or objects that "exist on almost unthinkable timescales [and] confound our limited, fixated, self-oriented frameworks" (2010, 19). Climate change confronts us with planetary rhythms and cycles that—unlike Abram's "ever-shifting" forms—we struggle to know experientially. Our sensory apparatus is attuned to our immediate surroundings, not to atmospheric carbon dioxide or global sea levels. This abstraction inherent in climate change is, of course, one of the reasons why it is so difficult to find a concerted solution to the problem—and, in some areas of society, even to acknowledge the existence of the problem.

Likewise, consider the claim that we are living in the "Anthropocene," a term popularized by chemist Paul Crutzen in the early 2000s (Crutzen and Stoermer 2000) and that rapidly caught the imagination of cultural theorists and social scientists.[10] The Anthropocene is a geological epoch marked by the planetary impact of human activities, through various processes including the production of nonbiodegradable materials (in themselves hyperobjects), the acidification of the Earth's oceans, and the release of greenhouse gases into the atmosphere. Not only do these processes disrupt the balance of many ecosystems, triggering large-scale species extinction, but they jeopardize the environment in which our own species has flourished. Further, these dynamics seemingly elevate humanity to the role of a geological agent capable of shaping the biological and climatological future of the Earth and leaving durable traces on its crust. Scientific debates on the Anthropocene tend to revolve around two interrelated questions: Should "the Anthropocene" be adopted as the official name of the current geological epoch (following the Holocene), or should it rather remain a loose label? If the Anthropocene is formally inducted into the vocabulary of geology, when did it start? With the industrial revolution—that is, at the end of the eighteenth century, as Crutzen originally proposed? Or around 1950, with humanity's ability to harness nuclear power and alter the Earth system on a scale and at a speed unprecedented in geological history (the Great Acceleration hypothesis; see Steffen et al. 2015)? Or have the seeds of the Anthropocene been planted much earlier in the timeline of *human* history, with the introduction of agriculture (Ruddiman and Thomson 2001)?[11]

While this debate goes on in the Earth sciences, humanities scholars have embraced the concept of Anthropocene to critique scientific accounts. One of the problems with the Anthropocene, as has been noted by many commentators (Crist 2013; Malm 2018), is that it glosses over the significant differences between the industrialized societies in the West that are directly responsible for the ecological crisis and communities, especially in the Global South, whose impact on the Earth's climate is negligible. The latter groups are also more vulnerable to the consequences of the climate crisis, because poverty and inadequate infrastructure expose them to catastrophic events such as flooding or water and food shortage. Talk of "humanity" becoming a geological agent thus risks sidelining the moral responsibilities that come with our capitalist and neoliberal economic system, whose roots lie in Western colonialist practices and in various forms of exploitation of human and nonhuman subjects. Put otherwise, the "anthropos" in the word "Anthropocene" does not extend evenly across the human species, but rather reflects a set of global historical forces that originated in Western modernity. Hence, a number of alternative labels have cropped up in the humanities, from Jason Moore's "Capitalocene" (2017) to the "Plantationocene" discussed recently by a group of scholars including Donna Haraway and Anna Tsing (Haraway et al. 2016). These terms seek to name the real culprit of the climate crisis, shifting the emphasis from a universalizing "anthropos" to, respectively, capitalism and colonialism.[12]

It is only with keen awareness of this sociopolitical specificity of the Anthropocene that terms like "humanity" or the collective species "we" should be used (and will be used in this book). The concept of Anthropocene will be adopted as shorthand for the countless ways in which human activities are dramatically reshaping the planet and the species with which we share it. As noted by Adam Trexler (2015, 4) in a comprehensive study of what he labels "Anthropocene fiction," the word "Anthropocene" is semantically broader than the term "climate change," but its concreteness conveys the notion that ecological collapse is already here, and that it is a global, systemic phenomenon rather than a series of localized "changes." Thus, this book asks how narrative can afford insight into the complexity of the Anthropocene, where complexity is used (as outlined in the next chapter) to convey three key qualities of the present moment: the *nonlinearity* of human impact on the planet (i.e., how individual actions, cultural biases, and political decision-making can lead to surprising and unintentional results); the *interdependency* of human societies and nonhuman animals, objects, and processes, including the way in which exploitative practices such as colonialism intersect with geological and climatological phenomena; and *multiscalarity*, or how the effects of human activity ripple across scalar levels, from the microscale of quotidian actions (e.g., driving to work, flying frequently) to the planetary scale (e.g., rising sea levels).

Individual humans living in capitalist, industrialized societies are responsible for humanity's planetary impact, but they are certainly not aware of this collective impact on an experiential basis; as Chakrabarty puts it, we "humans never experience ourselves as a species. We can only intellectually comprehend or infer the existence of the human species but never experience it as such. There could be no phenomenology of us as a species"

(2009, 220). Our species is deeply intertwined with the nonhuman realities of geology, the climate, and the biological history of life on Earth. We are reliant on them—for instance, by burning fuels created by the decomposition of organisms millions of years before our evolutionary ancestors took their first, hesitant steps on this planet. But we (and certainly some of us more than others) have also developed technologies that are capable of changing these nonhuman realities fundamentally, typically in ways that bring about widespread harm and devastation. Suddenly, "nature" becomes an inconvenient word, one that presupposes a cultural history of separation (especially in the West) between human societies and a nonhuman world seen as available to human exploitation. Instead, we need language capable of capturing the constitutive embrace between humans and nonhuman realities—how human societies shape, and are in turn shaped by, biological, climatological, and geological forces. Morton (2010, 28–33) proposes the metaphor of the "mesh": a *form* alternative to linear and hierarchical ways of thinking about humans' relationship with nonhuman realities (including animals) and processes (such as climatological trends). The image of the mesh suggests fragile interdependence, but also formidable complexity of pattern and connection. How can narrative adequately evoke the mesh-like entanglement that defines our Anthropocenic condition? Shedding light on this question will require a further refinement of the concept of form.

ABSTRACTION AND ECOLOGICAL FORM

The realization of humans' invisible enmeshment with the nonhuman world becomes a major stumbling block for Abram's argument. The direct experience of "natural forms," as Abram understands them, is not nearly enough to confront humans with the sheer scale and ubiquity of their impact on the planet, because that impact is too abstract and distributed for our perceptual systems. Instead, only climate science, and related Earth sciences, can reveal this impact fully—and it is no coincidence that the label "Anthropocene" grows out of scientific debates. For Abram, Western science is deeply complicit in the environmental crisis, in that it is factually and conceptually bound up with the driving forces behind the exploitation of natural resources: today's dominant economic system (capitalism), belief in the possibility of unlimited technological progress and economic growth, and, ultimately, the notion of human mastery over the nonhuman world.[13] Yet, as we face climate change, we cannot afford to ignore the insights produced by science, either. Scientific models offer an important—and in some respects the sole—route into the global scale of the climatological processes triggered by human activity. Hence, Abram's outright rejection of Western science (articulated, as the reader will remember, before climate change came to the fore in public debates) is not a fully satisfactory response to our current predicament. We must remain aware of science's web of complicities with anthropocentric ideologies, which Abram justly highlights, but the next step cannot be a nostalgic retreat into a prescientific worldview, because that does nothing to address climate change or mitigate its consequences. Many of the pristine natural landscapes privileged by Abram's prose are disappearing. We must learn from Abram's phenomenological method while seeking to reduce the gap between experience and scientific models; we must strive to translate science into the human-scale, embodied language of everyday perception. The central thesis of this book is that narrative has the tools to perform such work of translation—and that these are, fundamentally, *formal* tools: strategies, at the level of plot dynamics, character, consciousness representation, and metaphor, that mirror or integrate contemporary science in order to unsettle the primacy of the human-scale world.

In anthropology, a similar appeal to form is made by Eduardo Kohn in *How Forests Think* (2013). For Kohn, who bases his account on fieldwork in Ecuador's Upper Amazon, form straddles the human/nonhuman divide: the form of the nonhuman landscape (e.g., the configuration of waterways in the Amazon) intersects with the constraints on the production of rubber, which are in themselves a formal pattern, but in human terms. Taken together, these interlocking forms give rise to the emergent macroform of the economy of rubber trade (2013, 170). Kohn's discussion of form differs from Abram's because it is not geared toward forms that are phenomenologically available to the senses. Indeed, Kohn insists that the invisibility of form is both at the root of its "effortless efficacy" (2013, 187) and the main reason why anthropology has struggled so far to pay sustained attention to it: form "largely lacks the palpable otherness . . . of a traditional ethnographic object" (2013, 185). We begin to see here how uncoupling the concept of form from immediate perception offers better purchase on the complexity of today's ecological crisis, how human and nonhuman realities are folded together (enmeshed) within it. This realization also explains why the relative abstraction of narrative form is such a valuable resource in bridging the sensory and the invisible. At one level, narrative art is a concrete practice that involves the imagination of sensory patterns similar to those highlighted by Abram—for instance, through rich experiences of immersion in a story, or through the affective organization of plot.[14] At another level, narrative—for Levine and other new formalists, a capacious macroform—is able to implicate more abstract patterns of the kind discussed by Kohn. In this formal integration that narrative can perform (though, of course, not all narratives are equally adept at it), the intangibility of scientific models of climate change can be productively positioned vis-à-vis everyday experience.

To fully understand this process, we need to remember that science itself builds on a variety of forms. Philosopher of science Nancy Nersessian (1992) highlights two ways in which scientists employ forms as they abstract from individual cases to more general laws. These forms reflect more general cognitive propensities in human beings, particularly our tendency toward concrete thinking in problem-solving. The first "abstraction technique" identified by Nersessian is one with which all literary scholars are closely familiar: the use of analogy as a heuristic device allowing researchers to model phenomena that cannot be accounted for within the current scientific paradigm. A classic example is Charles Darwin's parallel between artificial and natural selection in *On the Origin of Species*. Darwin started by observing that the "diversity of the breeds [in domesticated animals] is something astonishing" (1970, 41): human breeders have selected animals for specific traits, thus increasing natural variability in species such as dogs or pigeons. Natural selection operates along similar lines, but on a much grander scale. This intuition is driven by analogy, but the analogy soon breaks down, yielding one of the central ideas of Darwin's theory—the difference between human (intentional) breeding and nature's "blind" concern with usefulness (that is, fitness-enhancing traits): "Man can act only on external and visible characters: Nature . . . cares nothing for appearances, except in so far as they may be useful to any being" (1970, 56).[15] Analogy is the cognitive pattern that makes this realization possible.

The second technique discussed by Nersessian is the use of imagistic models, such as diagrams or charts. These models allow researchers to visualize data, thus turning intangible data points into an external, sensory representation that enables further inferences. Again, we can turn to Darwin's work for an example: the famous "tree of life" diagram we find in his notebooks.[16] In itself the result of an analogy, the tree is the visual form of the evolutionary succession of species ("speciation"). Such visual representations abound in both the scientific method and in attempts to communicate science to the general public.

This interest in form is particularly evident in theories of ecological interconnectedness between organisms and their environment. Ernst Haeckel, the German naturalist who coined the term "ecology," wrote in his 1866 treatise *Generelle Morphologie der Organismen* (*General Morphology of Organisms*), "By ecology, we mean the whole science of the relations of the organism to the environment including, in the broad sense, all the 'conditions of existence.' These are partly organic, partly inorganic in nature; both, as we have shown, are of the greatest significance for the form of organisms, for they force them to become adapted" (quoted in Egerton 2013, 226). Whenever there is a system of relations, there is a configuration—and therefore a form. Ecological form can be expressed in an abstract, historical way (as in Darwin's tree of life) or through morphology, as in the physical coupling posited by Haeckel between an organism and its environment.[17] It is not a coincidence that Haeckel, one of the foremost advocates of Darwin's theory of natural selection in his times, is also known for a series of sketches that display the opulence of visual forms in the natural world. Adapted by lithographer Adolf Giltsch, these sketches appeared in 1904 under the title *Kunstformen der Natur* (*Art Forms in Nature*; see fig. 1).

Just as the sciences, and the science of ecology in particular, deploy an enormous variety of analogical and imagistic forms, cultural practices encapsulate and remediate these scientific forms: "All art—not just explicitly ecological art—hardwires the environment into its form," as Morton puts it (2010, 11). This is certainly true of narrative art. Although verbal narrative doesn't have the visual immediacy of Haeckel's sketches, it can *implicate* visual forms in the audience's imagination.[18] Narrative forms are conceptual and temporal as well as spatial, and they always manifest themselves in emotional terms. Through their affective patterning, stories can integrate scientific models—from analogies to visual representations—and stage their encounters or clashes with other forms active in human culture and society.[19]

A basic opposition that is brought into play by narrative form is between linear and mesh-like ways of thinking about the nonhuman. Linear models tend to involve a vertical organization, like the ancient "scala naturae" (see Lovejoy 2001). Implicit in the linearity of this "great chain of being," as it is also known, is a metaphysical hierarchy, with inanimate matter at

Figure 1. Jellyfish from Haeckel's 1904 *Kunstformen der Natur*.

the bottom of the "scala" (ladder), followed by plants, nonhuman animals, and—finally—humans, in close proximity to God. A mesh-like organization, by contrast, suggests metaphysical parity between human and nonhuman realities. This enmeshment is *complex* in the technical sense of complex systems theory, which will be detailed in chapter 1: it emerges from the way in which human activity interlocks and interferes with the cycles of climatological and biological processes.[20] Accordingly, chapters 1 and 2 will examine narratives that resist linear models by assimilating spatial forms such as the discontinuous line, the loop, the network, and the rhizome. These nonlinear narrative forms constitute templates for rethinking human-nonhuman relations in more mesh-like ways, even when the narratives do not explicitly engage with ecological themes. Diagrams (more visual forms) will feature in chapters 3 and 5: in the former, my approach to postapocalyptic fiction is inspired by an optical illusion first discussed by Italian psychologist

Gaetano Kanizsa; in the latter, a key passage in Rivka Galchen's novel *Atmospheric Disturbances* revolves around a meteorological model of a storm lifted from a scientific journal.

In other instances the discussion moves beyond a visual and spatial approach to form but still front-loads narrative's affective engagement with the conceptual form of scientific knowledge. In that vein, stories can resist a widespread anthropocentric template (a human-like subject acts on an inanimate object) by placing the nonhuman in the position of an agent (chapter 4); moreover, an insight into human-nonhuman enmeshment can emerge from within the experiential patterns of a character's psychology (chapter 5). Chapters 6 and 7 focus on metaphorical language as the closest verbal equivalent to Nersessian's analogical thinking. Through these devices, narrative has the potential to create formal bridges between the imaginative situations it evokes and the abstract nonhuman realities investigated by science. Throughout this discussion, it will be essential to remember that the conceptual form of human-nonhuman relations—and how it can be channeled by narrative—are never merely *formal* issues, if we take the word "formal" in the sense of conventions separate from the substance of a problem. On the contrary, form is the premise of an *ethics* of human-nonhuman relations, because seeing human societies as hierarchically superior to the nonhuman world—or as horizontally entangled with it—entails dramatically different ways of understanding our ethical responsibilities toward it.

NARRATIVE (THEORY) BEYOND THE HUMAN

In broad strokes, this book is positioned within what Richard Grusin (2015b) terms the "nonhuman turn," which refers to current approaches in the humanities and social sciences that are engaged "in decentering the human in favor of a turn toward and concern for the nonhuman, understood variously in terms of animals, affectivity, bodies, organic and geophysical systems, materiality, or technologies" (2015a, vii). Within this area of discussion, scholars frequently invoke the productivity of narrative in imagining the nonhuman. For instance, in *The Mushroom at the End of the World* (2015), anthropologist Anna Tsing examines the precarious coexistence of human societies with nonhuman species whose fate is tied to globalization and industrialization. The titular mushroom is the matsutake, highly prized in Japan, which in Tsing's book serves as a symbol of the fragility of human-nonhuman interactions. At the level of both conceptual framework and anthropological method, narrative is crucial to appreciating what Tsing calls the "contaminated diversity" of our environments: "Contaminated diversity is everywhere. If such stories are so widespread and so well known, the question becomes: Why don't we use these stories in how we know the world? One reason is that contaminated diversity is complicated, often ugly, and humbling" (2015, 33). As we'll see in chapter 4, Jane Bennett also tells a series of "speculative onto-stories" to illustrate the agency of the nonhuman world in *Vibrant Matter* (2010). Despite their promising focus on story, however, neither Tsing nor Bennett address the question of what makes narrative suitable to this exploration of human-nonhuman entanglement. All we have is the—undoubtedly powerful—example set by their own storytelling.

In laying the foundations for the field of "material ecocriticism," Serenella Iovino and Serpil Oppermann similarly foreground the role of narrative: "Taking matter as a text, material ecocriticism broadens and enhances the narrative potentialities of reality in terms of an intrinsic performativity of elements" (2012, 459). Iovino and Oppermann build on insights growing out of "new materialism": matter should not be thought of as passive and inert, as it tends to be in the Western world; material things are inherently efficacious and productive in ways that can unsettle human agency, as the climate crisis (with the devastating impact of, for instance, sea level rise) demonstrates powerfully. For material ecocritics, this productivity manifests itself in narrative terms: "Storied matter . . . is inseparable from the storied human in existential ways, producing epistemic configurations of life, discourses, texts, and narratives with ethico-political meanings" (Oppermann 2014, 34). Story thus serves as a conceptual springboard for understanding the efficacy of materiality and its entanglement with human societies. For example, in Iovino and Oppermann's discussion, the realities of the urban waste crisis in Naples are connected to economic forces and political debates by narrative threads that are inherent in matter itself, rather than imposed or projected externally by human agents: the land, polluted by the uncontrolled burning of waste, tells stories of mindless exploitation driven by greed and organized crime (2012, 458). But Iovino and Oppermann's work doesn't go very far in specifying the strategies through which stories can channel materiality, or what it means to accept the seemingly paradoxical idea that nonhuman matter can take on narrativity. How can story—a quintessential and, for all we know, uniquely human practice—convey a notion of "thing-power," to lift Bennett's phrase (Bennett 2010, xvi), uncoupled from human intentionality and agency?

These are the open questions that this book addresses by building on work in the field of narratology, which over the years has developed sophisticated tools (theoretical as well as analytical) to examine the forms of narrative.[21] Of particular relevance are discussions within what David Herman (1997) calls postclassical narrative theory, which seeks to renovate the vocabulary and framework of structuralist narratology by opening up the concept of story to interdisciplinary influences. Thus, narratological insights into formal strategies will here be supplemented by complex systems theory (chapter 1), cognitive literary studies (chapters 2, 3, and 5), ecolinguistics (chapter 4), the combined quantitative and qualitative analysis of metaphorical language (chapter 6), and a more theoretical discussion of anthropomorphizing or organismic metaphors for the nonhuman (chapter 7). Within the field of postclassical narrative theory at large, this book has particular affinity with Erin James's effort in *The Storyworld Accord* (2015) to develop an "econarratology," a theory of narrative that foregrounds the interplay between stories and the environmental imagination.[22] Equally pertinent is work by Nancy Easterlin (2012), Herman (2014; 2018), and Alexa Weik von Mossner (2017), who bring insights from cognitive narrative theory to bear on narrative's negotiation of ecological questions. These writers have started to move narrative theory beyond its anthropocentric framework—its narrow focus on human-scale space and time, or anthropomorphic voice and character. Easterlin engages with the evolutionary dimension of the organism-environment coupling in ways that, she argues, call for a reappraisal of the relationship between mind, storytelling, and ecocritical approaches to place. Herman explores narrative's power to probe the ways of being of nonhuman animals, while Weik von Mossner focuses on how environmental stories—in literary fiction as well as film—can involve readers in affective and embodied terms.

This book builds on these insights, proposing that thinking with and about narrative form, in its intersection with scientific models and patterns of affectivity, is a critical step in the econarratological project. My core contribution lies in exploring three pathways through which narrative can render, in formal terms, the complexity of our Anthropocenic moment. In the next chapter, these pathways will be discussed under the headings of nonlinearity, interdependency, and multiscalarity. This conceptual triad—which also inspires the book's subdivision into three parts—captures key dimensions of human-nonhuman enmeshment in the Anthropocene: *Narrating the Mesh* shows how narrative can integrate them at a formal level and translate them into a lifelike imaginative experience rich in affect. Each chapter will offer examples and a detailed account of this narrative conversion of the abstract into the concrete and embodied. This interest in formal devices also promises to overcome the "form blindness" that affects large swathes of ecocriticism, a field that has long tended to favor literary texts and genres, such as nature writing, that speak directly (i.e., at the level of plot and themes) to environmental issues.[23]

There are some notable exceptions: Astrid Bracke (2018) has offered formally sophisticated readings of contemporary British novels that confront climate change, while Pieter Vermeulen's work (2015; 2020) emphasizes the significance of literary and novelistic form vis-à-vis the Anthropocene. Thus, Vermeulen writes that "an emphasis on *form* can help us make a case for the enduring relevance of literature in debates over the environment. Literary *form* can enrich interdisciplinary discussions by providing patterns, connections, structures, and descriptions that other kinds of knowledge production are less free to generate" (2020, 47; italics in the original). If Vermeulen aligns form with literary writing, I place it on a continuum with cultural and scientific practices that involve a variety of conceptual and imagistic forms (although, arguably, they use these forms in less self-conscious and innovative ways than literary texts). Narrative occupies a unique position on this continuum, in that it straddles the divide between everyday life (in which stories play a central role, as I will explain in the next section) and experimentations within the artistic practice that we call "literature." The narrative templates (e.g., genres, tropes) that underlie our society's attitudes toward the nonhuman are also ideological forms complicit with an anthropocentric, extractive mindset.[24] By building on and questioning these forms, literary storytelling can clarify, nuance, and subvert dominant ways of thinking about human-nonhuman relations. Therefore, if one wants to explore the contribution of form to the cultural understanding of the ecological crisis, narrative is an excellent place to start.[25]

A NOTE ON NARRATIVE IMPACT

Coming to terms with form is a crucial step toward gaining a better understanding of how narrative can affect readers in imaginative and emotional terms. In a now classic study of reader response, David Miall and Don Kuiken (1994) show that stylistic foregrounding predicts affective involvement in literature, where foregrounding is defined as formal patterns that deviate from readers' expectations. Put otherwise, stylistically creative solutions are more likely to elicit emotional responses in readers than conventional ones. In turn, studies of "narrative persuasion" in social psychology (Green and Brock 2000) have revealed a correlation between emotional involvement and belief change in response to narrative: emotional responses, not conceptual information, drive narrative's impact on audience members' worldview. These findings demonstrate, powerfully, that form is not an arcane subject for literary scholars, but one that should concern anyone who has personal or professional stakes in people's perception of the ecological crisis.

As Timothy Clark discusses in *Ecocriticism on the Edge* (2015, 18–20), one of the fundamental premises of ecocriticism is that the immense challenges raised by climate change are not only political, but also cultural and imaginative, and that they can be solved through the cultural interventions staged by humanities scholarship. For Clark, this position reflects an idealistic overstatement of the "sphere of cultural representations" (2015, 20) of the environment at the expense of the material realities that are shaping the climate crisis. Clark's skepticism is important, but the present book attempts to go beyond representation, investigating the *cognitive and affective form* of human-nonhuman relations that underlies it: the entanglement of the mesh is directly opposed to linear and hierarchical ways of understanding humanity's position vis-à-vis the nonhuman, where linearity is culturally bound up with notions of human mastery and exploitation (in linear models of economic growth or scientific progress, for instance).[26] It is by promoting a cognitive shift from linear to mesh-like thinking that narrative strategies can provide key affective impetus to the ecocritical project. Hence, the formal complexity of literary fiction serves as a repertoire of narrative strategies that, when understood and framed adequately, could have profound repercussions on societal awareness of environmental issues.

Even within the field of ecocriticism, formally challenging narratives could hold more promise than narratives with a straightforward environmentalist agenda. In a discussion of how storytelling can be used to channel scientific knowledge (including findings about climate change), science communication expert Michael Dahlstrom argues that one "of the few factors that has been found to hinder narrative persuasion is when the persuasive intent becomes obvious and audiences react against being manipulated" (2014, 13616). Put otherwise, stories with an overt message are more likely to elicit skepticism than stories that enable readers to draw their own conclusions. The resistance observed by Dahlstrom is compounded by the fact that explicitly "green" literature is often not radical enough in putting pressure on the underlying form of human-nonhuman relations: it tells stories that may resonate with an ecocritical approach but are ultimately consistent with conventional (i.e., linear) ways of thinking about narrative and its possibilities, because they feature a stereotypical hero or embrace predictable trajectories such as the protagonist's environmental coming of age. The upshot is that these stories (and the ecocritical discussion thereof) carry a concrete risk of preaching to the converted—that is, of confirming environmentalist views that were already in place before the reading started.

Narrative can also teach more obliquely, by showing rather than by telling, but the effects of prolonged exposure to narratives that take this oblique approach are also broader in scope, and potentially more long-lasting. In *How to Do Things with Fiction* (2012), Joshua Landy has written insightfully about "formative fictions," which do not carry a straightforward message but "fine-tune our mental capacities" through protracted engagement (2012, 10). This fine-tuning is, precisely, the cognitive shift in the imagination of the nonhuman that challenging narratives can help us achieve. To promote such a shift, narrative has to deploy the affective resources of form in ways that reveal and disrupt entrenched assumptions about patterns of human-nonhuman coexistence. These assumptions are fully operant in more conventional instances of narrative—for instance, through a preference for linear plotting or anthropomorphic characters. That is what all the case studies in this book attempt to resist, whether or not their formal experimentation correlates with an overt ideological message.

It is worth pausing here to explain why articulating these ideas in terms of *narrative* specifically—and not of fiction, for instance—is essential to bringing about a shift in the form of human-nonhuman relations. It is almost a narratological cliché to refer to the cultural ubiquity of narrative, not only in artistic practices but also in oral interactions and media discourse (see Barthes 1975, 237). Narrative is an important tool in establishing cultural as well as personal identity and even selfhood (Brockmeier and Carbaugh 2001; Hutto 2007): stories, in both traditional and industrialized societies, convey invaluable cultural information and play a major role in a group's self-understanding. At an even higher level of abstraction, stories contribute to the very definition of the human by helping establish and maintain the boundary between our species, other life forms, and the physical world. Synthesizing a large body of work in cognitive psychology and narrative theory, Herman argues that narrative is a "basic and general resource for thought" (2003, 170) involved in five widespread problem-solving tasks: breaking down (or "chunking") the flow of experience; establishing causal relations between events; distinguishing between routine occurrences and exceptional ones; sequencing human behavior by correlating overt actions with mental states (such as beliefs and intentions); and, finally, distributing social knowledge within a certain intersubjective context. At all these cognitive levels, narrative as we know it in the West is deeply complicit in a worldview that places considerable emphasis on human agents acting for reasons within a human-scale time frame. Ultimately, in most modern instances of storytelling, the criteria for what counts as an exceptional occurrence and therefore what deserves being told are *human* criteria.[27]

To a large extent, the dualistic separation between human agency and a passive, inert material world is subsumed within a wide gamut of narrative practices. This covert dualism is an aspect of what Monika Fludernik (1996, 13) discusses under the rubric of narrative's "anthropomorphic bias" (see chapter 2). There are clear evolutionary and psychological reasons for this bias, having to do with the role of stories in transmitting information that may have enhanced the survival prospects of its recipients (see Scalise Sugiyama 2001). Because humans are a highly social species, it is hardly surprising that narrative itself is geared toward social interactions among human or at least anthropomorphic agents. Hence, narrative takes on the fundamental cognitive function of interpreting social behavior in terms of mental states, as discussed by Herman.[28]

Moving from cognitive to cultural predispositions, it also seems plausible that, in a Western context, narrative's close alignment with the genre of the novel has had the effect of deepening the anthropocentrism of story: the triumph of the novel is, after all, tightly linked to industrialization and therefore to the exploitation of the nonhuman world.[29] Addressing this question in *The Great Derangement*, Indian writer Amitav Ghosh draws attention to "the peculiar forms of resistance that climate change presents to what is now regarded as serious fiction" (2016, 9)—that is, the novel. But the vitality of formal experimentation—in the novel and in other narrative practices—gives more reason for optimism than Ghosh admits. As the case studies in this book show, formal strategies can remedy the novel's biases, turning it into a narrative practice more attuned to the nonhuman realities of the climate, biology, and the planet's geological history. This expansion of the novel's narrative repertoire is likely to involve dialogue with older forms of storytelling as well as with subgenres, such as science fiction or fantasy, that Ghosh dismisses as "generic outhouses" distinct from "the manor house" of serious fiction (2016, 24).[30]

The broader point is that the cognitive and cultural pervasiveness of narrative form, along with its privileged position in the definition of our species, provide a solid foothold for literary interventions—much more than the "cultural representations" favored by ecocritics (and critiqued by Clark). Through the network of storytelling practices, strategies developed within the seemingly rarefied domain of fiction have the potential for trickling down to concrete cultural attitudes toward the nonhuman. *Narrating the Mesh* argues that the possibility of conceptualizing narrative impact on environmental awareness depends, centrally, on scholarly efforts to identify narrative *form* as a site for negotiating the multiple divides between scientific knowledge, human cultures, and the material realities in which cultures are embedded.

DEFINING THE ARCHIVE

Like every contribution to a theoretical understanding of narrative, this book seeks to find a middle ground between the general and the particular. The theoretical framing developed in this introduction is admittedly broad: it provides a backdrop for my engagement with a far more specific set of narratives, in the genres of the short story and the novel, that convey the many facets of our Anthropocenic moment. Thus, before proceeding, a few words on the historical situatedness of this book's archive are in order. Most of my examples fall comfortably within contemporary fiction, with only a handful of stories—by Ray Bradbury, Julio Cortázar, Ursula K. Le Guin, and Kurt Vonnegut—stretching the timeline by a few decades. This focus is dictated by the pragmatic constraints of this study and does *not* imply that earlier narrative was inherently linear and anthropocentric. On the contrary, premodern narrative (in the Western world, but also and perhaps particularly in non-Western contexts) offers powerful ways of evoking humanity's interconnectedness with the nonhuman world. The same can be said about narrative modes, such as the romance, the Gothic, the fantastic, or magical realism, that attempt to subvert the dominance of literary realism and its claims to scientific objectivity.

Contemporary fiction often turns to these models for inspiration: A. S. Byatt's *Ragnarok* (2011) is a retelling of Norse mythology; Alexis Wright's *The Swan Book* (2013) grafts Aboriginal folklore onto a postapocalyptic scenario explicitly linked to climate change; at its best, Jeff VanderMeer's "new weird" fiction is reminiscent of the ambivalent and enigmatic qualities of Franz Kafka's works.[31] Crucially, it is through references to premodern or non-Western mythology as well as genres that resist the conventions of realist fiction that the contemporary novel blurs the demarcating line between the social world and natural processes. It is, of course, not surprising that the novel—a genre whose rise is deeply indebted to the industrial revolution (Watt 1957)—has to resort to these alternative modes of storytelling to destabilize anthropocentric concepts.

Further, the narratives I examine display a distinctive interest in issues of affect, ethics, and historical responsibility. They confront readers with the limits of the human not by deploying language in a self-reflexive or ironic mode, as postmodernist fiction tended to do (McHale 1987; Hutcheon 1994), but by attempting to channel the materiality of humanity's entanglement with nonhuman others. This renewed engagement with reality is one of the distinguishing features of twenty-first-century fiction, and the texts in this book's archive pursue it—more or less explicitly—in connection with ecological issues.[32] While *Narrating the Mesh* does not examine these historical links systematically, it proposes tools that can be used to further probe continuities and discontinuities between contemporary narrative practices and earlier engagements with the nonhuman in narrative form.

OVERVIEW OF CHAPTERS

Chapter 1 does most of the theoretical heavy lifting in this book, grounding narrative form in discussions on complex systems—that is, physical systems capable of "emergent behavior" across scalar levels. Drawing on work by Terrence Deacon and others, the chapter suggests that the Anthropocene can be understood as a complex system that entangles multiple layers of emergence, from physical and biochemical cycles to the advent of life on Earth and human intentionality. Further, I show—discussing examples drawn from literary fiction but also contemporary film and comics—that narrative has the formal resources to capture three major features of complex systems: their nonlinear nature, their high degree of interdependency, and their multiscalarity. Those headings serve as a conceptual guide throughout the book, structuring its three parts.

Part 1, devoted to "nonlinearity," explores texts that deviate from the goal-driven temporality that underlies prototypical stories. Chapter 2 focuses on the effects of narratives that either follow a circular logic (with short stories by Julio Cortázar and Ted Chiang, "The Night Face Up" and "Story of Your Life," respectively) or embrace puzzling discontinuities over a *longue durée* (*The Great Bay*, by Dale Pendell). By undermining expectations of linearity, those formal devices challenge notions of technological and economic progress and capture humankind's imbrication in a more-than-human world. Chapter 3 turns to the genre of postapocalyptic fiction, discussing the significance of "negative strategies" in novels by Emily St. John Mandel (*Station Eleven*), Cormac McCarthy (*The Road*), and Colson Whitehead (*Zone One*). Negative strategies put the storyworld under erasure, superimposing two temporalities (those of the pre- and the postapocalyptic world) in readers' imagination. In different ways, these narratives question the possibility of linear storytelling after an environmental cataclysm.

Part 2, "Interdependency," addresses the formal enmeshment of human and nonhuman forces in narrative head-on. Chapter 4 revisits Greimas's structuralist account of narrative, which admitted the theoretical possibility of nonhuman entities becoming "actants." The chapter critiques Greimas's model in light of contemporary work in ecolinguistics, arguing that Greimas—despite his promising expansion of the notion of character—builds on a conception of language fundamentally complicit with subject/object dualism. Instead, I explore five ways in which nonhuman entities can nondualistically drive narrative progression, touching on examples such as Jim Crace's *Being Dead*, Jeff VanderMeer's Southern Reach trilogy, and Kurt Vonnegut's *Galápagos*. After positioning the nonhuman at the core of narrative agency in chapter 4, chapter 5 suggests that strategies of consciousness evocation may embed it in the minds of full-fledged human characters. The recent "neuronovel" offers three compelling case studies, with the mesh emerging, with varying degrees of awareness, in the characters' mental processes: Richard Powers's *The Echo Maker*, Rivka Galchen's *Atmospheric Disturbances*, and Bruno Arpaia's *Qualcosa, là fuori* (Something, out there). These narratives bring into view a broader convergence between the nonhuman turn and cognitive models of the mind emphasizing the embodied, extended, and enactive nature of human cognition.

Part 3 turns to metaphorical language as the formal strategy that enables narrative to achieve "multiscalarity" as the third defining feature of complex systems. Chapter 6 presents the results of a computer-aided investigation of metaphorical patterns in three novels that address the climate crisis: Margaret Atwood's *Oryx and Crake,* Jeanette Winterson's *The Stone Gods,* and Ian McEwan's *Solar.* This chapter is based on work conducted in collaboration with Andrei Ionescu and Ruben Fransoo. Our analysis, which combines quantitative methods and qualitative (interpretive) engagement with the novels, brings to the fore the complexity of metaphorical bridges between human-scale and nonhuman realities in narrative. These bridges work in highly specific ways in each novel, reflecting the interaction between metaphorical language and other narrative strategies such as irony (Atwood), looping temporality (Winterson), and the grotesque (McEwan). Finally, chapter 7 takes a step back and examines the workings of metaphor in a more theoretical vein, with emphasis on anthropomorphization and the parallel between the Earth and a superorganism (in James Lovelock's "Gaia hypothesis"). I argue that the value of metaphor lies in the multiple strands of emergent meaning it creates as it brings together a source and a target—a point that complicates the discussion of direct source-to-target projections in the previous chapter. "Vaster than Empires and More Slow," a short story by Ursula K. Le Guin, and *As She Climbed across the Table,* a novel by Jonathan Lethem, demonstrate how anthropomorphic and organismic metaphors can trouble, through their emergent meanings, the human-scale notions of sentience and agency that are central to narrative practices. Through formal strategies, narrative offers a wealth of imaginative resources to embrace the conceptual and affective trouble that defines our Anthropocenic times. The coda illustrates this point with a close reading of excerpts from an interview with an environmental activist conducted as part of NARMESH, the research project from which this book develops. That discussion begins to show how the tools for narratological and stylistic analysis outlined here can be employed beyond the domain of literary fiction—and beyond literary scholarship itself.

CHAPTER 1

Complex Narrative in the Anthropocene

The previous chapter introduced the idea of the "mesh," by which Morton captures the constitutive entanglement of humans and nonhuman things and processes. Quoting from the *Oxford English Dictionary*, Morton argues in *The Ecological Thought* that "'mesh' can mean 'a complex situation or series of events in which a person is entangled; a concatenation of constraining or restricting forces or circumstances; a snare'" (2010, 28). This chapter takes seriously the idea of the mesh as an inherently *complex* system: its first goal is to develop a vocabulary to think about human societies' enmeshment with the nonhuman world as complex not just in Morton's loose sense of a complex situation, but in the more specialized sense of "complexity science" or "complex systems theory." The framework of complexity underlies this book as a whole, while the first chapter offers an initial reconnaissance of the three conceptual foci that will orient my discussion: nonlinearity, interdependency, and multiscalarity. Work by physicist Michel Baranger (2000) and cognitive anthropologist Terrence Deacon (2006) suggests that these features give rise to the emergent patterns of self-organization typical of complex systems, including humanity's enmeshment with nonhuman things and processes. Taken as *concepts* and applied to narrative practices, nonlinearity, interdependency, and multiscalarity reveal a set of formal resources through which storytelling may encapsulate the human-nonhuman mesh in the Anthropocene.

Complex systems theory is a highly diverse, interdisciplinary field, which can be traced back not only to developments in cybernetics, physics, and biology (Maturana and Varela 1980) but also to Niklas Luhmann's sociology (1996). Through its rich intellectual history, the notion of complexity straddles and problematizes the nature/culture divide.[1] Against the backdrop of these theoretical discussions, this chapter makes a more focused use of the concept of complexity. Recent work in narrative theory has investigated the relationship between complexity and narrative form.² This complexity is both intrinsic and extrinsic: intrinsic, because of the sophistication of the formal resources of narrative, and extrinsic, because narrative is embedded in sociocultural as well as material contexts that can be construed as complex. The question, then, is: Given narrative's intrinsic and extrinsic complexity, how can it do justice to the complexity of the Anthropocene?

The question has important ramifications, well beyond literary studies or even interdisciplinary work on narrative. For legal scholar Jens Kersten, the "concept of the Anthropocene calls for a new political anthropology that focuses on human enjoyment of a complex world" (2013, 39). To foster this kind of enjoyment, we need both a conceptual grasp of complexity and the capacity to build emotional interest in it. Narrative can offer both. As science communication scholars have not failed to notice, stories are an effective way of packaging science in human-scale form, translating scientific insights into a language that can be readily understood by lay audiences (Dahlstrom 2014). Furthermore, enjoyment is central to people's engagement with stories: as scholars in literary and media studies have persuasively argued, narrative is driven by emotional values that feed into enjoyment.³

Thus, narrative seems particularly well positioned to foster appreciation for the complexity of the Anthropocene and back up the new "political anthropology" envisaged by Kersten. But whether narrative is successful in this operation depends on a number of factors, including its capacity to capture the complex, emergent nature of the Anthropocene. Not all narratives are equally complex: a casual narrative exchanged at work is likely to be less formally complex than the narratives that can be found in, for instance, Joseph Conrad's novella *Heart of Darkness* or Christopher Nolan's movie *Memento*.⁴ Establishing whether and under what conditions narrative can have an impact on people's understanding of the Anthropocene is, necessarily, an interdisciplinary endeavor. Narrative theory can contribute to that endeavor by bringing into focus the formal strategies that enable stories to adequately model and convey the complexity of the Anthropocene. The next section turns to the definition of complexity and discusses the possibility of applying this concept to the human impact on geological and climatological phenomena.

COMPLEX LOOPS

Physicist Michel Baranger (2000) usefully lays out the defining features of a complex system. First, complex systems are based on components that interact nonlinearly—that is, in ways that are difficult to predict with absolute certainty, given the large number of factors involved. This kind of nonlinearity raises a challenge to a purely deterministic understanding of causation, whereby every effect can be straightforwardly assigned a cause (see Deacon 2006, 117). The second feature of complex systems is interdependency: it is impossible to remove a factor without influencing the system as a whole. Further, complex systems display multiscalarity and emergence: they involve multiple spatiotemporal scales, with structure existing at all scales and "new" phenomena emerging, unpredictably, as one moves across these scales.[5] In the human domain, a perhaps imperfect example of nonlinearity, interdependency, and emergence might be group dynamics: the decisions made by a group (whether of friends or colleagues or members of parliament) are the result of interpersonal factors that cannot be reduced to the beliefs and desires of the group's individual members, yet removing a single member can sometimes lead to profoundly different, and unpredictable, outcomes.

Finally, for Baranger complex systems also involve two kinds of interplay. Their components are in a state of fragile equilibrium; they fall into a dynamic (and relatively orderly) pattern, but are always at risk of tipping over into a disordered state ("interplay between chaos and non-chaos"). Also, the components of a complex system oscillate between cooperation (on scale n) and competition (on a larger scale, $n + 1$). Baranger's analogy is illuminating: "Consider the bourgeois families of the 19th century, of the kind described by Jane Austen or Honoré de Balzac. They competed with each other toward economic success and toward procuring the most desirable spouses for their young people. And they succeeded better in this if they had the unequivocal devotion of all their members, and also if all their members had a chance to take part in the decisions" (2000, 11).

Another way to conceptualize complex systems is to say that they are capable of *self-organization* through constant interactions ("feedback loops," to use a more technical term) with the environment: there is complexity when dynamic patterns emerge from a chaotic ensemble of elements and forces, with an apparent violation of the second law of thermodynamics (see Deacon 2006, 117–18). This law states that disorder in a closed system ("entropy") is bound to *increase* over time, whereas complex behavior results in an increase of order, even though this order is never static but remains dynamically coupled with a chaotic environment.

Complex systems exist at multiple levels of reality, from the microcosm to the macrocosm. A cell or the behavior of fluids (e.g., in a whirlpool) can be described as a complex system, but also an entire organism or evolution by natural selection or meteorological patterns. To account for these major differences in complex systems, researchers have attempted to distinguish between *types* of emergent behavior (and, by extension, classes of complexity). Deacon (2006) proposes three categories. In first-order complexity, molecular properties determine a higher-level feature of a system; for instance, surface tension in liquids is the macroscopic result of the cohesive force between molecules that, taken in isolation, do *not* display surface tension—a basic kind of emergence known as "supervenience." In second-order complexity, there is an *amplification* of emergence due to what Deacon calls "morphodynamics," the constraints imposed by the spatial configuration of a system. Deacon's example is that of the processes underlying the formation of snow crystals over time: "Reciprocally-reinforcing biases of molecular configuration and the contingencies of crystal growth together determine their macroscopic patterning" (2006, 134). The result is not just supervenience but a more advanced form of complexity that is generally found in atmospheric and geological phenomena. Morphodynamics is thus a form of self-organization based on gradual changes in spatial configuration within large-scale systems.

Finally, Deacon's third-order complexity encompasses living processes that are capable of retaining information—not only through conscious memory but also, at a biologically more fundamental level, through DNA structure. For instance, "haemoglobin, and indeed any complex structure within an organism, has the structure and properties it does because it is embedded in a vast elaborate evolutionary web" (2006, 140). As Deacon discusses, any purely physical description of hemoglobin, no matter how detailed, would not be able to explain why hemoglobin is so widespread in nature; hemoglobin can be properly understood only by reference to its *function* in living organisms, which in turn depends on a highly specific evolutionary history. This kind of historical self-organization—the complexity of life—builds on both supervenience and morphodynamics but cannot be reduced to them.

For Deacon, the evolution of mind and of complex semiotic systems, such as language, displays this third kind of emergence. Just as DNA is a form of evolutionary, superindividual memory, certain living systems can remember previous external and internal events and engage with the world in ways that can be properly called mentalistic and symbolic. This representational ability gives these systems enormous power over the supervenient and self-organizing dynamics of the physical world: "A symbolizing mind has perhaps the widest possible locus of causal influence of anything on earth. Minds that have become deeply immersed in the evolving symbolic ecosystem of culture—as are all modern human minds—may have an effective causal locus that extends across continents and back millennia, and which grows out of a locally least-discordant-remainder dynamic involving hundreds of thousands of individual communications and actions" (2006, 149). Nor does the chain of complexity stop at the level of individual minds. As Deacon implies in the quotation, the dynamics of culture and society are complex in their own right, their self-organizing history being entirely beyond the control of individual agents (and yet emerging from their actions). Deacon's typology thus brings into view the sheer magnitude and diversity of the processes involved in the Anthropocenic enmeshment of humankind with the nonhuman world. There is complexity—that is, supervenience and self-organization—at all levels of this entanglement, starting from physical and chemical phenomena that shape the macroscopic realities we call "the weather" and "the climate." But the distinctive self-organization of life and mind adds a further layer to the complexity of these processes. At the time of writing, a new study had recently appeared in *Nature Communications* (and attracted considerable attention in the popular-science press) suggesting that a rise in global temperatures during the early Cambrian period may be linked to the spread of tiny invertebrates that burrowed into the seabed. Through this burrowing behavior, these animals caused changes in "global geochemical cycles of carbon, sulphur, phosphorus and oxygen" (Van de Velde et al. 2018, 2). Put otherwise, humans are far from being the only species capable of triggering global warming—even as, of course, the *speed* with which industrial activity is driving changes in the Earth's ecosystems is unparalleled. This speed is a direct consequence of the uniquely complex possibilities offered by semiotic systems, which enable and "scaffold" human minds, societies, and technologies, including those involved in large-scale industrialization.[6] Let us not forget that, as I pointed out in the introduction, the anthropos that becomes a planetary force in the Anthropocene cannot be taken for granted as a species-level concept, being the result of concrete historical and sociopolitical dynamics—particularly the rise of Western capitalism as the world's dominant economic system and the main driver of anthropogenic climate change.

In an influential article, historian Dipesh Chakrabarty thus conceptualizes global warming as the "collision—or the running up against one another—of three histories . . . : the history of the earth system, the history of life including that of human evolution on the planet, and the more recent history of industrial civilization (for many, capitalism)" (2014, 1). Deacon's typology of emergence allows us to appreciate the staggering complexity implicated in each of these histories and their sudden Anthropocenic collision. Each history builds—with eerie precision—upon the previous one: human history (and its current cultural setup in a Westernized and globalized world) develops the third-order complexity of natural evolution, which in turn extends the self-organizing (second-order) complexity of physical phenomena ("the history of the earth system"). This is not a mere unidirectional hierarchy, however, because—through global warming and the manifold traces left by human activities on Earth—the complexity of human culture folds back into the physical complexity of geology and meteorological phenomena. Deacon's discussion of complexity thus puts minded agents and human societies on a continuum with self-organizing patterns in the physical world. It is striking that theorists as wide apart as Morton and Deacon conceptualize this continuum in terms of the same spatial form, that of the loop: Morton (2016, 7) talks about the "strange loop" of humanity's enmeshment in the ecology, while Deacon proposes the similarly looping image of the "ouroboros" (the mythical serpent biting its own tail; see Deacon 2006, 124).[7] If the image of the loop emerges repeatedly in this book (chapters 2, 5, 6), it is because narrative's engagement with the nonhuman, as discussed in the introduction, is grounded in formal patterns, and the loop constitutes a culturally salient and highly effective alternative to linear, hierarchical models of human-nonhuman relations. Both the loop and the mesh are figures of nonlinear entanglement.

It is important to keep in mind that loops are not a unique feature of narratives staging ecological questions. In *Postmodernist Fiction* (1987, 119–21), Brian McHale discusses narrative loops as a manifestation of postmodern self-reflexivity: the loop suggests metalepsis or the blurring of ontological boundaries, as in McHale's reading of Julio Cortázar's famous short story

"Continuity of Parks," where the ending violates the ontological distinction between the reader and the textual world set up by the beginning.[8] Such narrative loops remain internal to the human subject and culture; they do not unsettle the primacy of these anthropocentric categories, unlike the loops I will be exploring in the following pages. Of course, it is impossible to deny the postmodernist inspiration of these loops (my corpus includes another short story by Cortázar, after all). But the kind of looping I am interested in pushes in an entirely different direction from McHale's account of postmodernist fiction: rather than reflecting quintessentially postmodern concerns over the limits of language and the human subject, it foregrounds the material entanglement of human societies and nonhuman realities.

How can narrative form capture the complexity of this entanglement? This is where Baranger's account of complex systems comes into play. The following treatment singles out the first three traits of complex systems, as discussed by Baranger, because they are a precondition for emergent behavior as well as various dynamics within complex systems: nonlinearity, interdependency, multiscalarity. How can narrative integrate these features at the formal level? And how can it work to connect these features to a vision of Anthropocenic enmeshment of humans and nonhumans? The next sections examine each of these concepts and propose ways to make them viable in narrative analysis. This discussion is grounded in examples drawn from contemporary fiction but also from film and comic books. While the following chapters will restrict the focus to prose narrative in the genres of the novel and the short story, the account of complexity in this chapter deliberately casts a broad net to demonstrate that stories in a variety of media can create understanding of, and appreciation for, the complexity of the Anthropocene. Certainly, the verbal nature of prose fiction creates highly specific formal possibilities, which will be explored extensively in the rest of the book. But these possibilities are always projected against a background of shared concepts and constraints on storytelling, which this chapter seeks to map out through its transmedial scope.[9]

NONLINEARITY

At a basic level, narrative establishes connections between events in temporal, causal, and thematic terms. These connections are at the heart of narrative sequentiality. Consider E. M. Forster's famous example of plot: "The king died, then the queen died of grief" (1955, 86). This story is an effective illustration of how, in narrative, linkage involves simultaneously temporal, causal, and thematic relations between events: death here is the theme of the narrative, just as the queen's death follows, and is caused by, the king's demise. But even in a story as simple as Forster's the linkage is never completely predictable. It is, of course, an overstatement to speak of full-fledged "suspense" or "surprise" for this microstory. Yet it still implies that the queen could have survived or died of other causes. The emotional punch line of Forster's example derives, at least in part, from readers' latent awareness of these unrealized possibilities, and from the relative unpredictability of the outcome. Thus, John Pier sees complexity as inherent in any narrative sequence: "The global narrative cannot be predicted on the basis of its sequences, any more than the sequences can be formally deduced from the global story" (2017, 558). From this perspective, all narratives can be said to be nonlinear to the extent that the reader cannot determine their outcome from the outset.

Specific narratives may maximize this background of unpredictability. Typically, this happens when stories create tensions and rifts between temporal sequence, causation, and thematic unity, which are no longer bound up as they are in Forster's example. This point will be discussed in more detail in the next chapter, focusing specifically on the *psychological* causation that underlies prototypical instances of storytelling: the causation of characters' desires and goals, which usually serves as a trigger of narrative action (and thus of plot). A frequent pattern in nonlinear narrative is that the temporal and thematic logic of narrative sequentiality becomes uncoupled from psychological causation—that is, from the protagonist's long-term plans and goals. The more the connection between the temporal, causal, and thematic dimensions of narrative sequentiality is problematized, the more nonlinear a story becomes.[10] A case in point is *Le quattro volte* (*The Four Times*), a 2010 film by Italian director Michelangelo Frammartino set on the rural hills of Calabria, in the southern tip of the Italian peninsula. It is a slow, philosophical film, whose narrative weaves together a human character, an old goatherd, and his goats, as well as the material world in which they are embedded. Human dialogue is scarce and mostly inaudible; goat bleats, dog barks, and rustling leaves fill the soundtrack. The film foregrounds the cyclical nature of life through its four protagonists (see fig. 2). We first experience the daily routine of the goatherd, who appears to be seriously ill; after the goatherd dies, a goat is born; the goat finds shelter under a fir tree, which is later felled and turned into a greasy pole,

Figure 2. The four "protagonists" of Michelangelo Frammartino's *Le quattro volte* (2010).

becoming the main attraction of a country festival; finally, wood from the tree is turned into charcoal. This fourfold structure suggests ancient notions of metempsychosis or Buddhist reincarnation, but the film is remarkably agnostic and evokes the interconnectedness of life through narrative form rather than religious belief.

Importantly, these episodes seem to be arranged in a temporal sequence, but the causal linkage between them is extremely loose: the goat's birth is not causally related to the goatherd's death, and the connection between the goat and the fir tree is a matter of mere coincidence—the goat takes shelter under the tree during a storm. The interdependency of the film's human and nonhuman protagonists is emphasized in thematic and affective terms. The overall impression is highly nonlinear, and indeed the global organization of the plot evokes circularity, not linear progression.[11]

An even more radical example of nonlinearity can be found in an influential comic strip by American artist Richard McGuire titled *Here* and originally published in 1989.[12] *Here* is set in a room, which is always presented from the same spatial viewpoint, with the corner falling in the middle of the panels. While the narrative has a fixed spatial perspective, it keeps moving back and forth in time, showing what was happening at that precise location at different points. Consider the sequence in figure 3: in the left panel, we see a mouse squeaking in front of a mouse trap in 1999. An insert in the bottom right corner shows a child playing with a dinosaur

Figure 3. Narrative logic in Richard McGuire's *Here* (2006, 91). (© 1989 Richard McGuire, used by permission of the Wylie Agency [UK] Limited)

toy in 2028. There is some degree of temporal sequentiality here, since the latter scene follows the former, but no causal or thematic connection we can make sense of. The following panel greatly complicates this logic by multiplying—as well as differentiating—the narrative connections. The main portion of the panel is set, with a flashback, over a hundred million years ago; it shows a dinosaur roaring (just as the mouse was squeaking) at the location that will be occupied by the room in the distant future. Here the logic is thematic: the dinosaur resembles the toy dinosaur the child will play with in 2028. At the same time, the central inset is chronologically related to the previous panel: the mouse has entered the trap, in 1999. Finally, a new sequence is opened: in another insert, we see a man laughing in 1986. This temporally free-floating scene reads like a pun on the dinosaurs' extinction and subsequent transformation into toys; these mighty creatures have been superseded, in the course of evolutionary history, by the mammalian ancestors of the mouse that falls into the trap in 1999.

What has happened here? Simply put, McGuire's style—like Frammartino's formal choices—challenges the usual convergence of temporal, causal, and thematic linkage in narrative. But, while Frammartino's movie evokes the image of a circle, the logic underlying McGuire's work can be called "rhizomatic" in Deleuze and Guattari's sense (1987), in that it favors a plurality of nonoverlapping and largely divergent connections over linear progression. Deleuze and Guattari use the rhizome as a botanical metaphor for a model of horizontal, decentralized linkage, which they oppose to the vertical, hierarchical organization of roots and trees. By articulating time in this decentralized way, McGuire maximizes the unpredictability of narrative sequentiality and thus strongly suggests the nonlinearity of complex systems. This nonlinearity is inherently mesh-like in that it doesn't display a "definite center or edge" (Morton 2010, 8); instead, it is up to readers to connect the dots and infer narrative sequences out of the multiplicity of visual and verbal stimuli offered by McGuire's comic strip. Yet these reader-created sequences remain localized and defeasible. The proposed evolutionary connection between the mouse and the dinosaur exemplifies this "do it yourself" approach to narrative sequentiality: these fleeting resonances between panels and inserts are extremely suggestive but don't offer sufficient foothold to impose coherence on the whole text.[13] Furthermore, through the staging of geological scales prior to the rise of humanity, McGuire (indirectly) raises the specter of the Anthropocene. *Here* thus powerfully suggests the coexistence of temporal scales within a single spatial location.

INTERDEPENDENCY

Interdependency can be realized in narrative in multiple ways. The discussion offered in chapters 4 and 5 focuses on interdependency as a function of narrative *agency* and *consciousness evocation:* how fictional stories can sever the link between characters and the human mind, by foregrounding nonhuman actants (chapter 4) or by embedding nonhuman materiality into the mental lives of human protagonists (chapter 5). The complex interdependency of human societies (e.g., cultures, psychologies) and nonhuman things and processes thus emerges as character—one of the main components of narrative—is uncoupled from an anthropocentric understanding. But stories may also flaunt their interdependency at the level of plot. This effect is particularly well illustrated by narratives featuring plotlines that, while seemingly independent, come together in a surprising convergence. Arnaud Schmitt (2014, 84) calls the confluence of distinct plotlines a diegetic "knot": for instance, a plot can track the parallel lives of two characters for a certain period, until they cross paths and establish a romantic relationship. This overlap is a knot in Schmitt's sense. The combined use of multiple story lines and knots is particularly common in a strand of contemporary fiction and film that foregrounds the interconnectedness of societies, and individual lives, in a globalized world. Rita Barnard discusses a number of recent movies and novels in this light, as "attempts to devise new and more cosmopolitan narrative forms" (2009, 208). The challenge tackled by this strand of contemporary fiction is that of creating a sense of global interdependency between characters and plotlines that are separated by a significant spatial, and typically also sociocultural, gap. A case in point is *Babel*, a 2006 movie directed by Alejandro González Iñárritu. Here three story lines unfold in different parts of the world, straddling the divide between the Global North and the Global South: Morocco, the US-Mexico border, and Japan.

Two American tourists, Richard and Susan, are traveling in Morocco when Susan is accidentally hit by a stray bullet fired by Yussef, a Moroccan boy who was testing a Winchester rifle given to him by his father. In the aftermath of the life-threatening accident, Richard and Susan have to postpone their return to the United States, where a Mexican nanny, Amelia, is looking after their children. Amelia's son is soon getting married in Mexico; waiting for Richard and Susan's return would mean missing the wedding. Thus, Amelia decides to take Richard and Susan's children with her. Everything goes smoothly until, on the way back from the wedding, Amelia is questioned by the US border police after failing to prove that she had Richard and Susan's permission for the trip. In a botched attempt to escape arrest, Amelia and the children find themselves stranded in the desert, where they narrowly escape death from dehydration. The result is Amelia's expulsion and deportation to Mexico. Susan's wounding in Morocco functions as the knot that sets in motion the Mexican subplot: narrative interdependency is shown at work on a global scale. The third subplot, set in Japan, focuses on a rebellious Japanese teenager, Chieko, whose father was the former owner of the Winchester rifle involved in the accidental shooting in Morocco. In fact, we discover that Chieko's father gave the rifle to Yussef's father during a hunting trip in Morocco: this is the second plot knot foregrounded by the movie.

Presented in chronological order, *Babel*'s main plot knots are as follows: the rifle is given to Yussef's father (story line 1) → Yussef unintentionally shoots Susan (story line 2) → Amelia decides to travel to Mexico with Richard and Susan's children (story line 3). Each story line is causally dependent on the previous one; what brings the plot together thematically and generates a profound sense of *inter*dependency is the history of a material object, the rifle. In a Latourian vein, the rifle can be read as a stand-in for the efficacy and quasi-autonomous agency of technology, which propels a narrative sequence largely uncoupled from human intentionality. In this global movie, interdependency is thus tied to a form of "object-oriented plotting" (see Caracciolo 2020c), in which an object shapes the narrative progression. (Two further instances of object-oriented plotting—the novels *Station Eleven* by Emily St. John Mandel and *A Tale for the Time Being* by Ruth Ozeki—will be discussed in chapters 3 and 4, respectively.)

In *Babel*, plot knots are threaded together in a relatively sequential way, even if viewers can only grasp the overall pattern retrospectively. By contrast, Richard Powers's novel *The Overstory* (2018) makes a far less centralized use of narrative knots to convey a sense of human-nonhuman interdependency. The novel presents an intricate plot in which nine characters from several US states develop a personal connection with trees, becoming aware of plants' ecological centrality and even of their shaping—if typically undetected—influence on human history. Formally speaking, the plot works along the lines of what, in the context of film theory, David Bordwell (2008, chapter 7) calls "network narratives." A network narrative is one in which "there are . . . several protagonists, but their projects are largely decoupled from one another, or only contingently linked" (2008, 192). This is certainly the case in the first part of Powers's novel, which consists of eight chapters, each devoted to and titled after one character from the novel's cast (with the exception of the chapter "Ray Brinkman and Dorothy Cazaly," which focuses on a married couple in suburban Saint Paul). These chapters introduce the characters, their socioeconomic background, and the way trees became part of their lives. For instance, Nick Hoel continues a family tradition of taking monthly pictures of the chestnut tree on an Iowa farm—one of the few surviving specimens after the blight that decimated American chestnuts in the early twentieth century. Another character, Neelay Mehta, is wheelchair-bound after falling off an oak tree; he goes on to launch a highly successful video game company named "Sempervirens" after the redwoods of northern California. Patricia Westerford, a scientist, discovers trees' extraordinary ability to communicate with one another via fungal networks, but her theories are initially considered improbable and met with skepticism in the scientific community.

While the first part of the novel traces the lives of these and other six characters as separate from one another, the plotting of the following parts brings the cast together in a highly nonlinear pattern. For five characters, we have a series of diegetic knots (in Schmitt's sense): one by one, they meet and their lives become increasingly intertwined. As is typical in network narratives, these encounters are generally governed by a logic of contingency and not tied to the psychological causation of the characters' long-term goals (Bordwell 2008, 199). Olivia, a student at a Midwestern college, experiences near-death after a severe electric shock. When she miraculously regains consciousness, she starts hearing voices that urge her to travel to California to join demonstrations against widespread logging. Driving through Iowa, she stops by a farm that turns out to be Nick's; on a whim, Nick decides to join her on her trip to California, where they spend months together living on the branches of a threatened redwood. Adam, a psychology graduate student, makes their acquaintance while doing fieldwork for his dissertation on the psychology of environmental activism. Initially a skeptic, Adam is soon converted to the environmentalist cause. Meanwhile, Douglas and Mimi have had separate plant epiphanies. While serving as an Air Force loadmaster during the Vietnam War, Douglas's plane is shot down; his catastrophic fall is broken by a banyan tree, which saves his life. Mimi, a senior engineer in a ceramics company, develops an obsession with the smell of the Ponderosa pines wafting through her office window. Douglas and Mimi meet in Oregon, in the radical environmentalist community of Cascadia. When Adam, Olivia, and Nick are forcibly removed from the redwood forest, they decide to move north, and they also wind up in Cascadia. Together, the five characters transition from peaceful protest to ecoterrorism: they start burning down buildings and machinery used for logging. They disband after Olivia's accidental death, at the end of the novel's second part. Some of them meet again as they face the moral and legal consequences of their actions.

It is important to note that this summary gives a far more orderly impression of the plot than the novel itself. After the first part, the chapters no longer focus on a single character. There are no chapter subdivisions; the narrator summons and dismisses the characters in short sections separated only by the stylized image of a tree trunk. It is up to the reader to work out the connections and construct an increasingly coherent intersubjective network. In this way, the novel steers clear of a sense of predestination and does not present these five characters' union as an inevitable outcome of the plot: the five environmentalists' converging pattern does emerge in the course of the novel, but the plotting retains a fragmentary and haphazard quality, rather than a clear teleological orientation. The four remaining characters (Patricia Westerford, Neelay, Ray, and Dorothy) are integrated into the plot by way of looser knots. As in *Babel*, the connections revolve around a physical artifact: Patricia Westerford's popular-science book *The Secret Forest*, in which she outlines her groundbreaking studies on the social cognition of plants. Echoes of Patricia's book ripple through the novel, reaching, at different times and in different contexts, all the characters. The first lines of Patricia's book—"You and the tree in your backyard come from a common ancestor" (2018, 132)—are quoted three times in the book, serving as a verbal knot; Neelay, Ray, and Dorothy are deeply affected by Patricia's work, which draws them further into the network of the plot. Finally, the ending pulls the strands together by increasing the frequency of knots that connect the peripheral characters to the five environmentalists' group. Patricia plans to stage her suicide during a talk that is jointly attended by Mimi and Neelay; shortly before Ray's death, Ray and Dorothy read about Adam's arrest in a newspaper; and, in the novel's final scene, Nick's landscape art is observed by Neelay's latest creation, an artificial intelligence based on machine-learning algorithms.

The form of network narrative, as film scholar Maria Poulaki (2014) has argued, is an inherently complex one.[14] It is mesh-like, though perhaps not as mesh-like as the rhizomatic structure of *Here* (I will return to this point at the end of the next chapter). Poulaki's analysis focuses on what she calls "complex causality" of network narrative: "a cumulative, nonlinear and emergent effect rather than as an event-sequence of causes and effects" (2014, 393). The complexity of a network narrative relies on the author's ability to orchestrate multiple story lines in such a way that the emerging pattern is satisfyingly coherent without yielding to a deterministic, cause-effect reading. This pattern, not front-loaded in the narrative but dynamically assembled by the audience, is what gives network narratives their distinct sense of interdependency. This point explains why Powers needs the more "peripheral" characters, along with the five environmentalists whose lives do intersect in a significant way: the external plotlines enter a dynamic tension with the environmentalists' lives, disrupting an overtly teleological reading of the events in which they become involved. At the same time, these plotlines offer thematic justification (largely through Patricia's theory of plant sociality) but also the vague possibility of a resolution (through the artificial intelligence developed by Neelay, which, in the novel's ending, appears to take control over the future of our planet).

This complex structure is, in many respects, comparable to the network films discussed by Bordwell and Poulaki. What distinguishes Powers's novel is how it puts the characters' social network in the service of another, more-than-human network. *The Overstory* channels humans' mesh-like interdependency with plants: it suggests that our species is dependent on plants for its survival, and yet we are dramatically blind to them—a shortcoming that Powers explicitly frames by reference to the current ecological crisis. The clearest articulation of this view can be found in one of Patricia's public lectures: "Trees stand at the heart of ecology, and they must come to stand at the heart of human politics" (2018, 454). Even as it draws attention to humans' interdependency with plants at the thematic level, the novel foregrounds and probes another mode of interdependency—namely, the nine characters' entangled life trajectories. The conceit of Powers's novel is that these distinct modes of interdependency—the human-nonhuman and the intersubjective—are blended together by way of formal devices. From the very title of the novel, "story" is both a canopy of leaves and a practice of human sense-making. The first part of the novel is titled "Roots," the second "Trunk," the third "Crown," and the fourth "Seeds": the physical structure of trees is superimposed on the organization of the novel, and of the intertwined life stories that it contains. The apparent linearity of the progression from roots to crown is complicated by the final reference to seeds, which suggests the life cycle of plants and thus circularity: in *The Overstory*, the characters' network is enriched by circular patterns, evoking nonlinearity in addition to interdependency. Compared to the rhizomatic structure of *Here*, however, the network of *The Overstory* appears less openended, more focused in both diegetic and thematic terms.

Crucially, Powers's novel implies that its cast of characters can be analogically mapped onto the nonhuman communities explored by Patricia's scientific work, the "mycorrhizal networks" formed by plants and fungi. These underground networks are responsible for sharing resources such as water or nutrients.[15] We read that trees "care and feed each other, orchestrating shared behaviors through the networked soil" (2018, 217). Likewise, the human characters' "lives have long been connected, deep underground. Their kinship will work like an unfolding book" (2018, 132). The plotting of the novel, with the multiple knots of human vicissitudes, thus serves as an imaginative aid for readers, on two levels: first, the human characters become an anthropomorphic stand-in for the physical mesh formed by trees and fungi; and, second, the analogy between a human group and the nonhuman form of the mycorrhizal network channels human societies' reliance on biochemical cycles that depend on plants. The concrete, and highly tellable, situations of human intersubjectivity thus model a far more abstract notion of *human-nonhuman* enmeshment.

MULTISCALARITY

As a key element of human intersubjectivity, narrative favors social interactions taking place in human-scale reality. But this does not mean that narrative cannot integrate realities well below, or above, the human scale.[16] David Herman makes a case for the possibility of "multiscale narration" in the last chapter of *Narratology beyond the Human* (2018). Among other formal strategies for achieving multiscalarity, Herman focuses on what he calls "allegorical projection," which "bridges, with greater or fewer intermediary layers or 'rungs,' the meso and macro levels of creatural life on earth" (2018, 282). Put otherwise, a human-scale phenomenon can point—by way of allegory—to a process that is not human-scale.

This discussion of allegory suggests that analogical thinking plays a pivotal role in opening up narrative to nonhuman-scale realities. "Analogy" refers, broadly, to a process of establishing similarity across distinct semantic domains—"cross-domain mapping" is the technical term used by cognitive linguists. Both allegory and metaphorical language are linguistic manifestations of an analogical mapping.[17] Such mappings, as we'll see in chapters 6 and 7, are not limited to human-scale phenomena; on the contrary, they can push narrative beyond its home field of human interaction by bringing out what Katherine Hayles characterizes as "recursive symmetries between scale levels" (1990, 13)—that is, the ways in which nonhuman-scale realities resemble human-scale ones. In this way, analogy enables narrative to mirror the multiscalar workings of complex systems. We have already encountered a multiscalar use of analogy in Powers's *The Overstory*, which draws inspiration from the structural symmetry between the biochemical network of trees and fungi and the interlaced life trajectories of nine characters. This is the macroanalogy that shapes the plot, straddling the divide between the human lifeworld (the characters' vicissitudes) and the largely invisible—but biologically indispensable—contribution that plants make to the Earth's ecosystems.

We can turn to two further examples of multiscalar analogy, one in the audiovisual medium of film and another in the verbal medium of prose narrative. The preamble of Stanley Kubrick's "proverbial good science-fiction movie" *2001: A Space Odyssey* (1968) is set in prehistory and shows a group of ape-like creatures (clearly, the ancestors of Homo sapiens) making their first steps in the use of tools: for the first time in human history, animal bones are employed as weapons to drive off a rival group.[18] This sequence builds up to the famous scene in which one of the hominids, Moon-Watcher, throws a bone into the air, apparently to celebrate the death of the rival leader. A close-up shot tracks the bone as it ascends through the air and later starts falling, but the fall is suddenly interrupted by images of a satellite orbiting around the Earth, with an unexpected leap in both space and time. In one of film history's best-known match cuts, the satellite resembles, in shape and downward trajectory, the bone hurled by Moon-Watcher (see fig. 4).

The match cut establishes a visual analogy, but also a metaphorical link of a more conceptual nature: on the one hand, the editing conveys, by way of ellipsis, a history of technological progress that led from rudimentary weapons to advanced technology; on the other hand, just as the bone-weapon is an expression of the hominids' desire to master other animals and their own conspecifics, the satellite becomes a stand-in for space exploration and shows that human efforts in space participate in, and extend, our quest for domination. Strictly speaking, then, the match

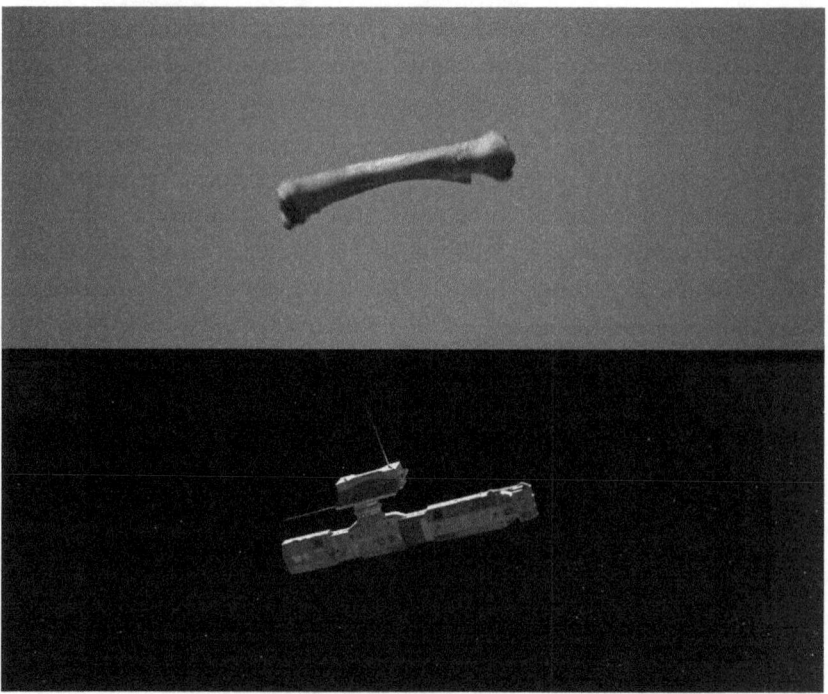

Figure 4. Bone-satellite match cut in Stanley Kubrick's *2001: A Space Odyssey* (1968).

cut involves *both* a metaphorical mapping between two distinct technologies and metonymic associations between, first, the bone and warfare and, second, the satellite and space exploration. Crucially, this analogical device allows Kubrick to bring together a human-scale object—the bone—and the far more intangible realities of outer space and evolutionary history. The bone thrown into the air by Moon-Watcher is an object that affords direct, embodied manipulation; from the perspective of embodied cognition, spectators echo its rotating movement in their bodies as they watch it climbing, and then falling, through the air.[19] By contrast, outer space and natural evolution are phenomena whose spatial and temporal scales (respectively) far surpass the range of direct embodied experience. The multiscalar mapping facilitates the imagination of these more-than-human realities by bringing them down to a human-scale object, the bone, even as the bone-satellite juxtaposition calls attention to the vastness of the conceptual leap involved. The surprise engendered by Kubrick's editing builds on this conceptual tension between imaginative facility and dramatic scalar difference.

To transition to the verbal domain, we find numerous instances of multiscalar analogy in *Flight Behavior,* a novel by American writer Barbara Kingsolver. *Flight Behavior* focuses on Dellarobia, a woman living in rural Tennessee, who comes into contact, for the first time in her life, with the world of science. Due to the effects of global warming, a population of butterflies changes its usual migration pattern and flies to Tennessee instead of Mexico. A group of researchers arrive to investigate the butterflies and strike up an acquaintance with Dellarobia. In one key scene, Ovid, the lead scientist, explains to her the genetic blending that occurs when the whole butterfly population comes together in our place. The woman responds through another kind of blending—a metaphorical one. She draws an analogy between genetic dynamics and her own experience of selling and buying clothes: "I get that. Okay. Like mostly swapping your goods at the secondhand store in town, and then once a year doing the international-trade thing at the dollar store" (2012, 439). The "international-trade thing" is, of course, a nod at the global scale of trade—how clothes produced far from the United States end up in dollar stores across the country. Through this elaborate analogy, the narrative integrates three levels of reality: ecosystemic variations tied to climate change, the globalization of international trade, and Dellarobia's human-scale, quotidian experience of buying and selling clothes.

Nor is this an isolated phenomenon: Kingsolver's novel is rich in metaphorical language that bridges between human-scale and nonhuman realities, foregrounding—like Kubrick's match cut—the continuities between these scales but also the jarring tensions between them. While surrounded by a dense swarm of butterflies, for instance, people are compared to "human boulders in the butterfly-filled current" (2012, 76). A few pages earlier, we read: "The trees had lost their leaves early in the unrelenting rain. After a brief fling with coloration they dropped their tresses in clumps like a chemo patient losing her hair" (2012, 67). These sophisticated metaphors weave together the human and the nonhuman, reminding us of their fundamental similarity even as, implicitly, they reveal how everyday language tends to compartmentalize boulders, trees, and cancer patients. Compared to the extraordinary nimbleness of a swarm of butterflies, humans can seem as isolated and static as boulders; ailing trees and patients are revealed in their shared suffering. Metaphor thus serves what Gerard Steen (2008) would call a "perspective-changing" function, inviting readers to take a novel perspective on entrenched linguistic categories (human vs. nonhuman and animate vs. inanimate). In turn, the blurring of conceptual boundaries is bound to create affective tensions as readers are nudged outside of the familiar human-scale world in which trees are far less significant than cancer patients. Through this pattern of similarity and affective resistance, which will be explored more extensively in part 3 of this book, metaphor enters an open-ended (and fundamentally nonlinear) relationship with the human-centered events that underpin the plot. Thus, analogical mappings are crucial to multiscale narrative: they unsettle the focus of plot on human-scale happenings by capturing, in metaphorical or allegorical form, the complexity of the mesh.

This chapter has shown that narrative has the means to integrate and illuminate key features of complex systems: their nonlinearity, interdependency, and multiscalarity. Most relevant in this context, this power of narrative extends to human societies' enmeshment with geological, climatological, and biochemical processes—the enmeshment that is currently expressed by the concept of Anthropocene in its various embodiments (as discussed in the introduction). The Anthropocene should be understood as a highly complex phenomenon, emerging from interlocking and cross-cutting loops of biochemical and physical processes, human intentionality, and socio-economic dynamics.

My examples, drawn from contemporary fiction but also from film and comics, are a first step in this book's sustained engagement with the repertoire of forms and strategies through which narrative can model the complexity of the Anthropocene. It is essential to highlight that fiction doesn't have to speak to the Anthropocene *directly*, at the level of themes and plot, to deploy pertinent formal resources. Among the examples discussed in this chapter, only Powers's and Kingsolver's novels address climate change explicitly; the other case studies either pre-date or seem tangential to contemporary discussions on the Anthropocene. Yet the formal sophistication displayed by, for instance, Kubrick's match cut or McGuire's rhizomatic narrative demonstrates that fiction can package complex dynamics in a language that requires limited technical knowledge and is far more emotionally impactful than scientific models. Formally challenging narrative is at ease with complexity and affords an opportunity to sidestep the reductionism of scientific thinking in engaging with the human-nonhuman mesh, opening up science to issues of broader social and ethical relevance (such as globalization or the cultural isolation of Appalachia in *Flight Behavior*).

The following chapters continue this exploration of formal strategies, using as a guide the concepts of nonlinearity, interdependency, and multiscalarity. However, before embarking on that discussion it is critical to stress that my focus on formal resources is necessarily only one half of the equation. The other half is, of course, the reader, and the manifold factors, psychological as well as sociocultural, that modulate the effects of fiction. Not every reader will respond to the formal devices examined in this book; only readers who possess certain competences and prior knowledge are likely to appreciate complex patterns. Thus, we can hypothesize that fictional narrative may serve as a platform for fostering what Kersten, in the article discussed above, describes as "enjoyment of a complex world" (2013, 39). But we must remain aware that the psychological effects of fiction are, in themselves, a deeply complex matter, and no linear relationship can be established between engagement with narrative and people's worldview. Raymond Mar, Keith Oatley, Jacob Hirsh, and Jordan P. Peterson (2006) and David Comer Kidd and Emanuele Castano (2013) have published path-breaking work on the psychological impact of reading literary fiction; however, those studies concentrate on the effects of literary reading on intersubjectivity and social cognition, rather than on the appreciation of complexity outside of the social domain. More empirical work is needed to probe the link between formal complexity and the complexity of contemporary social and political challenges, including climate change. One thing is clear: sensitizing audiences to the complexity of the Anthropocene, and to the large-scale ramifications of our everyday actions, is likely to require more than mere exposure to fictional narrative, no matter how complex. Various institutions, from the educational system to the media and the scientific community, have to be involved in that effort, as well as in translating conceptual knowledge into a sense of ethical responsibility toward the nonhuman.[20] But fictional narrative, through its formal resources and imaginative and affective impact, should play an important part in that project.

PART I

Nonlinearity

CHAPTER 2

The Form of the Butterfly

The hallmark of complex systems, as we know from the previous chapter, is their emergent, self-organizing nature. Emergent behavior can lead to "butterfly effects": outcomes that seem highly unlikely from the standpoint of a linear, deterministic understanding of reality. An apparently inconsequential event in one area of the system, such as a butterfly flapping its wings in Brazil, can trigger dramatic consequences elsewhere in the system, such as a tornado in Texas. This phenomenon stems from both the interdependency of complex systems and their multiscalarity: a local occurrence travels upward in scale and brings about dramatic system-wide changes. The term "butterfly effect" has an intricate history, which Robert Hilborn (2004) reconstructs in detail. Edward Norton Lorenz, an American meteorologist and one of the fathers of chaos theory, used the phrase at a conference paper he gave in December 1972. However, in earlier writings Lorenz had talked about a seagull's—not a butterfly's—possible effects on the weather. The butterfly was apparently suggested to Lorenz as a more effective label by another meteorologist, Philip Merilees, the organizer of the session in which Lorenz presented his work in 1972. It was at this conference of the American Association for the Advancement of Science that Lorenz introduced the term as well as the now famous example of the causal link between a butterfly in Brazil and the weather in Texas. A butterfly also plays a central role in "A Sound of Thunder," a time travel narrative by American science fiction writer Ray Bradbury. "A Sound of Thunder" appeared in *Collier's* magazine in 1952 and seems eerily prescient of chaos theory, yet, as Hilborn points out, neither Lorenz nor Merilees were familiar with Bradbury's text when they named the effect.

There is a certain irony, of course, in this apparently fortuitous convergence on the image of the butterfly. Perhaps Bradbury's short story itself is a minor disturbance that rippled through culture and emerged, twenty years later, in a scientific theory, gaining increasing popularity also outside of scientific circles. What is certain is that "A Sound of Thunder" is a striking demonstration of the nonlinearity at the heart of complex systems. In Bradbury's story, a group of explorers embark on a very special safari: they travel back in time to hunt a dinosaur. The rules of engagement are extremely strict; with the now familiar science fiction trope, the time travelers are warned that, if they leave behind even a minute trace during their visit to prehistory, they run the risk of altering the future forever: "A dead mouse here makes an insect imbalance there, a population disproportion later, a bad harvest further on, a depression, mass starvation, and, finally, a change in *social* temperament in far-flung countries" (Bradbury 2004, 79). This is precisely the cumulative, exponential effect across great spatiotemporal distances that Lorenz described as a butterfly effect. To avoid triggering this potentially catastrophic chain reaction, the hunters can't stray from a prearranged metal walkway and have been instructed to kill a specific animal, which was bound to die shortly independently of the time travelers' intervention. However, at the sight of a T. rex, Eckels, one of the explorers, loses his nerve and steps off the path. Later, in the time machine, he examines his boots, discovering—to his companions' dismay—that he has crushed a butterfly.

Back in the present, everything seems in order at first, but Eckels detects that "there was a thing to the air, a chemical taint so subtle, so slight, that only a faint cry of his sublimal [sic] senses warned him it was there" (2004, 85). When Eckels turns around and sees the sign on the door, the change becomes far more palpable; it is embedded in the spelling of the English language:

TYME SEFARI INC.
SEFARIS TU ANY YEER EN THE PAST.
YU NAIM THE ANIMALL.
WEE TAEK YU THAIR.
YU SHOOT ITT. (2004, 85–86)

The time travelers also learn that the United States has a different president, one ideologically close to fascism. These twists are so surprising because Bradbury, like the story's readers, works from the perspective of a nature/culture binary in which language and politics are seen as insulated from the ecosystemic effects triggered by a butterfly's death. But, while in Lorenz's butterfly example emergent behavior manifests itself across a spatial distance (from Brazil to Texas), in Bradbury's short story it is narrative *time* that takes center stage. The timeline of the story captures the strange circularity of how a human character can bring about cultural and political changes by acting on the nonhuman world. This circular enmeshment takes a form reminiscent of the "strange loops" theorized by Douglas Hofstadter in *Gödel, Escher, Bach:* a phenomenon that "occurs whenever, by moving upwards (or downwards) through the levels of some hierarchical system, we unexpectedly find ourselves back where we started" (1999, 18). The system, in Bradbury's tale, is primarily that of narrative time, with its bifurcation between story (the implied chronology of the represented events) and discourse (the narrative presentation of that chronology).[1] The story level traces a loop through time travel, by going backward and then forward along the timeline of evolutionary history. Even more interesting, the discourse of Bradbury's narrative also loops back on itself. The text of the sign on the office door appears twice in the short story: on the first page, in standard English spelling, and, in the story's ending, with the strangely altered spelling. Likewise, the titular image of the "sound of thunder" is repeated twice in the text: it is the narrator's characterization of the T. rex's roar (2004, 81), and it describes—in the story's last line—the blast of a rifle as Travis, the expedition leader, shoots Eckels for changing the course of history (2004, 86). These echoes from prehistory to the modern world complicate the pattern traced by the narrative: the repercussions of Eckels's unintentional killing of a butterfly travel in unexpected directions, leading to cultural and political shifts but also to Eckels's own death. Put otherwise, the story's causality works toward amplifying the background unpredictability of narrative sequence (as discussed in the previous chapter): the plot operates in an emergent and looping fashion, insofar as Eckels gets caught up in the deadly consequences of his own inadvertent action. The linearity of the narrative is thus challenged, an impression reinforced by the fact that the progression of the story is not goal-oriented: the outcome (Eckels's death, a fascist is elected president of the United States) emphatically and unpredictably deviates from the character's intentions. Underscored by the strategic repetitions in Bradbury's language, this narrative form becomes a stand-in for the integratedness of nature and culture—the impossibility of drawing a clear-cut line between the physical footprints left by Eckels on prehistoric soil and the structure of human language and culture.

These formal butterfly effects that disrupt the linearity of narrative time and causality are the focus of the present and the following chapter.

Linearity can break down either through plot organization (as in Bradbury's short story) or (as discussed in the next chapter) via negative devices that shatter the reader's imagination of the narrative into multiple possibilities and temporal planes. Such formal strategies can provide templates for thinking about the distinctive temporality of living in the Anthropocene. The link between the butterfly effect and the changing climate is anything but far-fetched. In an entry on the science website RealClimate, we read that Edward "Lorenz's discoveries and their implications played a central role in climate modelling efforts and in the most recent IPCC [Intergovernmental Panel on Climate Change] report" (2008).[2] At the time of writing, Europe and much of the Northern Hemisphere were in the throes of a historic heat wave that scientists agree (Schiermeier 2018) was made more likely by climate change. In a world of extreme weather events of increasing intensity and frequency—in a world of "global weirding," to use the term popularized by Thomas Friedman (2007) in a *New York Times* opinion piece—the impact of human industrial activity is emerging, and dramatically altering our lives, when and where we would least expect it.[3] This "weirdness" is also an aspect of the human-nonhuman mesh theorized by Morton. Narrative offers formal resources to model these surprising effects via strategic variations on the linear temporality and causality that we associate with storytelling.

An important reference point here is Manuel De Landa's *A Thousand Years of Nonlinear History* (1997), which takes up the concept of nonlinearity and the framework of complex systems to rethink world history since 1000 AD. In three dense chapters focusing, respectively, on geology, genetics, and language, De Landa explores the structural entanglement of human events with material processes. Even as De Landa's critique of linear and teleological models of progress is highly persuasive and relevant in the context of this book, the distinction De Landa draws between the notion of nonlinearity and its textual presentation is less convincing: "A nonlinear conception of history has absolutely nothing to do with a style of presentation, as if one could truly capture the nonequilibrium dynamics of human historical processes by jumping back and forth among the centuries" (1997, 15). This kind of form/content dualism is perhaps appropriate in a philosophical study (even though it is worth observing that De Landa's style departs repeatedly from his explicit statement), but form/content dualism is certainly not compatible with the new formalist agenda and literary corpus of this book. On the contrary, the epistemological value of nonlinearity can be demonstrated only by formally bending the linear presentation of narrative in ways that—like Lorenz's butterfly effect—elicit surprise and puzzlement. Thus, this chapter starts out by discussing how the notion of narrative nonlinearity can be systematized in light of scholarship in both narrative theory and cognitive literary studies. After this theoretical discussion, two formal strategies of plot organization will be examined—namely, "looping temporality" (a device related to the pattern at work in Bradbury's short story) and "discontinuous sampling." Both strategies destabilize narrative linearity and hold particular promise for an investigation of how story can figure human-nonhuman enmeshment. My case studies are Julio Cortázar's "The Night Face Up" (1956) and Ted Chiang's "Story of Your Life" (1998) for looping temporality, and Dale Pendell's *The Great Bay* (2010) for discontinuous sampling. The chapter closes by reexamining two examples discussed in the previous chapter (Richard Powers's novel *The Overstory* and Richard McGuire's comic strip *Here*) to present further spatial models of plot organization that challenge linearity: the network and the rhizome.

GOALS, PATHS, AND IMAGE SCHEMATA

Narrative, as discussed in the introduction, is a practice calibrated to reflect the cognitive biases of human audiences. As fundamentally social animals, we take an intrinsic interest in other people's mental states, such as beliefs, desires, intentions, and long-term goals. A growing body of scholarship in psychology and the philosophy of mind suggests that stories are centrally involved in the negotiation of these mental states. Philosopher Daniel Hutto (2008) takes a developmental perspective, arguing that narrative is key to the constitution of a "folk psychology," in that it enables children to coordinate with the mental states of other individuals.[4] For psychologists Mar and Oatley (2008), narrative is a form of simulation—a vicarious enactment of social experience. Likewise, but from an evolutionary perspective, Michelle Scalise Sugiyama (2001) suggests that storytelling developed to help humans navigate increasingly complex sociocultural contexts, storing—in an external, public form—knowledge about the social world and its norms.[5]

Given narrative's embedding in the social world, the anthropocentric bias of storytelling practices comes as no surprise. Prototypical stories—those that strike audiences as highly significant or "tellable"—foreground the interactions of anthropomorphic subjects.[6] This is why E. M. Forster's "The king died, then the queen died of grief" (1955, 86), discussed in the previous chapter, works so well as an example of plot: it centers on characters linked by two attributes, mortality and emotional attachment, that have enormous psychological significance for animals like us. Mortality and attachment (with its close associate, sexual desire), as Peter Brooks argued in *Reading for the Plot* (1984), are the engines of narrative progression. Further, Forster's story is grounded in *mental causation:* the queen's death is caused by the king's death not in merely physical terms, but psychologically ("of grief").

In *Possible Worlds, Artificial Intelligence, and Narrative Theory*, Marie-Laure Ryan builds on this insight into the primacy of mental states in narrative to develop a comprehensive account of plot. In her words, a "network of mental constructs . . . [underlies] human action in general and narrative action in particular. Insofar as these constructs reflect on the history, past or future, of the narrative universe, they link states and events in a temporal sequence, and they present the same structure as the narrative of which they are a part" (1991, 147). What drives the progression of narrative is the interaction of characters' mental states—and particularly, for Ryan, of characters' desires and concrete plans to realize those desires. In Forster's minimal narrative, the progression is determined by a single mental state: the queen's attachment to the king. But, in longer and more complex narratives, the pattern of plot is based on the interplay of multiple characters' long-term goals—an interplay that typically leads to a conflict of some sort. For instance, the plot of "Little Red Riding Hood" (in Charles Perrault's version) unfolds as a function of two conflicting plans: Little Red Riding Hood's plan to deliver food to her grandmother (on her mother's instructions), and the wolf's desire to eat Little Red Riding Hood, which involves a carefully planned ruse. The story's outcome is directly tied to the wolf's goal and the girl's gullibility, both of which are a manifestation of their mental worlds. Extrapolating from this kind of analysis, Ryan suggests that the progression of narrative is closely coupled with the characters' intersecting desires, beliefs, and psychological dispositions. Of course, that coupling is not equally tight and salient in all instances of narrative. In general terms, the closer the match between characters' (and, in particular, the protagonist's) mental world and the events and actions that advance a plot, the more clearly a plot will be perceived as linear, because it will be easier for readers to establish causal and thematic coherence; humans are such avid mind readers that it becomes much easier to follow a temporal sequence (a plot, in this case) when it involves the orchestration of mental states in emotionally charged circumstances.[7]

The anomaly of Bradbury's "A Sound of Thunder" is that, while we can discern a number of mental states in the story, they do not fall into a unidirectional pattern from characters' goals to the outcome of the narrative. The mental states involved are the following: Eckers's plan to travel in time and hunt down a dinosaur; the explorers' desire to leave no traces so as not to alter the course of history; Eckers's panic upon seeing the T. rex, which leads to an unintentional action (killing a butterfly by straying off the prearranged path) that contravenes the explorers' desire; and Travis's anger and decision to kill Eckers. Trivially, it was not Eckers's plan to be killed by Travis, but, less trivially, that outcome hinges on a violation that can be imputed to Eckers and yet is *not* coupled with his desires and goals. The verbal repetitions in Bradbury's text (the door sign and the "sound of thunder") underscore the challenge to linearity by introducing—in incipient form—a circular logic. In this account, linearity in narrative is not an either/ or phenomenon, but it is scalable based on the closeness of the coupling between psychological causation and temporal progression.[8]

To better capture the loosening of the link between plot and characters' mental life, we can draw on the language of what cognitive linguists call "image schemata." A term introduced by philosopher Mark Johnson and linguist George Lakoff in the 1980s (Johnson 1987; Lakoff 1987), an image schema is a protoconceptual template that is derived from sensory experience and used to package abstract ideas in a convenient, readily intelligible format. For instance, the expression "work-life balance" does not refer to balance in the sense of "physical equilibrium," but it employs that embodied experience of balance, metaphorically, to conceptualize something much more abstract—namely, the ease of dividing one's time meaningfully between professional obligations and family life. "Balance" is, thus, an image schema in Johnson's and Lakoff's sense.[9] Image schemata help us think and talk about temporal experience, which is far more intangible than our physical interactions with space. Just as we use physical movement in space (i.e., of the sun or a clock's hands) to track the passage of time, we build on spatial image schemata to position events in time. For psychologist Lera Boroditsky (2000), there are two alternative systems for conceptualizing time through spatial movement: the "ego-moving" system, in which the subject is traveling through the medium of time ("we are approaching the Christmas holidays"), and the "object-moving" system, in which an event is seen as traveling toward or away from an unmoving subject ("the Christmas holidays will be here soon"). The image schema involved in both conceptualizations is "path," which proves to be an immensely useful way of expressing not just the passage of time but also structured temporal processes.

As narrative theorists of all stripes have long acknowledged, narrative is our primary means of capturing temporal experience in semiotic form: narrative is "the semiotic articulation of linear temporal sequence" (Walsh 2017, 473).[10] Richard Walsh's use of the word "linear" reflects the quasi-inevitability of conceptualizing not just time but *narrative* itself as a line or path connecting an initial state of affairs with a certain outcome. Narrative is at its most linear when the path it builds upon can be directly mapped onto a character's (usually, the protagonist's) plan. Of course, the path traced by narrative can be more or less winding. In most stories, and certainly in most interesting or nontrivial stories, the path-like progression of the protagonist toward his or her goal is obstructed: it can clash with other characters' plans (the wolf's desire to eat Little Red Riding Hood) or it can face other hurdles, such as an apparently insurmountable social barrier (e.g., Romeo and Juliet's marriage is made impossible by the history of rivalry between the two families).

Crucially, not only is the ideal goal-oriented movement of narrative based on the path image schema, but the factors that slow down or otherwise impede this movement can also be conceptualized as image schemata. If the embodied view of language and narrative comprehension is on the right track, audiences' engagement with narrative is grounded in somatic modes of interaction with the world.[11] Thus, just as the experience of goal-oriented movement in space structures our understanding of linear progression in time, our understanding of *deviations* from that ideal linearity will also be grounded in bodily interactions. Image schemata that reflect our perceptual experience of physical objects interacting and colliding in space (known as "force-dynamic" image schemata) are especially useful to describe those deviations: for instance, image schemata like "blockage," "counterforce," and "compulsion" (Evans and Green 2006, 188) capture well the dynamic of the complications that hinder or delay the protagonist's plan.

Producers and recipients of narrative will rarely be consciously aware of these image-schematic structures and how they shape their experience. In fact, the role of image schemata is mostly unconscious; they underlie audiences' experience, and (in a scholarly context) they can be used productively to analyze the dynamics of that experience. What does emerge in awareness, however, is the affective patterning created by characters' goals and how they bump into—and obstruct—one another. To understand this affective dimension, we can return to the conflict between Little Red Riding Hood's plan and the wolf's desire: readers form certain expectations as they engage with the tale (e.g., "Little Red Riding Hood will deliver the food to her grandmother"; "the wolf will kill Little Red Riding Hood"; "Little Red Riding Hood will realize that the wolf is not her grandmother"); these expectations are updated as readers read, changing emotional valence in the process and creating a distinctive affective trajectory. Put otherwise, we may not experience image schemata directly, but we generally experience what Michel Kimmel (2009), who also discusses literary narrative in terms of image schemata, calls their "affective contour": the emotional curve created by readers' changing expectations as they engage with a story.

This cognitive linguistics-inspired discussion suggests that talk about linearity in narrative is more than a mere figure of speech: it has to do with how plot, through the implication of characters' goals and plans, can fall into an affective pattern whose spatial form reflects physical motion along a "path." Narrative can—and does—complicate this progression, but, as highlighted by Ryan (1991), the plot remains typically tied to the goals of one or more narrative agents, so that the path schema rarely drops out of the picture completely. By contrast, in the narratives that will be examined in the following sections the path image schema is actively challenged as the progression becomes uncoupled from the characters' goals and the mental states that underlie them. This process leads to surprising situations and outcomes—the equivalent of the butterfly effect in narrative form. Bradbury's "A Sound of Thunder" offers a first example of this nonlinear strategy through the dramatic consequences of Eckers's unintended killing of a butterfly. The text, as we've seen, also foregrounds Eckers's entanglement in the effects of his action through strategic linguistic repetitions at the beginning and at the end of the text; one way to express this idea is to say that the "loop" image schema takes precedence over "path." The next section turns to two short stories that embrace this looping logic to an even greater extent than Bradbury's: "The Night Face Up" by Julio Cortázar and "Story of Your Life" by Ted Chiang. Both texts follow a circular schema that unsettles ontological and temporal distinctions, as well as the expectation that the progression of narrative is linearly driven by the protagonist's mental states. The section that follows discusses a different case of nonlinearity: one in which the path of story does not loop back on itself, but is interrupted by unexplained temporal gaps that create a sense of both fragmentation and repetition, with a complete breakdown of linear progression. The case study in that section will be Dale Pendell's postapocalyptic "chronicle" *The Great Bay*. The conclusion expands on two spatial schemata encountered in the previous chapter—the network and the rhizome—that also challenge linear models of plot, with the rhizome being the most radical and mesh-like instance of narrative nonlinearity.

LOOPING TEMPORALITY IN "THE NIGHT FACE UP" AND "STORY OF YOUR LIFE"

Through image schemata, our basic understanding of time and causality is grounded in the experience of moving our bodies and interacting with objects in space. But concepts of time and causality are also fundamentally shaped by culture.[12] In an article that reappraises arguments on linguistic relativity (the "Sapir-Whorf" hypothesis), Boroditsky (2010) offers a number of fascinating examples of the influence of language on cognition, via the experience of time: native speakers of Arabic or Hebrew (languages that are written from right to left) understand time to move in the same right-to-left direction, opposite to the perceived direction of time in the Western world. For speakers of Aymara, the language of an indigenous people of the Andes, the future is behind their back, because they can't see it yet, and the past is in front, because they can remember and therefore experience it. For members of the Pormpuraaw community in Australia, time flows from east to west, like the sun; the direction of the future is thus adjusted according to their spatial position. If they face south, time goes from left to right; if they face north, it travels in the opposite direction, right to left; if they face east, time travels through their body, westbound.

The conceptualization of time we have examined in the previous section is based on a universal experience, that of physical movement along a *path*. However, the idea of the "movement" of time as fixed and unidirectional is anything but a cultural universal. It is widely known that Western views of time have come to privilege the sequential, irreversible model that Stephen Jay Gould (1987, 11), among many others, discusses under the heading of "time's arrow." Notions of progress and technological or social advancement in the West are bound up with this linear way of thinking about temporality and history. Yet ideas of cyclicity—now largely dormant in the West—have structured the temporal experience of many cultures.[13] In "The Night Face Up" and "Story of Your Life," Cortázar and Chiang draw on an imaginary non-Western culture (pre-Columbian, in Cortázar; extraterrestrial, in Chiang) to inscribe a cyclical schematization of time into the formal logic of narrative. This strategy destabilizes a linear understanding of progression in a way that opens up intriguing formal (as well as thematic) possibilities.

"The Night Face Up" begins with an unnamed character riding a motorbike through an unnamed city. Unexpectedly, a woman dashes onto the road in front of him; it is too late to brake, and, in an attempt to avoid a head-on collision, the biker veers left and falls off the bike. He doesn't seem to be hurt too badly, but he is still taken to the hospital, where he is given a sedative while lying on a stretcher—face up, as in the story's title. As soon as the protagonist starts dreaming, he realizes that "it was unusual as a dream because it was full of smells, and he never dreamt smells" (1985, 69). He also grasps the situation instantly: a member of the Moteca tribe, he is in a forest being pursued by the Aztecs as part of a ritual war; he is running for his life. The dream is vivid and unsettling enough, but soon the character wakes up in the hospital, surrounded by other patients and all the comforts of modernity. Yet, surprisingly, when he falls asleep again the nightmare continues from where it left off; after two of these cycles (from the hospital to the pre-Columbian forest, and back), the short story effectively establishes two parallel plotlines. The plotlines are defined by three semantic oppositions: historical (modern vs. pre-Columbian world), cognitive (reality vs. dream), and emotional (safety of the hospital vs. deadly pursuit in the forest). What provides continuity between the two plotlines is the character's subjectivity—relayed by Cortázar's internal focalization—and soon also his spatial position: when he is taken prisoner by the Aztecs, the protagonist is bound face up, mirroring exactly the way in which he lies on the hospital bed. In the dream story line, his fate is clear: he is being taken through an underground passage; when "the stars came out up there instead of the roof and the great terraced steps rose before him, on fire with cries and dances, it would be the end" (1985, 74).

Soon the anxiety of the looming execution starts seeping into the reality of the hospital: the nightmares are more and more frequent, and we see the character struggling to remain awake in order to escape death in the dream world. In the story's final twist, the opposition between dream and reality is inversed, and the character suddenly realizes "he was not going to wake up, that he was awake, that the marvelous dream had been the other, absurd as all dreams are—a dream in which he was going through the strange avenues of an astonishing city, with green and red lights that burned without fire or smoke, on an enormous metal insect that whirred away between his legs" (1985, 76). Just as the revelation comes as a shock to the protagonist, readers have been tricked into assigning ontological priority to what came first in the text, seeing the pre-Columbian story line as a nightmare grafted onto a reassuring—to us, and to the character—modern world. The inversion builds up to the defamiliarizing vision of the motorbike as an "enormous metal insect," which blatantly contradicts the familiarity with modern technology that the story's first scene suggests.

The story is thus an instance of what Cornelia Klecker (2013) calls "mind-tricking narrative," which features a final twist prompting the audience to fundamentally revise their interpretation of the events. Of special interest in "The Night Face Up" is the narrative form that the trick takes. Considered in itself, each story line clearly traces a path-like pattern, complete with explicit character goals and plans (recovering from the accident and later avoiding sleep, in the hospital; escaping capture in what is initially presented as the protagonist's nightmare). The two story lines are interlaced throughout most of the story, but the final inversion disrupts the linearity of the pattern, turning it into far more than a formal juxtaposition: what we experience is a character gradually becoming entangled in his dream world as his attention and anxieties shift from the motorbike accident to the pre-Columbian chase. The spatial form of the character's entanglement is that of a strange loop, with his physical position in space (his lying "face up") occupying the center of the loop—the place where the temporal-causal pattern bends on itself. The loop schema is reinforced by how the ending prompts a reinterpretation of the beginning, sending readers "back" to the first scene. Importantly, in this ending, the spatial and formal logic of the loop overrides any concern over psychological realism: If the city of the beginning is but a dream, why did the character seem so at ease in that modern world? The question misses the point: the protagonist's mental states are not the primary factor in the organization of plot, because a twisted (and in that sense fully dreamlike) logic trumps the teleological coherence of goals and intentions.

Cortázar's choice of a loop schema was perhaps inspired by the fact that the story's events take place during a *ritual* war. The epigraph reads as follows: "At certain periods they went out to hunt enemies; they called it the war of the blossom" (1985, 67). The entangled form of the text encodes something essential both about the cyclicity of the rite and about the ghastly experience of physical capture that the Aztecs' enemies undergo. Also central to the text is the coupling between human societies and the natural world: in the pre-Columbian story line the protagonist engages with his physical environment (its odor, its colors, the protection it affords) in a fully embodied way, marking a sharp departure from the human-made bubble of the hospital. In the reader's experience, this embodied loop between the human subject and the nonhuman world becomes blended with the nonlinear plot pattern.

In "Story of Your Life," Chiang goes a step further, building the challenge to linear notions of time into the very premise of his narrative. Adapted by Denis Villeneuve into the movie *Arrival* in 2016, "Story of Your Life" belongs to the popular science fiction strand of narratives of first contact with an alien species. The tentacular "heptapods" land on Earth for no apparent reason other than establishing communication with humans. The narrator, a linguist, is contacted by the US Army to help decode the aliens' mysterious language. In a series of encounters with the aliens, the narrator realizes that writing is a more viable channel of communication than speech. The aliens' writing system, while baffling at first (it looks like "fanciful praying mantids drawn in a cursive style, all clinging to each other"; 2016, 112), follows a logic that the narrator feels confident she can reverse-engineer. In the process, she comes to understand a great deal about the aliens' way of thinking about time and causality. The heptapods' writing uses highly complex and integrated signs whose most striking feature is that, from the very first stroke, the aliens seem to know what the pattern will look like in the end. The strokes are "so interconnected that none could be removed without redesigning the entire sentence" (2016, 123). The narrator's inference is that this way of writing reflects an essential feature of the aliens' time consciousness—their understanding situations holistically and not in terms of cause-effect sequentiality. For instance, in the case of a ray of light being refracted by water in a glass, the aliens see the light as "wanting" to travel through the water in the most efficient way—which means that the light has to "know" from the beginning where it will end, just as the alien writer has to know from the outset how each stroke will fit into the structure of the sign it is about to create.

On the one hand, then, the aliens ascribe intentionality to the inanimate world, perceiving it in terms of teleological goals instead of mechanical causes and effects. On the other hand, they experience teleology itself in a way that is profoundly different from the human "path" image schema (an ideal trajectory connecting an intention with a desired outcome). The aliens' teleological thinking has no "orientation" in time; it involves a simultaneous vision of the events falling into a temporal sequence, as well as their interrelation. As the narrator describes this fundamental cognitive difference, humans "had developed a sequential mode of awareness, while heptapods had developed a simultaneous mode of awareness. We experienced events in an order, and perceived their relationship as cause and effect. They experienced all events at once, and perceived a purpose underlying them all" (2016, 134). Heptapod time is self-contained and highly integrated, like the aliens' writing; it is organized around circles of time, with the final state determining the initial state. Chiang's story spells out that this circular time consciousness directly matches the aliens' physical makeup: we learn that their bodies display "radial symmetry," that they "have no 'forward' direction, so maybe their writing doesn't either" (2016, 105).

The narrative thus resonates with contemporary arguments on the embodiment of our cognitive makeup (A. Clark 1997; Gibbs 2005). Culture—in this case, the aliens' writing system—is both shaped by their physical bodies and fundamentally bound up with their perception of the physical world, which offers an experience of teleological circularity instead of the cause-effect sequentiality typical of human thinking. Recall how the ideal direction of time is from right to left for individuals used to writing in Arabic or Hebrew: the aliens' time consciousness in "Story of Your Life" is a radical example of that coupling between experience and writing technologies. Recall also, in a different context, how Bradbury's time travel story reveals the interrelation between the history of the nonhuman world and human language, via the shift in English spelling brought about by the protagonist's action in prehistory.

In Chiang's story the butterfly effect of culture's integration with the material world is anything but a local conceit; on the contrary, it permeates the text by informing a secondary plotline, which focuses on the narrator's daughter and counterpoints the first-contact narrative. The text begins, in the present tense, with the narrator conjuring up the moment in which she was asked by her partner if she wanted to have a child: "Your father is about to ask me the question. This is the most important moment in our lives, and I want to pay attention, note every detail" (2016, 91). The addressee, the "you," is the narrator's daughter, whom we will get to know through a series of passages interspersed into the main plot. Some of the most important events in the daughter's life—from her childhood to college graduation via her parents' separation—are narrated in this oblique way. Gradually, it emerges that the narrator's daughter died at twenty-five in a rock-climbing accident, a revelation that sheds new light on the second-person sections: a grieving narrator is reexperiencing her daughter's life as she comes to terms with her premature death. Yet, even though these events apparently presuppose retrospective knowledge of how the story of the daughter's life will end, the text alternates present and future tense, creating a striking contrast with the more conventional past tense of the heptapod story line: for instance, "I remember one day during the summer when you're sixteen.... You'll have a friend of yours, a blond girl with the unlikely name of Roxie, hanging out with you, giggling" (2016, 102). The anomaly of the present- and future-tense narrative conveys the mother's disorientation at the sudden loss of her daughter, but it also suggests that, through prolonged exposure to the heptapods' writing, the narrator has partly integrated their time consciousness. "My worldview is an amalgam of human and heptapod," she remarks (2016, 140). Ultimately, we may wonder: Are these sections truly retrospective, as a naturalistic reading of the story would suggest, or are they rather prospections of a narrator who has nonhuman knowledge of future outcomes? The question remains undecidable, just as the tense system of human languages, with the present wedged between a knowable past and an uncertain future, ceases to matter: the narrator comes to experience her own life, and her daughter's, as an integrated whole.[14]

The resulting "amalgam" gives particular poignancy to the narrator's grief. In the heptapods' floating time consciousness, the daughter's birth and death are copresent in a simultaneous apprehension of her life. That much the narrator can conceive, or at least begin to understand. But it is much more difficult for the narrator to reconcile her loss (whether located in the past or in the future) with the teleological nature of that temporal pattern—the knowledge that, from a heptapod perspective, death was not an accident tragically interrupting a trajectory that should have continued into the future; rather, it was an outcome inherent in every moment of her daughter's life. Death is spliced into life, creating a loop-like pattern that the final paragraph of the story makes explicit, with a return to the situation captured in the beginning: the daughter's father-to-be asking the narrator, "Do you want to make a baby?" (2016, 146).

The narrative thus breaks with the path image schema at multiple levels: it rejects an understanding of human life whereby premature death is seen as a dramatic deviation from an established path; it destabilizes the idea of grief itself as a linear process marked by specific stages (a popular, if increasingly contested, idea introduced by Kübler-Ross in 1969); finally, it undercuts the identification of narrative progression with meaningful goals, plans, and outcomes. Even the aliens' departure is abrupt and inexplicable: "We never did learn why the heptapods left, any more than we learned what brought them here, or why they acted the way they did" (2016, 144). This is the central irony of Chiang's story: it foregrounds, through engagement with the aliens' consciousness, a teleological explanation of time even as it prevents readers from imposing a meaningful *human* teleology on the narrated events themselves. If there is teleology at work here, it is a deeply nonhuman one, and that is the crux of both the narrator's grief and the reader's puzzlement.

The loop schema that displaces linear temporality is analogous to Cortázar's narrative technique in "The Night Face Up," and it also involves two story lines that fold back into one another in a surprising way—a "strange loop," in Hofstadter's sense (1999). But the exact position of the fold is less easily identifiable in Chiang's story than it is in Cortázar's: there is no recognizable "trick" here, no moment that suddenly reconfigures the reader's understanding and affective experience of the plot. Indeed, the daughter's death is implied multiple times before the narrator confirms our growing suspicions. Instead, the loop is demonstrated throughout the text by the shifting verb tenses and undecidable temporality as the narrator tries to gain a perspective on the events that approximates—uncomfortably—the aliens' simultaneous time consciousness.

DISCONTINUOUS SAMPLING IN *THE GREAT BAY*

Neither "The Night Face Up" nor "Story of Your Life" uses form to obvious ecological ends, but their challenge to the path image schema as a structuring principle for narrative bears a striking resemblance to the loop of humanity's entanglement in the nonhuman world. With Dale Pendell's *The Great Bay: Chronicles of the Collapse* we enter the domain of explicitly ecological narrative, within a postapocalyptic framework (a genre that will be discussed in more detail in the next chapter).[15]

While presented as a "novel" on the frontispiece of my edition, the term "chronicles" in the subtitle is perhaps a more accurate categorization of this text, which lacks the narrative continuity associated with the genre of the novel. These chronicles trace a fictional history of the catastrophic consequences of an epidemic that, compounded by global warming, decimates the human species in 2021.[16] What kind of history is a "chronicle"? For Fludernik, who discusses the relationship between history and narrativity in *Towards a "Natural" Narratology*, "as soon as history started to become more narrative, improving on the early forms of the annals and chronicles with their unrelated presentation of 'one thing after another,' it was the pattern of the great life, and hence of regal biography, that flourished with much success, and this was a pattern that allowed for a skilful combination of the personal and the historical (i.e. political)" (1996, 18).

Fludernik argues that annals and chronicles—unlike later forms of historiography—should *not* be considered narrative because they do not display what is, for her, the defining feature of story: namely, a centralized focus on the experience and evaluations of one or more characters (Fludernik's "experientiality"). We may or may not agree with Fludernik's equation between narrativity and experientiality (for discussion, see Caracciolo 2014b, 47–48), but she seems fundamentally right to say that the "unrelated presentation of 'one thing after another,'" as in a mere list of discrete events, is unlikely to tell a compelling story. *The Great Bay* is a case in point: we find no "pattern of the great life" in Pendell's text—indeed, we struggle to find an overarching pattern at the level of story. Yet, because the text constantly plays with the reader's expectation of narrative continuity (partly through the paratextual reference to the novel as the narrative genre *par excellence*), narrative theory remains a productive framework for analyzing these chronicles. Weik von Mossner (2014) has already engaged with *The Great Bay* in an article where she remarks on the ambitious scope of Pendell's vision, but also on its inability to sustain the reader's interest—largely, because of the absence of a human protagonist. However, what Weik von Mossner treats as an artistic shortcoming seems to me central to the book's radical disruption of narrative teleology: the slow pace and even the monotony that may accompany the experience of reading *The Great Bay* underpin that aesthetic agenda. As we'll see, Pendell asks us to read in a significantly different way from prototypical narrative (and novelistic) practices, as a step toward distancing ourselves from anthropocentric assumptions.

The presentation of *The Great Bay* is highly fragmentary. The text begins with a "Memorandum for the Colleagues of Thermocene Studies" announcing the discovery of a cemetery dating to the time before the catastrophe. "Colleagues of Thermocene Study," we find out at the very end of the book, is the name of a historical society active sixteen thousand years after the collapse of the world as we (contemporary readers) know it. The "Memorandum" is followed by an excerpt, dated 2021, from "the last issue of the *New York Times,*" whose headlines announce the extreme measures taken by the US government to curb the catastrophic epidemic. The twelve chapters of *The Great Bay* continue in this haphazard vein, building on a mixture of genres.

Every chapter is introduced by a section titled "panoptic" that relates, in a quasi-scientific register, broad geological and sociopolitical developments in the period covered by the chapter, as well as more local events. Within the chapters, most sections focus on the character they are named after; the section headings indicate that these materials come from various sources, including Janet Conway's book *Stories of the Collapse* (published by the "Archives of the Scholar's Guild, Berkeley"), the "Library of the Order of Antiquities," and the already mentioned "Colleagues of Thermocene Studies" (in the last chapter). The first four chapters contain interviews conducted by Janet Conway, whose death is announced in a telegraph-like insert in chapter 4. The interviews are discontinued after chapter 5. After the panoptic, chapter 6 consists in entries from the journal of Solomon, a Buddhist monk, who is traveling through California.

Taken in isolation, most of these sections do show a high degree of narrativity—with chapter 6 being the most sustained narrative exercise in the book. There are also thematic echoes and diegetic "knots" in Schmitt's sense (2014) between the character-focused sections: for instance, a character in chapter 5 is presented as the "great-great-great-granddaughter of Inez Vallejo" (2010, 108), whose interview with Janet Conway appears in chapter 3. However, these knots are too minor and occasional to crystallize in a plot through-line or in a tight character network like the one created by Powers in *The Overstory*. In this way, *The Great Bay* mounts perhaps the most radical challenge to the path schema we have seen so far: there can be no linear teleology in Pendell's chronicle, no overarching sequence of intentions and actions, because the text stubbornly resists foregrounding characters whose beliefs and goals could drive the progression of the whole text. Partly, this is due to the fact that the time frame covered by each chapter increases gradually: a single decade for chapters 1 and 2, three decades for chapter 3, half a century for chapter 4, and so on until chapter 9 (a thousand years), chapter 10 (three thousand years), and chapter 11 (five thousand years). Chapter 12, the last one in the book, is vaguely titled "The Far

Millennia." Given the magnitude of the time periods involved, the absence of a central character or coherent character network appears justified by the disparity between the novel's timeline and the human life span.

The textual fragmentation also reflects a fundamental feature of the world portrayed by Pendell's chronicles. With the collapse of civilization, human communities have returned to a pretechnological state in which communication across vast distances is impossible. "Languages began diversifying, and people often had trouble understanding the speech of those who lived on the other side of a mountain pass" (2010, 216), leading to pockets of political and cultural isolation that the text explores in great (and at times lurid) detail. The proliferation of characters and also of genres and text types is a direct equivalent of this breakdown of linguistic and cultural authority.

The text proceeds by sampling characters, time frames, and episodes within these time frames, but no attempt is made to spell out the logic of the sampling. The only meaningful coordinates are provided by the chapters' expanding chronology and by the spatial setting—the titular Great Bay, formed by the flooding of coastal California (whose evolving geography is displayed by the maps that punctuate the book). Yet these coordinates are incidental to the characters' efforts. *The Great Bay* thus flaunts the haphazardness of its own plot organization, resulting in a marked affective distance from the subject matter—a distance that, for some readers, can easily tip over into boredom. Certainly, most of the characters we encounter are dismissed, often summarily and violently, before readers can develop an emotional connection with them. Nowhere does that distanced perspective on human affairs emerge more clearly than in the panoptic chapters, where the narrator discusses, in the same breath and with no apparent concern for coherence, the planetary changes that mark each epoch and various inconsequential bits of information about the life of human communities: "In 2150 Greenland was bare. Much of the Arctic ice was gone and it was still getting warmer" (2010, 97) is followed, within the same section, by "In 2180 a chess craze spread across the Bay, with championship matches held at the Mechanics Club in San Francisco" (2010, 103–4).

It is legitimate to wonder about the identity of the narrator responsible for the montage of the chapters—and for voicing these panoptic interludes. At times, the narrator appears to articulate a deeply biocentric point of view that we can identify with the Great Bay itself, which is perhaps the book's only true protagonist (see chapter 4 on what I call "promotion of place to character"): "Grasses flourished in the new valley, and during the winter months tens of thousands of sand hill cranes filled the meadows and wetlands. People imitated their dances" (2010, 262). People fuse with the natural world in a way that suggests that the human-nonhuman distinction ceases to matter from the vantage point of large-scale, geological time. But at other times the narrator's voice takes on recognizably human tones—for example, when remarking ironically that, by avoiding outright extinction, "class *Mammalia* had dodged a bullet and everyone knew it" (2010, 268). That informal idiom, "dodging a bullet," stands out from the flat scientific tone of these pages, almost as an in-joke directed at the contemporary reader (in Pendell's postapocalyptic world, humanity quickly runs out of ammunition). The indeterminacy of the narrator's figure, along with the vagueness of the "Far Millennia" in the last chapter, contribute to challenging expectations about the linearity and teleology of the telling: there is no recognizable endpoint to the organization of the book, no obvious retrospective position from which we can view, and evaluate, the expanse of human history.

Teleological progression gives way to discontinuous sampling; the only pattern we can discern, partly replacing the stringent logic of narrative, is the abstract geometry of the book's timeline, coupled with the constantly shifting coast line of California. Instead of a path with a clear destination or the precise (if disorienting) loop of Cortázar and Chiang, this pattern is something like a "golden spiral," a curve whose sections become wider (by a fixed factor) after each turn: every chapter increases the temporal distance from anthropogenic catastrophe by a larger time frame, from the ten years of chapter 1 to the five thousand years of chapter 11. This progression, which is nonlinear in mathematical terms, culminates in the temporally open ending of chapter 12 (whose complete title reads "The Far Millennia: Beginning Ten Thousand Years After the Collapse"). The book thus implies that the end of the world is only a new "beginning," and that the spiral will continue unfolding, indefinitely, into the future.

However, the temporal expansion is accompanied by moments of unexpected return of humanity's past—butterfly effects produced as the spiral of time bends on itself. In the last character-focused section (titled "The Caribou Hunters" and set sixteen thousand years after the catastrophe), a sparse humanity has gone back to cave painting. Yet, as the narrator notes, their art "lacked the magical optimism and the sense of unlimited power that had characterized the paintings of their predecessors forty and fifty thousand years before them" (2010, 267–68). Perhaps this is a hopeful note, a suggestion that humans have learned their lesson about how easily that "sense of unlimited power" can backfire. The arrow of technological progress (and of path-like narrative teleology) breaks down, making room for a sense of cyclicity that is strikingly demonstrated by the mythical tone of the last novel's episode. While the chapters closer to the disaster don't shy away from the trappings of postapocalyptic fiction (ruthless rulers, widespread violence, desperate attempts at rebuilding a social order), as time advances the atmosphere becomes more rarefied. The preapocalyptic reality with which the book's actual readers are familiar is transfigured into myth: "When the First World had burned, according to the stories, there had been so much smoke that the people had all turned dark—not on the outside, but on the inside—so that their dreams were dark" (2010, 227). Realism is displaced by a logic that is both metonymic and metaphoric: the smoke that caused the catastrophe—the burning of fossil fuels that polluted the atmosphere and raised global temperatures—blends metonymically with the smoke *caused* by the catastrophe, which is in turn metaphorically internalized, made into the stuff of people's dreams. Such displacements are the distinctive feature of myth, and Pendell's book gradually but resolutely embraces them.

In "The Caribou Hunters," the last section, a character named Sengimet kills a reindeer without knowing "that it was his younger wife who was out looking for the deer herd" (2010, 269). Sengimet and his second wife, Ridiwyn, grieve for so long that "the gods took pity on them and changed both of them into reindeer" (2010, 270) so that they could continue searching for Jennith, the slain wife-deer. As the book's last sentence explains, Sengimet and Ridiwyn "wandered far to the north to the frozen country and then they climbed into the sky, and that's where they still are [with Jennith]—those three bright stars, Vega, Deneb, and Thuban, that circle around the pole, chasing each other and marking the way north" (2010, 270). The closing image of the book is, thus, a circular chase, and it offers an interpretive key—steeped in myth—to the organization of the episodes contained in the book.

The circular schema stands for a prescientific conception of history as "eternal return" (Eliade 2005), but also points to the "feedback loops" of the climate announced by the narrator in the panoptic section of chapter 6. It is also significant that the book's most extended narrative, in chapter 6, is a diary composed by "a Buddhist monk of the Zen persuasion" (2010, 142), given the centrality of the cycle of life in Buddhist doctrine. *The Great Bay* encourages a reading strategy reminiscent of what Jan Alber, in a different context, calls "the Zen way of reading," which "presupposes an attentive and stoic reader who repudiates . . . explanations and simultaneously accepts both the strangeness of unnatural scenarios and the feelings of discomfort, fear, worry, and panic that they might evoke in him or her" (2016, 54). The explanations that Pendell's book asks us to discard are the teleological ones; feelings of deep discomfort and even boredom emerge as we are exposed to so many disconnected narratives without a full-fledged human protagonist coming to the fore and driving—through his or her experiences—the narrative progression. But the benefits of this Zen way of reading are remarkable. From the vantage point of millennia after the catastrophe, climate science and myth seem to fuse: characters live and die in an eternal chase, just like the geological epochs whose scale gradually spirals out of the narrator's control. Ultimately, the form of Pendell's book remediates this chase through a dialogue with both science and myth, disrupting path-like structures in an attempt to keep readers from thinking linearly and teleologically about the Earth's history.

Butterfly effects—"freak" events that pop up across spatiotemporal scales—challenge a linear, deterministic understanding of reality. The science of complex systems has started to grasp such anomalous events; literary writing can help make them more readily imaginable. Plot is normally coupled with characters' beliefs, evaluations, and intentions in a way that privileges a linear structure; in the terminology of cognitive linguistics, narrative tends to follow a "source-path-goal" image schema centered on the characters' mental world. However, by disrupting the spatial conceptualization of narrative progression as a path, literature can create formal equivalents of butterfly effects across scalar levels.

The narratological analysis in this and the previous chapter has brought into view four spatial models of plot organization that resist the path schema. The first is the discontinuous progression of Pendell's novel, which can be compared to a dotted line. This model resists linearity *from within,* building on a linear (sequential) structure but also disrupting it via a highly fragmentary organization. Pendell uses discontinuous sampling to effectively distance plot from expectations of teleology and emotional relevance, fostering a Zen-like mindset in readers who are willing to put up with the chronicle's lack of a central character. The second nonlinear spatial model is the loop in Cortázar's and Chiang's short stories: a structure that undercuts teleology, as we have seen, but also creates a paradoxical sense of closure. These narratives loop into their own beginnings, destabilizing ontological distinctions between dream and reality (in the former text) and temporal sequentiality (in the latter)—and eliciting puzzlement and disorientation in the process. Frammartino's film *Le quattro volte*, examined in the previous chapter, also embraces a looping structure, but here the effect is contemplative distance rather than puzzlement. Thirdly, linearity can be disrupted by way of a network-line plot organization, as in Richard Powers's *The Overstory*, where the lives of nine characters, first presented as independent from one another, converge and become increasingly intertwined. The novel develops a complex character system, centered, diegetically, on five characters who become involved in ecoterrorist activities and, thematically, on an insight into the ecological importance of plants. Powers's virtuoso ability to weave together these strands throughout the novel and sew them up in the ending is highly satisfying, as discussed in the previous chapter. Finally, the most radically nonlinear of these spatial models is the rhizome of McGuire's comic strip *Here*, which employs a highly decentralized form of narrative organization: because temporal sequentiality and causal coherence exist only at the local level (between specific panels or inserts), the text fosters a plurality of connections and a sense of playful open-endedness.[17] As a narrative setup, the rhizome offers perhaps the closest formal approximation to the human-nonhuman mesh theorized by Morton.

A visualization of this typology is offered in figure 5.[18] While the difference between discontinuous progression and the loop should be straightforward, the distinction between the network and the rhizome calls for clarification. Both forms foreground multiplicity, but the network displays a more compact, centralized structure (hence Powers's focus on a "core" group of five characters) and a more closed ending than the rhizomatic organization found in *Here*. It should be noted that the distinction between these four spatial forms, and between linearity and nonlinearity itself, is not a categorical one, and several nonlinear forms may coexist within a narrative: Powers's *The Overstory*, for instance, combines a network with linear as well as loop-like elements. The decision as to what counts as the *dominant* form in a plot is certainly subjective. Some readers may see *The Overstory* as a more open plot than the previous chapter suggested, aligning it with the rhizome and not the network. Likewise, readers may emphasize the circular logic

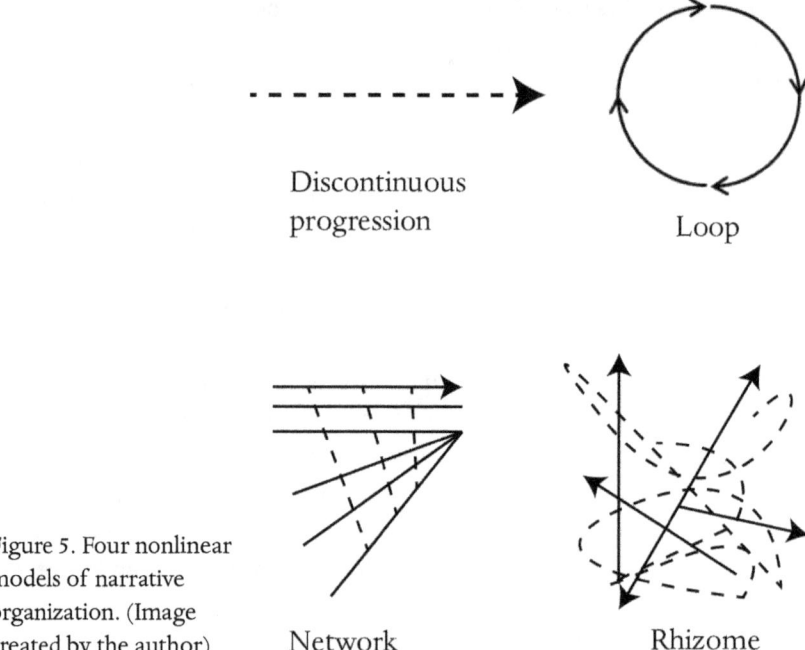

Figure 5. Four nonlinear models of narrative organization. (Image created by the author)

implicit in the mythical "chase" of Pendell's ending over discontinuities in presentation. These interpretive disagreements about the exact spatial form foregrounded by nonlinear narrative are less important than the overall impression of nonlinearity they project, and how that impression aligns with affective qualities (e.g., puzzlement, contemplative distance, or amazement at the complexity of the narrative architecture).

Nonlinear narrative can work against our basic propensity to think about temporality and causality in linear terms. This tendency has deep roots in human cognition and evolution. Work in developmental psychology (Baillargeon 2004) shows that children's capacity to reason about the physical world develops at an early stage: infants are surprisingly quick to grasp the "naïve" physics of bodies bumping into one another, objects falling to the ground, or liquids being poured into containers. These "small spatial stories," as cognitive literary scholar Mark Turner (1996, 14) calls them, form the basis for our understanding of causality as direct manipulation of the world. The physical manipulation of objects is *linear* in the sense that it is frequently goal-oriented and produces immediate consequences. However, if this model of causation is uncritically extended to spatiotemporal processes beyond the human scale, the linearity of embodied interaction will bias our thinking and prevent us from fully appreciating the behavior that emerges from human-nonhuman enmeshment: a sufficiently large number of everyday actions can have unforeseen consequences at a spatio-temporal remove—for instance, in the environmental impact of producing plastic or burning fossil fuels.

In a Western context, this cognitive predisposition toward linear cause-effect thinking is greatly enhanced by culture. According to De Landa, "Western thought has been dominated by notion of linear (nonreciprocal) causality for twenty-five hundred years" (1997, 67). Seen in this light, linearity is deeply bound up with the sequential model of technological progress and with an economic mindset that favors consumption over reutilization of resources. It is no coincidence that the image schema of the loop figures prominently in symbols for recycling. The Fifth Assessment Report released by the Intergovernmental Panel on Climate Change in 2014 points to linearity as one of the psychological biases responsible for the inadequacy of current responses to the ecological crisis. Linear heuristics lead people to misrepresent environmentally relevant metrics such as miles-per-gallon ratings in car; the result is that linearity encourages "wait-and-see behavior on policies that mitigate climate change" (IPCC 2014, 164). Thanks to the close link between linearity of form and affective impact, narrative has considerable potential to reshuffle these patterns of thinking, conveying to lay readers inherently "loopy" and complex phenomena such as humanity's entanglement in the current ecological and political predicament of the Anthropocene. By obstructing source-path-goal progression through formal schemata such as the discontinuous line, the loop, the network, and the rhizome, narrative can challenge the linear understanding of temporal processes in a way that—given appropriate framing—can have real-world implications for readers. The next chapter turns to *negation* as another affect-laden strategy through which narrative may promote nonlinear thinking about human-nonhuman relations.

CHAPTER 3

Negative Strategies and Nonlinear Temporality in Postapocalyptic Fiction

Literary scholars love catastrophe. From Maurice Blanchot's seminal *The Writing of the Disaster* (1986) to more recent work in ecocriticism (Rigby 2015), the subjects of catastrophe and disaster have been discussed extensively in literary scholarship. But the formal challenges raised by catastrophe have not been investigated as thoroughly or systematically; having introduced some of them with my reading of Pendell's postapocalyptic *The Great Bay*, this chapter takes a closer look at how the complex and nonlinear causality involved in catastrophic events can impact narrative practices.

Catastrophe consists, essentially, in an event that causes a radical instance of what David Herman (2009, 133–36) calls "world disruption." For Herman, world disruption and narrative worldmaking are two sides of the same coin: narrative worldmaking is triggered by events that destabilize the status quo of a world and are therefore surprising and highly tellable. Catastrophe owes its inherent tellability to the scale of the destabilization it brings about. In postapocalyptic fiction, catastrophic destabilization is built into the very structure of a storyworld: by definition, postapocalyptic fiction implies and foregrounds a catastrophic rupture between a preapocalyptic and a postapocalyptic state.[1] The former is typically aligned with present-day reality, while the latter is a dystopian world in which the few survivors face extremely harsh conditions and new social structures. At the same time, the postapocalyptic scenario reveals something about the preworld: as James Berger writes in *After the End*, the "apocalyptic event, in order to be properly apocalyptic, must in its destructive moment clarify and illuminate the true nature of what has been brought to an end" (1999, 5). More specifically, postapocalyptic fiction holds considerable potential for revealing the fundamental interdependency between human societies and the biological, geological, or climatological phenomena that led to the apocalyptic event. Thus, the genre raises formal questions that are both distinctive and indicative of the broader stakes involved in capturing the human-nonhuman mesh in narrative form.

The storyworlds constructed by postapocalyptic fiction are closely related to what Lubomír Doležel calls "dyadic worlds" (1998, 128–29), which are split into two domains characterized by distinct and often diametrically opposed conditions. But, whereas Doležel conceives of these domains as fundamentally *spatial* (they are distinct parts of a storyworld, as in Franz Kafka's *The Castle*, one of Doležel's examples), postapocalyptic fiction is dyadic in its temporal extension: its setting is rich in traces of the world before the catastrophe, which may be only implied or may be shown directly, through strategic flashbacks. Pendell's *The Great Bay*, for instance, implies the preworld through references such as the initial statement about the discovery of a cemetery pre-dating the catastrophe. The key narratological challenge raised by the genre is, then, evoking a preapocalyptic state via the *outcome* of a catastrophe. This challenge, as we'll see, unsettles at multiple levels the linear model of narrative temporality that builds on the "path" image schema. In a discussion of contemporary postapocalyptic fiction, Vermeulen takes issue with the genre for downplaying the difference between quasi-instantaneous nuclear annihilation and the gradual devastation wrought by climate change: "Post-apocalyptic fiction misrecognizes the differences between nuclear war (short and fast) and Anthropocene attrition (long and slow)" (2020, 154).[2] Vermeulen is right to draw attention to the slow pace of the ecological crisis, but his statement downplays the inherently dyadic temporality of postapocalyptic fiction, which can serve as a decelerating device. In this chapter's case studies, the preapocalyptic world emerges in unexpected ways and becomes blended nonlinearly with the postapocalyptic world, thus complicating and slowing down the reader's temporal experience of disaster.

The genre of postapocalyptic fiction has a long history. Mary Shelley's *The Last Man*, originally published in 1826, is typically hailed as the first postapocalyptic novel, inaugurating a rich strand of "last man" stories in which only a handful of humans are left on Earth, like latter-day Adams and Eves. In Shelley's novel, a plague outbreak kills all of humanity apart from three characters (including the narrator, Lionel Verney); unlike more recent instances of postapocalyptic narrative, however, there is no indication in *The Last Man* that the epidemic is of anthropogenic origin. The same is true for influential postapocalyptic stories written at the turn of the twentieth century by H. G. Wells ("The Star," an 1897 short story) and M. P. Shiel

(*The Purple Cloud,* a 1901 novel in the "weird" tradition), in both of which a mysterious cosmic force devastates humanity. In the second half of the twentieth century, the postapocalyptic imagination was fueled by Cold War anxieties of nuclear annihilation and started to engage with the possibility of human-induced cataclysm.[3] J. G. Ballard's *The Drowned World* (1962), for instance, is considered a particularly influential prefiguration of contemporary novels addressing questions of climate change.[4] Nor is postapocalyptic fiction limited to the novel: today, the genre has a significant presence in comic books and TV (*The Walking Dead*), video games (the *Fallout* franchise), and film (the *Mad Max* series). The novels explored in this chapter build on the catastrophic imaginary created by these widespread cultural representations, even as they approach postapocalyptic motifs with distinctive formal sophistication and self-consciousness: Cormac McCarthy's *The Road* (2006), Colson Whitehead's *Zone One* (2011), and Emily St. John Mandel's *Station Eleven* (2014).

These novels are certainly not unique in their literary take on the postapocalyptic genre, but they offer a convincing demonstration of how the representation of catastrophe calls for increased formal complexity, as is made evident by the novels' nonlinear handling of narrative temporality. While, as we have seen, *any* narrative in this genre presupposes a temporal rupture between a pre- and a postworld, the case studies in this chapter probe this divide as a means of engaging with the psychological consequences of catastrophe: the emphasis falls not on apocalypse as a trigger for a conventional plot structure, but on its power to disrupt the linearity of the protagonists' experience of reality, and particularly their sense of a sharp demarcation between human societies and nonhuman things and processes. This conceptual destabilization is an effect of what I call "negative strategies": the postworld emerges as the narrative negates (i.e., subtracts or pares down) some of the salient characteristics of the preworld—features with which readers are familiar through their everyday reality. Thus, famine negates the availability of food and other resources, the postapocalyptic wasteland negates the organized urban environments of the pre- period, widespread violence contradicts the rule of law, and so on. This may sound like a schematic process, but it is central to the genre of postapocalyptic fiction, and it leverages important structural features of readers' imagination. In the novels by McCarthy, Whitehead, and St. John Mandel, negative strategies are deployed in a particularly sophisticated way, in order to foreground psychological rupture and maximize its impact on readers.

Each of these novels creates nonlinearity by combining negation with a specific formal device: spatial descriptions in McCarthy, the evocation of the narrator's self in Whitehead, the use of lists in St. John Mandel. The effect of these negative strategies can be brought into focus by adopting a "second-generation" cognitive approach to narrative, which highlights the reader's share in making sense of narrative affectively and imaginatively (see Kukkonen and Caracciolo 2014).

NEGATION IN LANGUAGE AND MENTAL IMAGERY

Narrative theory has so far addressed negation in the form of "denarration," to use Brian Richardson's terminology.[5] The kind of narrative negation that this chapter explores—and that plays a key role in postapocalyptic fiction—works differently from denarration: it does not revoke previous narrative information but conveys the hiatus between two temporal frames within the storyworld's chronology. Nonlinearity does not result from overarching image schemata for narrative progression, as discussed in the previous chapter, but from how readers are asked to simultaneously entertain and imaginatively blend two temporal planes of the fictional reality.

Consider the Kanizsa triangle, from the name of the Italian psychologist who first described this optical illusion in the 1950s (see Kanizsa 1955 and fig. 6). We see a triangle brighter than the background, even though we know—or even after we've been told—that, strictly speaking, there is no triangle, because the background and the area at the center of the figure are exactly the same color. Technically, this is known as an "illusory contour."

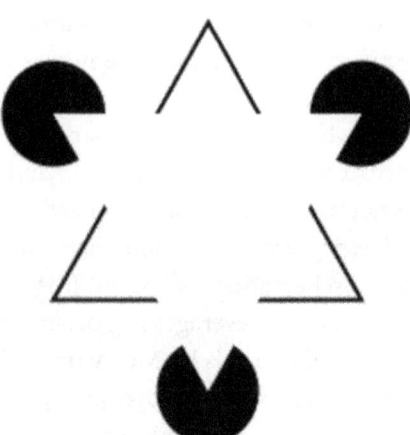

Figure 6. The Kanizsa triangle.
(Fibonacci, CC BY-SA 3.0,
https://commons.wikimedia.org
/w/index.php?curid=1788215)

Central to the experience of this figure is the simultaneous, and therefore paradoxical, awareness of something (the triangle) and its absence. Negative strategies in postapocalyptic fiction work in a fundamentally similar way: they conflate the imagination of something and the poignant awareness of its absence. This dynamic builds on some more general features of the psychology of negation, which we can examine along two dimensions. The first is concerned with how people process negation as a *linguistic* phenomenon; the second turns to negation as an intrinsic feature of mental imagery, including the imagery that arises while reading narrative.

"The bird is alive" and "the bird is not dead" mean, logically speaking, the same thing. But, in terms of how they are processed psychologically, these statements are quite different. Referencing Laurence Horn's *A Natural History of Negation* (1989, 168–75), Daniel Gilbert puts this point as follows: "To comprehend a denial (*armadillos are not herbivorous*), a listener must first comprehend the core assertion (*armadillos are herbivorous*) and then reject it" (1991, 113). This means that, when we process a negative statement, we entertain its affirmative counterpart before fully parsing its negative meaning. We do so in an unconscious way, without any awareness that we are considering the affirmative statement. But the repeated use of negation in the novels by McCarthy, Whitehead, and St. John Mandel can "fix" the reader's imagination on the realities that are being negated, so that they come into full awareness: for a moment, a statement and its opposite appear to coexist. These narratives evoke the postworld as a negation of the preworld—a strategy that, as a matter of fact, *affirms* the preworld while foregrounding its absence in affectively charged terms. In readers, this gives rise to a sense of nonlinearity comparable to the experience of the Kanizsa triangle: just as the triangle oscillates between presence and absence, mentally entertaining two states of a storyworld disrupts temporal sequentiality by conflating readers' imagination of the pre- and the postapocalyptic scenario.

This idea can be better understood by taking into account work on the phenomenology of the imagination. When we talk about mental imagery, we usually focus on the substantive contents of our imagery: the *things* that we experience as part of an imaginative act. Yet phenomenological analysis complicates this commonsensical view of mental imagery significantly. For instance, Evan Thompson writes that we "visualize an object or scene by mentally enacting or entertaining a possible perceptual experience of that object or scene" (2007, 138). Thompson adds that mental imagery is different from perception: while in perception we experience objects or scenes as physically present, mental imagery allows us to experience them *as absent* (2007, 151). Mental imagery thus operates analogously to perception, minus the sense of presence that accompanies perceptual experience. This is, fundamentally, an instance of negation that is part and parcel of the experiential structure of mental imagery. Jean-Paul Sartre raises this point in his seminal work *The Psychology of Imagination:*

> The [mental] image also includes an act of belief, or a positional act. This act can assume four forms and no more: it can posit the object as nonexistent, or as absent, or as existing elsewhere, it can also "neutralize" itself, that is, not posit its object as existing. Two of these acts are negations, the fourth corresponds to a suspension or neutralization of the proposition. The third, which is positive, assumes an implicit negation of the actual and present existence of the object. This positional act—and this is essential—is not superimposed on the image after it has been constituted. The positional act is constitutive of the consciousness of the image. (1948, 16)

Not only are imagined objects by definition absent from our immediate surroundings, but we can *experience* their absence within the act of imagination itself. When this happens, in Sartre's third case, we imagine objects or scenes under erasure: we bring them to life through the imagination but at the same time we negate their presence, precisely as seeing the Kanizsa triangle involves an awareness of the triangle's absence, or as the comprehension of negative statements involves entertaining *both* their affirmative counterpart and its negation.

This is a structural feature of mental imagery that postapocalyptic fiction can use in particularly effective ways, because of the constitutive absence of the preworld. Scholars working in cognitive approaches to literature have suggested that the imagery elicited by fiction can be exceptionally vivid and can result in a sense of embodied presence: thanks to the stylistic qualities of literary narrative, readers may physically feel part of the storyworld that is being evoked by a text.[6] In narratives of catastrophe, the preworld haunts readers' imagination of the postworld, increasing its vividness, affective impact, and potential for embodied involvement. At the same time, the core of absence probed by readers' imagination evokes the complex, nonlinear causality of catastrophe itself: how catastrophe results from, and reveals, the deep entanglement of human and nonhuman realities. It is time to exemplify these claims, beginning with *Station Eleven,* which deploys negative strategies in an exceptionally straightforward way, and then moving on to the more indirect uses of negation in *The Road* and *Zone One*.

ENUMERATING WHAT IS NO MORE: *STATION ELEVEN*

The first part of Emily St. John Mandel's *Station Eleven* is set in present-day Toronto, at a time when the news of a virus outbreak of unprecedented scale is beginning to emerge. One of the novel's main characters, Jeevan, "was crushed by a sudden certainty that this was it, that this illness . . . was going to be the divide between a *before* and an *after*, a line drawn through his life" (2014, 20–21; italics in the original). But, while this temporal hiatus is only foreshadowed in the first five chapters, chapter 6 changes gear and presents the reader with what the narrator characterizes as "an incomplete list." This list takes up four pages (the entirety of the chapter) and begins as follows:

> No more diving into pools of chlorinated water lit green from below. No more ball games played out under floodlights. No more porch lights with moths fluttering on summer nights. No more trains running under the surface of cities on the dazzling power of the electric third rail. No more cities. No more films, except rarely, except with a generator drowning out half the dialogue, and only then for the first little while until the fuel for the generators ran out, because automobile gas goes stale after two or three years. (2014, 31)

The multiplication of negative statements describes, indirectly, how the virus outbreak reshaped the reality of those who survived. This enumeration evokes a postapocalyptic world by subtracting things with which both the novel's readers and the inhabitants of the fictional Toronto of the previous chapters are intimately familiar.[7] Crucially, this negative strategy can create vivid, and hauntingly persistent, mental images, just as the Kanizsa triangle is strongly perceived as present despite our awareness of its absence. This effect depends, in part, on the skillful use of what Elaine Scarry (2001, 77–88) calls "radiant ignition": many of the sentences in the quoted passage allude to light and light sources, such as the water "lit from below," the "porch lights," or (indirectly) the light of the film projector. References of this kind, Scarry suggests, set the reader's imagination in motion; through the chiaroscuro-like contrast between light and darkness ("the trains running under the surface of cities"), they infuse the represented world with dynamic, lifelike qualities. The fact that the passage teems with objects that are both concrete and quotidian—and therefore can be easily visualized by readers—heightens this overall imaginative effect. The three-word sentence about the vanished cities marks an abrupt shift in spatial scale, which serves a strategic purpose: it communicates the scope of these negative statements, how they operate not only on individual objects but on a planetary scale. What the passage conveys, therefore, is a deep sense of nostalgia for a world that does not exist anymore, and whose absence is vividly evoked through a series of negative statements.

Not only does the storyworld's temporally dyadic structure inflect the reader's imagination, but it underlies the organization of the narrative as a whole. The novel's multiple story lines straddle the dividing line between the "before" and the "after": chapters 1–5, 13–15, 17, 25–30, 32, 34, 36, 39–41, and again 53–54 are set before and in the immediate aftermath of the outbreak, with the other chapters taking place several years afterward. The protagonist of the latter chapters is Kirsten, a young woman who travels through the wasteland of North America with a company of actors. Kirsten owns a precious relic of the preworld, a science fiction comic book titled, like the novel, *Station Eleven*. This comic book was given to Kirsten by Arthur Leander, a famous actor who died during a Toronto performance of *King Lear*—a dramatic moment related in the novel's first scene. In parallel, the novel narrates both Kirsten's struggles in the postworld and the events that led to (and accompanied) Arthur's death in the preworld; several chapters focus on Arthur's first wife, Miranda, the author of the comic book now in Kirsten's possession.

In structural terms, the comic book brings together the plot's strands, so that the progression of the narrative appears to be controlled not by a single character's intentions but by the nonlinear circulation of an inanimate object. The comic book connects all the major characters, without them becoming fully aware of one another's lives; only the reader has a complete picture of the comic book's history. Like Iñárritu's *Babel* (discussed in chapter 1), the plot is object-oriented in the sense that it is driven by a material object. Remarkably, that plotting strategy builds on and integrates the thematic significance of the object, its being located at the intersection of pre- and postworlds, of human lives and the nonhuman event that disrupted them (i.e., the catastrophic virus outbreak). The narrative told in that comic book, which we only glimpse, centers on a lonesome physicist who lives on a space station built in the earth's image, after our planet has been taken over by an alien species. The setting is clearly dystopian and postapocalyptic, and the novel quotes repeatedly the following lines attributed to Dr. Eleven, the physicist: "I stood looking over my damaged home and tried to forget the sweetness of life on Earth" (2014, 214). This inability to forget the world before the catastrophe is the feeling that the novel conveys via the negative enumeration of chapter 6: that haunting presence-absence of the preworld, inscribed into the workings of the reader's imagination by the list, is perfectly encapsulated by Dr. Eleven's words.

Moreover, the negative experience of the preworld echoes many of Kirsten's own statements: "[We] are always looking for the former world, before all the traces of the former world are gone," she reflects (2014, 130). Later, she adds that "the people who struggle the most with [the postapocalyptic world] are the people who remember the old world clearly" (2014, 195). The same nostalgia for a world that is no more is mirrored, at the level of the formal organization of the novel, by the back-and-forths between the chapters, which follow the vagaries of the comic book, one of those rare "traces of the former world." The negation of familiar objects performed by the enumeration is thus made into a thematic focus *and*, concurrently, into a principle of formal organization: the nonlinear juxtaposition of temporal frames in the narrative keeps the preworld alive in the reader's mind just as linguistic negation foregrounds the absence of what is denied. In this way, the plot captures and models the characters' inability to *let go* of the preapocalyptic past. *Station Eleven* thus draws its affective power and distinctly elegiac tone from the way in which the negation of a recognizably contemporary world inflects the whole narrative.

NEGATING COLOR, NEGATIVE SPACE: *THE ROAD*

In Cormac McCarthy's *The Road*—perhaps one of the most influential postapocalyptic novels of the literary variety—an unspecified catastrophe has turned the world into a sparsely populated wasteland. The protagonists are a man and his son, both of them unnamed, who attempt to escape the devastation of what is repeatedly portrayed as a dying world. The storyworld's dyadic temporality is here implemented not via multiple story lines that interweave the pre- and the postworlds, but through passages focusing on the man's dreams, which hark back to his experiences before the disaster. These dream sequences are short inserts, often no longer than a couple of sentences—for instance: "Rich dreams now which he was loathe to wake from. Things no longer known in the world. The cold drove him forth to mend the fire. Memory of her crossing the lawn toward the house in the early morning in a thin rose gown that clung to her breasts" (McCarthy 2006, 131). The female character is the man's partner (and the boy's mother), who committed suicide in the aftermath of the disaster: she is among the memories brought back by the dream, one of the few strands still linking the man to the preapocalyptic world. The contrast between the present and the past evoked in the man's dreams is underlined by the fact that the dreams are "so rich in color. How else would death call you? Waking in the cold dawn it all turned to ash instantly. Like certain ancient frescoes entombed for centuries suddenly exposed to the day" (2006, 21). As the simile emphasizes, the transition between the dreams' preworld and the present is marked by a sudden perceptual change: while the dreams are in color, the postapocalyptic world only presents shades of gray.

The narrator's insistence on the monochromatic landscape is the main route through which negation operates in the novel. Whereas *Station Eleven* focuses on the denial of objects, technologies, and practices of the preworld, *The Road* embeds that denial into the perceptual features of the landscape that surrounds the protagonists. The world is progressively drained of its familiar chromatic qualities; the novel's beginning announces, "Nights dark beyond darkness and the days more gray each one than what had gone before. Like the onset of some cold glaucoma dimming away the world" (2006, 3). Throughout the novel, the wasteland in which the man and his son travel is so relentlessly characterized as gray and ashen that few readers will miss its colorlessness, as attested by several commentators: "The book is written in language almost like watching black and white TV which adds to the setting," writes an online reviewer (Lutz 2007).[8] The absence of color acts as a unifying backdrop to readers' mental imagery, making the narrative space more tangible and therefore more easily imaginable: the uniformity of the landscape eases readers into the storyworld, creating a strong sense of physical presence. To this end, McCarthy leverages the connection between color and affective qualities: through the denial of color, the dramatic contrast between the pre- and the postapocalyptic world is affectively realized in the novel (and, potentially, in readers' imaginations) even before the narrative registers—by way of direct representation—the consequences of the disaster. Grayness becomes a visual stand-in for the nonlinear history of the storyworld, a layer superimposed on familiar realities and signaling, through the negation and subtraction of color, the inescapability of disaster.

Even beyond this pall of grayness, the spaces explored by the characters are remarkably bare and empty. Consider, for instance, a passage in which the man enters a house in search of food or usable tools:

> He went through the house room by room. He found nothing. A spoon in a bedside drawer. He put that in his pocket. He thought there might be some clothes in a closet or some bedding but there wasnt [sic]. He went back out and crossed to the garage. He sorted through tools. Rakes. A shovel. Jars of nails and bolts on a shelf. A boxcutter. He held it to the light and looked at the rusty blade and put it back. Then he picked it up again. He took a screwdriver from a coffee can and opened the handle. Inside were four new blades. He took out the old blade and laid it on the shelf and put in one of the new ones and screwed the handle back together and retracted the blade and put the cutter in his pocket. Then he picked up the screwdriver and put that in his pocket as well. He walked back out to the barn. (2006, 119–20)

There is very little here in the way of concrete spatial references that may help readers imagine the house and the garage. Space is only seen as a physical container for objects that may ensure the protagonists' survival, and even these objects are captured through a list-like enumeration that emphasizes their scarcity ("Rakes. A shovel"). Yet, in the domain of readers' mental imagery, less is more: the rarer and more isolated these objects appear, the easier it becomes to visualize them against the background of the ghostly house and garage. This phenomenon has something in common with "verbal overshadowing" (see Schooler and Engstler-Schooler 1990), a well-known psychological interference between visual memory and verbalization: several studies have found that verbally describing a new face impairs the subsequent visual recognition of that face. While visual memory and mental imagery are not the same thing, it is at least conceivable that McCarthy's sparse style of spatial description *encourages* the production of mental imagery through the lack of verbalized details. The man's movements may also contribute to this effect: they lend a dynamic quality to readers' mental imagery, as if following the character through this environment compensated for the shortage of spatial information. This idea is consistent with Anežka Kuzmičová's argument (2012) about the role of object-directed movements in creating an illusion of "presence" in storyworlds. At the same time, the man's movements feel automatic and almost gratuitous, and the house even more empty and lifeless because of that: paradoxically, the description denies spatial detail and foregrounds absence ("He found nothing") even as it is likely to evoke vivid mental imagery in readers.

When, a few pages later, the protagonists discover a bunker miraculously replete with "crate upon crate of canned goods," the man remarks, "I found everything. Everything" (2006, 138). But this temporary abundance only reminds the man of the extent of the loss, and that it cannot be communicated to the child, who was born after the disaster: "He could not construct for the child's pleasure the world he'd lost without constructing the loss as well and he thought perhaps the child had known this better than he" (2006, 154). Material objects encode the catastrophic rupture between the time before and the time after the disaster, thus foregrounding the nonlinear temporality of the storyworld.

Negation is not only active in the visual and spatial domain, however, because absence defines this world at a deep, existential level. The narrator compares it to a "crushing black vacuum" (2006, 130) that swallows up the material comforts of the preworld as well as emotions and—especially—hopes of long-term survival and flourishing. Language itself is impacted: the world, we read, was "shrinking down about a raw core of parsible entities. The names of things slowly following those things into oblivion. Colors. The names of birds. Things to eat. . . . How much was gone already? The sacred idiom shorn of its referents" (2006, 88–89). As the world becomes sparser, the richness of language is pared down to a "raw core" of words. McCarthy's own style mirrors this depletion, with short sentences and monolithic words competing with the barrenness of the landscape: a degree of formal abstraction (reminiscent of the geometric structure of the Kanizsa triangle) serves to increase the vividness of the storyworld. The novel's thematic and stylistic strategies thus work in tandem with the negation of color and spatial detail that shapes readers' experience of this landscape.

UNDERCUTTING NARRATIVE CONTINUITY: *ZONE ONE*

Colson Whitehead's *Zone One* reappraises a genre that has been a staple of popular culture since George Romero's *Night of the Living Dead*: zombie fiction. Many of the elements that define zombie narratives are present, but packaged in an unapologetically challenging text, one in which Whitehead's elaborate prose eclipses the plot-driven thrills of genre fiction. The premise is that a deadly virus has turned millions of Americans into zombie-like "skels" (as the novel calls them), with the exception of a handful of individuals who have been lucky enough to dodge the contagion. Sometime after the outbreak, the survivors begin to reorganize; marines and later paramilitary troops—among them the protagonist, Mark Spitz—sweep through the southern tip of Manhattan in order to clear its buildings of the remaining skels. A few blocks to the north, a concrete wall keeps other skels from entering the sanitized perimeter of what is known as "Zone One"— the first step in the reconstruction of a semblance of civil society.

While set for the most part in the postworld, the novel teems with flashbacks to earlier time frames, either the preworld of Mark's childhood or his perilous journey to New York City in the immediate aftermath of the virus outbreak. These flashbacks are quite unlike McCarthy's sentence-length dream sequences: they extend over several pages, and they tend to be left unannounced and unmarked. A striking example can be found in the opening of the novel, which, far from providing us with the basic coordinates of this postapocalyptic world, veers toward an episode of Mark's youth: "He always wanted to live in New York. His Uncle Lloyd lived downtown on Lafayette, and in the long stretches between visits he daydreamed about living in his apartment" (2011, 2–3). On a first reading of this opening, there is no way to know that the transition between the two sentences already implies a leap from the post- to the preworld: the first sentence—of the quotation and of the novel—is anchored to the protagonist's consciousness as he is making his way through an apartment complex in New York City and dispatching the remaining skels; the second sentence reflects Mark's recollection of his childhood impressions of New York. Readers realize that this is a flashback only much later, and retrospectively. This episode is representative of Whitehead's narrative method in *Zone One*, which favors a free-floating temporality that constantly blurs the distinction between the pre- and the postworld. In fact, these flashbacks are so frequent, and their signposting so elusive, that any sense of linearity breaks down: readers have a hard time following the narrative progression in "path"-like terms. To quote from an online review of the novel, "Flashbacks start and end without any warning—sometimes in the middle of a paragraph, or as part of a random observation—and major plot twists are both telegraphed and buried in other random pieces of information" (Anders 2011). The disorienting effect of this strategy is exacerbated by the scarcity of paratextual cues: the three-hundred-page novel is divided into three chapters, titled, respectively, "Friday," "Saturday," and "Sunday," which offer little help as the reader attempts to piece together the plot and the novel's expansive chronology.

Perhaps the closest literary parallel is Virginia Woolf's "tunnelling" method (see Showalter 1992, xxix), which enables the narrators of novels such as *Mrs. Dalloway* and *To the Lighthouse* to weave in and out of the characters' minds, through ad hoc flashbacks. In *Zone One,* just as in Woolf's seminal modernist works, these temporal shifts follow—or are at least inspired by—movements internal to the protagonist's consciousness: typically, remembering a salient episode of his (pre- or postapocalyptic) past. But Mark's past, unlike that of Woolf's characters, remains an incomplete patchwork, which is bound to frustrate readers' need for narrative as well as formal closure.[9] Surely, this resistance is in itself psychologically justified, because it reflects catastrophe-induced trauma, what the survivors of *Zone One* refer to as "PASD" (Post-Apocalyptic Stress Disorder, a not entirely unironic label). As one of the novel's characters emphasizes in a conversation with Mark (2011, 69), the pronunciation of this acronym makes it virtually indistinguishable from the word "past," thus further cementing the link between the character's traumatic memory of the past and the novel's loose temporality: the temporal structure of the novel mirrors the disruption brought about by catastrophe not just in the storyworld's external reality but—more important—in the protagonist's understanding of his life.

We have seen that St. John Mandel and McCarthy foreground the temporal rupture brought about by catastrophe through strategies of negation directed at storyworld objects and spaces. *Zone One* is not devoid of these moments: for instance, in a memorable episode the protagonist finds shelter in an eerily "prim and elegant" farmhouse that evokes the orderliness and material comforts of the preapocalyptic world, like McCarthy's bunker (2011, 210). But far more striking in Whitehead's novel is another negative strategy: *Zone One* consistently negates narrative continuity and closure as Mark, the protagonist, struggles to make sense of his life. Psychologists and philosophers working in the wake of Jerome Bruner (1991) have persuasively argued that narrative is a fundamental tool in the construction of a coherent personal identity.[10] Catastrophe denies the protagonist precisely the possibility of a linear life narrative. This denial registers in the novel not only through the disorienting flashbacks but also, thematically, through the multiplication of "Last Night stories"—the survivors' accounts of where they were and what they were doing on the night in which the disease broke out.

Mark, we are told, has three versions of his Last Night story, which are deployed according to the degree of intimacy he enjoys with his interlocutors: "The Silhouette was for survivors he wasn't going to travel with for long.... He offered the Anecdote, robust and carrying more on its ribs, to those he might hole up with for a night" (2011, 138). Finally, the aptly named "Obituary" was "nonetheless heartfelt, glancing off his true self more than once, replete with digressions about his lifelong friendship with Kyle, nostalgia for the old A.C. trips, the unsettling and 'off' atmosphere of that last casino weekend, and a thorough description of the tableau at his house and its aftermath" (2011, 139). The Obituary may "glance off" Mark's true self, but it is still unable to bring together the strands of his narrative identity. In the world of *Zone One*, the psychological centrality of narrative is repeatedly foregrounded, but so is its inevitably loose and fragmented nature: stories function like "interstitial narrative sequences ... in first-person shooters," as the narrator puts it (2011, 217). Stories punctuate the text, like sudden flashes of narrative meaning, but ultimately fail to mold the protagonist's life into a meaningful whole. Mark remains, as the text foregrounds, a postapocalyptic everyman whose nonlinear trajectory opposes the assumptions of exceptionality or predestination that characterize many survival narratives: "He was their *typical*, he was their *most*, he was their *average*, receiving hearty thumbs-ups from the gents in the black van parked a discreet distance across the street" (2011, 11; italics in the original).

The novel thus plays with the idea of a satisfying, and liberating, narrativization of catastrophe, and it impresses this need for narrative meaning-making on the reader. But, at the same time, it denies this possibility through its loose, erratic progression, which challenges readers' expectations of narrative linearity and closure. This dynamic is similar to how the Kanizsa triangle both creates and undercuts the illusion of a contour, and therefore of geometric closure. Whitehead's literary method thus translates the workings of the triangle—the imaginative coexistence of a shape and its absence—to the level of narrative coherence. In turn, the falling short of narrative can be seen as a result of what the "skels" (the zombies) embody in *Zone One* on a symbolic level: as we'll see in more detail in the next chapter, the skels are a collective agent that enters a reciprocal relationship with humankind. We are thus brought back to the question of how narrative can confront the interrelation between human societies and phenomena beyond the human. The novel raises this question by repeatedly suggesting that the skels are "a kind of weather" (2011, 221). When Mark finds himself in a farmhouse about to be overrun by hordes of skels, he pictures "himself underneath the news copter as the folks in more fortunate weather watched from home. He was on the roof, the brown floodwaters pouring around the house" (2011, 228). The skels' movements have the nonlinear but ruthless logic of extreme weather, a comparison that both stresses the haphazardness of their behavior and points to the equation between the zombie apocalypse and the real-world possibility of climate change-induced catastrophe. The novel's negation of narrative continuity is thus a literary response to the problem of imagining nonhuman realities: realities that (like the skels or, outside of the fiction, anthropogenic climate change) put pressure on narrative's built-in bias toward linearity through their unpredictable, emergent behavior.

The point of departure for this chapter was the tension—which Herman sees as fundamental to narrative—between stories' capacity to evoke experientially thick domains ("storyworlds") and the representation of disruptive events ("world disruption"). Catastrophe is a limit case of world disruption, in that it constitutes a radical, large-scale deviation from a state of affairs seen as normal or ordinary. This explains why catastrophe is, at the same time, so productive and so challenging for narrative. On the one hand, due to its inherent tellability catastrophe is likely to generate a profusion of stories, fictional as well as nonfictional. The link between narrative and catastrophe runs deep: some of the oldest written narratives (from the *Epic of Gilgamesh* to the book of Genesis and Greek mythology) place great emphasis on natural disasters and their consequences. But, while in these classical narratives catastrophe tends to be presented as the result of divine intervention in human history, in today's world catastrophic occurrences are widely conceptualized as the product of a nonlinear and inherently complex causal history, one that is "meshy" because of how it crisscrosses human and nonhuman factors.

This raises an important challenge for narrative. As part 1 of this book has argued, storytelling shows a marked bias for individual protagonists and linear progression reflecting the protagonist's beliefs, desires, and intentions. Plot is keyed to human or human-like intentionality, whereas modern catastrophe (unlike the premodern understanding of catastrophe as divine intervention) *denies* direct intentionality. Of course, the standard account of the Anthropocene positions humanity as the collective entity that has brought the planet perilously close to an ecological cataclysm.[11] While it may be tempting to see humanity as an individual protagonist in this Anthropocene narrative, this move results in a gross misunderstanding of the complexity of the causal and historical processes involved: there is no human-scale intentionality behind the Anthropocene, but rather the emergent agency of industrialized societies under a capitalist system. Because of the emergent nature of the current ecological crisis, capturing catastrophe puts pressure on the human-scale structures of narrative, a challenge that is central to the genre of postapocalyptic fiction. Particularly when a postapocalyptic scenario is married with formal innovation, the affective and conceptual dynamics of narrative can effectively probe human societies' enmeshment with geological or climatological processes.[12]

The three novels examined in this chapter bring to the fore this nonlinear interrelation by implementing negative strategies, which exploit basic features of linguistic comprehension as well as mental imagery in order to juxtapose two states of the storyworld: what preceded the catastrophic event and what came after it. The nonlinearity of catastrophe is a function of both its temporal scale—how it straddles several human generations—and of the psychological traumas it creates at the individual level, disrupting attempts at straightforward narrativization. In an effort to convey this temporally complex structure, negation is elevated to a formal principle: it underlies the enumeration of objects no longer in existence as well as frequent chapter-length flashbacks to the preworld (*Station Eleven*); it inspires McCarthy's approach to spatial description in *The Road,* with its gray landscapes and bare environments; and it shapes the protagonist's inability to bring satisfying narrative closure to his life in *Zone One.* Insights into readers' psychological processing of narrative explain how these negative strategies are able to evoke, and impress on readers, a sense of the preworld's absence, which accounts for the haunting quality of these novels and their lasting imaginative impact. The complexity of catastrophe is compressed into an affective experience that is shared by the protagonists and by readers alike. This emotional effect is heightened by the preworld's proximity to the real world, so that the novels, even when they do not explicitly foreground climatological processes, resonate symbolically with contemporary anxieties about climate change. Part 2 of this book homes in on the interdependency between humans and nonhuman things and processes, examining how it can be captured at the level of narrative agency (in chapter 4) and consciousness representation (in chapter 5).

PART II

Interdependency

CHAPTER 4

Five Ways of Looking at Nonhuman Actants

In *Vibrant Matter* (2010), a seminal contribution to the nonhuman turn, Jane Bennett makes a case for the autonomy and productivity of matter. For Bennett, inanimate things are constitutively entangled with, and participate in, human activities. As discussed in the introduction, in the wake of Iovino and Oppermann's work (2012; 2014b) material ecocritics have explored the ramifications of this idea for an understanding of literary practices; they point to narrative as a culturally privileged platform for exploring the vitality of nonhuman things. Not only does matter display efficacy, but it displays a specifically *narrative* form of efficacy, through the realization that things are profoundly entangled with stories—and that they can even become the *protagonists* of stories in which human characters are left on the sidelines. In the first chapter of *Vibrant Matter*, Bennett already employs narrative in this fashion. She writes as follows: "The strangely vital things that will rise up to meet us in this chapter—a dead rat, a plastic cap, a spool of thread—are characters in a speculative onto-story. The tale hazards an account of materiality, even though it is both too alien and too close to see clearly and even though linguistic means prove inadequate to the task" (2010, 3–4).

Bennett's appeal to the medium of narrative to bolster her case for the vital efficacy of matter is significant for several reasons. On one level, it testifies to narrative's power to demonstrate a philosophical argument in terms that are both concrete and affectively resonant. At the same time, Bennett is raising the possibility of using narrative against the grain of what Monika Fludernik (1996, 13) has called its "anthropomorphic bias" (see also the discussion in chapter 2). Bennett's "speculative onto-stories" suggest that narrative may be able to move beyond this bias. To understand how this is possible, we can consider one of Bennett's examples: a 1919 short story by Franz Kafka, "Cares of a Family Man." The protagonist of this narrative is a mysterious entity called Odradek, which at first sight would seem to be a literal "mesh" of assorted fabric: "It looks like a flat star-shaped spool for thread, and indeed it does seem to have thread wound upon it; to be sure, they are only old, broken-off bits of thread, knotted and tangled together, of the most varied sorts and colors" (2005, 428). But we soon discover that Odradek is able to hide, and even speak and laugh (its laughter sounding "like the rustling of fallen leaves"; 2005, 428), and that it will survive the narrator's children (hence the anxious "cares" hinted at by the title). For Bennett, Odradek blurs the boundary between subjectivity and materiality, agency and passivity: "This animate wood exercises an impersonal form of vitality" (2010, 7).

Figures like Odradek challenge the first and perhaps most important pillar of narrative's anthropomorphism: its bias toward human or humanlike characters. In an article coauthored with Lars Bernaerts, Luc Herman, and Bart Vervaeck (2014), we examined the cognitive and interpretive challenges raised by nonhuman characters and, more specifically, nonhuman first-person narrators. This chapter extends and deepens that argument, engaging with the notion of character head-on and discussing the ways in which narrative and narrative theory may attempt to extricate character from anthropomorphic conceptions. How can narrative elevate the nonhuman—material objects, but also large-scale processes such as globalization or the weather—to the position of a character, thus realizing the key material-ecocritical notion that matter itself is "storied" (Iovino and Oppermann 2014a)? What are the limits and the possibilities opened up by this expansion of narrative agency?

Engaging with these questions is a crucial step toward outlining a theory of narrative attuned to the human-nonhuman mesh in the Anthropocene. As Eileen Crist (2013) points out, it is only within multiple scare quotes that humanity is "promoted" to the role of geological "agent" in the Anthropocene. This is hardly a promotion, and humanity is not an agent in the sense of the autonomous, liberal subject that we inherited from the Enlightenment.[1] There are major socioeconomic discrepancies within the category of humanity, which create very different burdens of responsibility vis-à-vis the ecological crisis—for instance, between the wasteful Western world and underprivileged communities in the developing world. Like the knotted and tangled threads of Kafka's Odradek packed away in a conceptual box, the deceptively simple notion of humanity contains numerous feedback loops of genetics, biology, cultural practices, technologies (notably, those involved in large-scale industrialization), and sociopolitical structures (particularly capitalism). Likewise, the Anthropocene reveals that geological, climatological, and biological processes are causally efficacious in ways that theorists affiliated with the nonhuman turn have discussed under the rubric of "material agency" (see Iovino and Oppermann 2012). In an article on "Agency at the Time of the Anthropocene," Bruno Latour notes that "the Earth has now taken back all the characteristics of a full-fledged *actor*. Indeed, as Dipesh Chakrabarty has proposed, it has become once again an *agent of history*, or rather, an agent of what I have proposed to call our common *geostory*" (2014, 3; italics in the original). Latour goes on to ask: "The problem for all of us in philosophy, science, or literature becomes: how do we tell such a story?" (2014, 3).

Narrative strategies serve as a concrete answer, grounded in form, to Latour's question. If one seeks to understand how stories can convey the complex and interdependent "agencies" of humanity and the nonhuman world, the notion of character—a key concept of narrative theory, and a bulwark of anthropomorphism—would seem to be an obvious and perhaps inevitable starting point. Broadly speaking, narrative tends to place individual human characters in the position of agents, while nonhuman realities (including nonhuman animals and natural landscapes or processes) are relegated to the position of objects: tools to further human ends, or a backdrop to human-centered events. Through formal resources, narrative can put pressure on this anthropocentric setup and foreground nonhuman agency.

The resistance to an anthropomorphic understanding of character is not entirely new. In his pathbreaking study of the Russian folktale, originally published in 1928, Vladimir Propp (1968) was the first to develop a formal understanding of character, through the equation of character and "function"—namely, the role a given character plays within a narrative arc. For Propp, a character could be a hero, a dispatcher, a helper, or a prize: all roles defined by semantic relations that were largely (though not completely) abstract in the sense of being independent from psychological factors. Propp's work was immensely influential in structuralist narratology.[2] The culmination of that structuralist approach is A. J. Greimas's actantial model of narrative (1976), which does away with character as an inherently mimetic concept and prefers to talk about "actants"—a term that emphasizes the structural link between character and narrative-advancing actions. Effectively, this approach reduces character to a textual device, and therefore would seem to undermine the notion's inherent anthropomorphism.

Does this mean that a nonanthropocentric theory of character can simply adopt the structuralist model? Unfortunately, the answer is no. The problem is that the structuralist approach, although it may seem to do away with the human subjectivity of character, is in fact deeply committed to the subject/object binary that philosophical work such as Bennett's destabilizes. Put otherwise, structuralist theories, by seeing character as a mere textual function, tend to *objectify* it. By contrast, a nonanthropocentric theory of character should resist the whole subject/object split and move beyond *both* an anthropomorphic approach to character and its understanding as an inert textual mechanism.

Developing this argument will require delving deeper into Greimas's actantial theory of narrative and spelling out why it is based on a dualistic conception of the world, and of language in particular. Andrew Goatly's seminal work on "green grammar" in the field of ecolinguistics (1996) helps link dualism to a specific grammatical construction widespread in Indo-European languages—namely, the transitive sentence, with its clear-cut separation between a grammatical subject and a grammatical object. Greimas's actantial model relies on transitivity and therefore cannot be adopted in the context of this book without substantive modification. Goatly's ecolinguistics serves as a template for examining five ways in which narrative can deanthropomorphize character by moving beyond transitivity and therefore dualistic notions. The fictional narratives I will investigate in this connection include Richard Powers's *The Echo Maker*, Jim Crace's *Being Dead*, Ruth Ozeki's *A Tale for the Time Being*, Jeff VanderMeer's Southern Reach trilogy, and Kurt Vonnegut's *Galápagos*. Clearly, this inventory of strategies and texts is not exhaustive, and there are many overlaps among the formal devices discussed in the following pages. Further, a theory along these lines will not work for all narratives, and certainly not for the many narratives that (more or less deliberately) take on board anthropocentric ideas. It is a theory attuned to a particular corpus of literary texts that unsettle the human subject by inscribing human-nonhuman interdependency into the very formal logic of story. The notion of character—bound up as it is with human subjectivity—is key to this destabilization.[3]

STRUCTURALIST PRECEDENTS?

Greimas's actantial model of narrative builds on, and extends, the parallel drawn by Propp between the workings of story and the syntactic organization of natural languages. In an essay originally published in French in 1973, Greimas (1976, 106) distinguishes between actants and actors, the former being an abstract function comparable to subject and object in grammar, the latter being the instantiation of those roles in what we would informally call a narrative's characters. Greimas envisages two possible "elementary schemata" of actantial organization: subject → object and sender → object → receiver (1976, 108). In the first, a subject acts upon an object, whereas in the second a subject (the sender) *transmits* an object to the receiver. These roles are actualized in countless ways by narrative: for instance, the object transmitted in the second schema may be something material (a sword, a letter, an inheritance) or something intangible (knowledge, a tale).

At first glance, Greimas's schemata appear to be successful in uncoupling the actant from the human. It is no coincidence that Latour's actor network theory—an influential paradigm within the nonhuman turn—lifts the term from Greimas.[4] In broad strokes, actor-network theory argues for the role played by technology as well as sociocultural structures in producing what we normally think of as human societies, which in fact arise from complex interactions crisscrossing the human/nonhuman divide. Latour refers to the nonhuman entities that shape cultural practices as "actants"; the nonhuman, in this sense, takes on full-fledged agency. Greimas anticipates this view, in the domain of narrative theory, by suggesting that a material object or an abstract entity such as capitalism can be actants in narrative, just like human characters. In Latour's words: "[Literary] theorists have been much freer in their enquiries about figuration than any social scientist, especially when they have used semiotics or the various narrative sciences. This is because, for instance in a fable, the same actant can be made to act through the agency of a magic wand, a dwarf, a thought in the fairy's mind, or a knight killing two dozen dragons" (2005, 54).

Latour is correct to say that, in Greimas's model, human subjectivity and identity are relegated to a matter of "discourse"—a surface manifestation that does not reach into the deep actantial level of formal relations. Yet, even as it evacuates the human subject, Greimas's account does not go very far in exorcising the specter of anthropocentrism. The reasons for this are twofold. The first is more obvious and has to do with the problematic claim to scientific objectivity of structuralist models. In evacuating the subject from narrative's deep structures, Greimas effaces his own subjectivity: he construes narrative as an object "out there," instead of taking into account the deep entanglement between storytelling and human experience, which has been emphasized by more recent, mind-oriented models of narrative (D. Herman 2013; Caracciolo 2014b). The subject/object divide is thus built into Greimas's analytical method—a problematic assumption when viewed from the perspective of a theory of nonhuman characters. Second, and more important, in drawing an analogy between narrative and sentence structure Greimas implicitly treats as a universal of syntax a particular kind of sentence—namely, the transitive sentence. Both his actantial schemata are predicated on the possibility of distinguishing between a grammatical subject (or sender in the second schema) and a grammatical object (what is being acted upon, or what is being transmitted in the second schema). This is a transitive organization, and it is deeply bound up with a dualistic worldview, as the next section will detail.

BEYOND TRANSITIVITY

The point of departure of Goatly's influential article "Green Grammar and Grammatical Metaphor" (1996) is that transitive sentences tend to cast the agent into the position of a grammatical subject impinging on a grammatical object that is both inert and passive.[5] Goatly's intuition is that it doesn't matter if the grammatical subject is semantically a human, a nonhuman animal, a material object, or an abstract concept; the dualistic notion of agency as mastery is deeply implicated in sentence structure. Syntax is thus bound up with the view that passive matter can be shaped and exploited at the subject's will. As Goatly explains, paraphrasing the title of George Lakoff and Mark Johnson's well-known book on conceptual metaphor, "Transitive effective structures are conventionalized grammatical metaphors, metaphors we die by, language which perpetuates the myth of power" (1996, 558).[6] Goatly's suggestion is that, in order to dispel this myth, "our image of the world has to become one in which processes predominate and human Actors disappear" (1996, 554).

An example of a linguistic system that appears to implement this worldview is Blackfoot, an Algonquian language spoken by Native American tribes living in the northwestern United States and Canada: "A native speaker of Blackfoot . . . can speak all day long without uttering a single noun—and . . . this is the exception rather than the rule" (from an internet post quoted in Goatly 2011, 80). Instead, the processual view of reality that emerges from Blackfoot is, for Goatly, "in step with recent, scientific, post-relativity models of the physical and biological universe" (2001, 231), including, arguably, the notion of metaphysical parity between humans and nonhuman realities. Whether or not this is accurate with respect to Blackfoot, the lesson we can draw from this discussion is a theoretical one. By serving as grammatical subjects and objects, nouns give the subject/object split a firm linguistic foothold. Because verbs are the closest linguistic equivalent of events, a language that eschews nouns in favor of verbs implies that human subjectivity and nonhuman matter—and everything in between, such as the life of nonhuman animals—are equally transient, processual configurations of an unstable reality.[7]

To return to Greimas, the main problem with his structuralist theory of actants is that it reproduces—unwittingly—the dualistic power structure implicit in transitive sentences, with all that it entails ideologically. Put otherwise, a theory of character that is attuned to the causal efficacy of the material world will never get off the ground if we take syntactic transitivity as a starting point. What alternatives are available in the linguistic system, and how do they lay the groundwork for a new understanding of character qua actant? Goatly points out that, even if English is biased toward transitivity, it does not lack grammatical resources to question the separation between subject and object, and by extension human agency and the material world.

In particular, Goatly identifies five grammatical tools that challenge the dualism of transitivity (1996, 547–54). The first is the "ergative system," a sentence structure alternative to transitivity in that the grammatical object *participates* in the action initiated by the subject.[8] Examples are "John opened the door," or—perhaps even clearer—"John walked the dog," where the door and the dog are directly implicated in John's action. Goatly's second linguistic tool is the use of filler words like "it" and "there" in sentences like "it rains" and "there's been an accident on the highway." As Goatly puts it: "This structure makes it possible to state a proposition involving a process [such as rainfall or the accident, in my examples], without mentioning the participant . . . involved. . . . The use of relational processes instead of material ones is a gesture towards de-humanization of world view" (1996, 549). Thirdly, Goatly points to reciprocal verbs, which foreground interaction and therefore the bidirectionality of a causal process: for instance, "John and Mary met." The fourth antidualistic strategy is the promotion of a place or environment to the position of grammatical subject, in sentences such as "The bed was crawling with ants" (instead of "Ants were crawling all over the bed"). Finally, Goatly draws attention to nominalization, which turns a verb into a grammatical noun (e.g., "the condensation of water" for "the water condenses"). Nominalizations extrapolate from the agent responsible for a given action; thus, they can be used to call attention to the processual nature of reality.

Goatly hastens to add that none of these grammatical devices is, in and of itself, sufficient to undermine dualism and anthropocentric assumptions, but they at least point to a use of language that is more aligned with what both science and contemporary philosophy tell us about the deep imbrication of human and nonhuman realities. The next sections of this chapter explore, in a speculative vein, how these grammatical devices may serve as building blocks for an account of nonhuman characters in narrative. The goal is not to develop an all-encompassing theory of narrative (like Greimas's), but to identify strategies through which stories may deploy characters that resist notions of human mastery and exceptionalism. These strategies are thus to be seen as narrative-level equivalents of the syntactic structures described by Goatly.

NONHUMAN INSTIGATION

In the ergative system, agency is a matter not of direct causation but of "instigation," and it extends from the grammatical subject to the grammatical object, involving both. In the sentence "John walked the dog," for instance, John initiates ("instigates") the action, but he and the dog coparticipate in it. Something similar happens in the plot of *The Echo Maker*, the novel by Richard Powers that will be discussed more at length in the next chapter. At the forefront of the novel is the human drama of a car accident and its aftermath. The victim, a character named Mark, suffers brain damage and develops a psychiatric condition known as "Capgras syndrome": he views his sister, Karin, as an impostor, a lookalike of his real sister. The backdrop to these events is the Platte River in Nebraska, where thousands of sandhill cranes congregate every year, on their way from Central America to Canada and Alaska. In parallel with Mark's slow and uneasy recovery is the attempt, on the part of a group of corporate investors, to build a tourist resort on the banks of the river, which would seriously endanger the cranes. This subplot follows a standard transitive pattern, which places the human in an agentive position, and the nonhuman world (meaning both the river and the cranes) in the position of a disempowered object.

However, Mark's mysterious mental condition complicates and to some extent subverts this pattern. Not only are the cranes physically present when Mark's car skids out of control, but their fate seems intimately bound up with Mark's. In his delusion, he is convinced that the surgeons implanted a bird's brain into his skull during the operation that followed his accident. In this way, the cranes are symbolically implicated in the traumatic disruption of the character's subjectivity, which points to a more general instability of the human subject. Powers's narrative reinforces this effect by portraying the birds not as individualized agents but as a collective actant, endowed with a group mentality that conflicts with the presumed autonomy and singularity of human selfhood: "Then thousands of them lift up in flood. The beating surface of the world rises, a spiral calling upward on invisible thermals. Sounds carry them all the way skyward, clacks and wooden rattles, rolling, booming, bugling, clouds of living sound. Slowly, the mass unfurls in ribbons and disperses into thin blue" (2006, 429). Powers's metaphorical language blurs the dividing line between the cranes' coordinated behavior and the surrounding landscape, transforming them into a "flood," "a beating surface," or "clouds" that eventually merge with the "thin blue" of the sky. This image of the cranes as a collective actant affects the human characters as well; for instance, it defamiliarizes Karin's view of humanity, in a key passage in which she realizes that "the whole [human] race suffered from Capgras. Those birds danced like our next of kin, looked like our next of kin, called and willed and parented and taught and navigated all just like our blood relations. Half their parts were still ours. Yet humans waved them off: impostors" (2006, 347–48).[9]

The cranes are thus a full-fledged actant in Powers's novel insofar as they coparticipate in Mark's accident and determine its narrative and ethical stakes. Crucially, this does not happen by way of direct causation, but through the symbolic instigation of Mark's condition: "The cranes crashed Mark's car" would be the closest sentence-length equivalent of the plot. Through this ergative structure, with the cranes as a nonhuman actant, the novel is able to locate the human within a longer, evolutionary history that undermines any separation between human agency and an allegedly inert natural world.

DOING WITHOUT A HUMAN SUBJECT

Goatly's second device is the use of filler words like "there" or "it" in existential statements or to denote atmospheric phenomena. Because these words fulfill a purely grammatical function, their semantic emptiness draws attention to the processual nature of the scenario that is being verbally conveyed: in a sentence like "It is cold today," the "It" is not an agent or subject, but only stands in for meteorological conditions defined by a certain perceived temperature. In narrative terms, this device is reminiscent of what Ann Banfield (1987) calls "empty center texts": descriptive passages in which the subject position is left vacant, and a scene is verbally recorded despite the absence of any observers. The deictic center of this scene—the location that would normally be occupied by an experiencing subject—remains empty. Banfield takes as an example the interludes of Virginia Woolf's 1931 novel *The Waves*, which portray a sea landscape at different times of the day, without any character being present at the scene.

The emptiness of these scenarios serves as a window onto a world untouched by human presence.[10] This is something that Woolf herself strongly cues in the famous "Time Passes" section of *To the Lighthouse*, which registers material changes in a house during a ten-year period in which it is left uninhabited. Greg Garrard (2012) discusses Woolf's "Time Passes" as an instance of what he calls "disanthropy," a vision of the world without humans. Yet, for Garrard, attempts at disanthropy in verbal narrative are bound to fail: "The helpless allegiance of written genres to narrative voice and anthropomorphic characterization makes disanthropic literature conspicuously self-contradictory, and probably impossible" (2012, 43). Instead, Garrard turns to cinema as a medium that, due to the "ostensible impersonality of the camera" (2012, 43), is uniquely equipped to represent human absence. Garrard does not discuss Banfield's empty deictic center and appears to downplay the power of literary language to break its "helpless allegiance" with "anthropomorphic characterization." In fact, it can be argued that empty center passages like Woolf's capitalize on what Garrard calls their "self-contradictory" nature, inviting readers to undergo and value an experience of absence that exposes the rich vitality of the world without humans.

Jim Crace's novel *Being Dead* (1999) is a powerful example of how empty center descriptions can probe nonhuman materiality. The novel narrates the events that led to a couple's murder on a deserted beach. What takes center stage in the narrative—rather morbidly—is the material history of the two dead bodies, whose decomposition is described in painstaking detail even if there is no full-fledged character on the scene. Consider, for instance, this passage: "But the rain, the wind, the shooting stars, the maggots and the shame had not succeeded yet in blowing them away or bringing to an end their days of grace. There'd been no thunderclap so far. His hand was touching her. The flesh on flesh. The fingertip across the tendon strings. He still held on. She still was held" (1999, 102). The description features the equivalent of an "it" or an existential "there" where we would expect a human-like observer: it foregrounds process and the slow but inevitable decomposition of the bodies on the beach, conveying a cosmic and not entirely unironic perspective on the two characters' death. The absence of human spectators is made so salient by the narrative that it becomes an anomalous, ghostly (and ghastly) actant—a reminder of the nonhuman processes that enfold the human and constitute its fate.

EVOKING HUMAN-NONHUMAN RECIPROCITY

Reciprocal verbs place two subjects in an agentive role, stressing the reciprocity of an action without establishing a subject-object (and therefore inherently hierarchical) relation: "John and Mary met." A degree of reciprocity is present in all narratives that probe the interrelation between human and nonhuman realities. Narratives focusing on catastrophe are a particularly salient example of how reciprocity can be foregrounded and inscribed into the progression of plot, with nonhuman events and elements becoming actants.

We have seen that in Whitehead's *Zone One*, for example, the zombies ("skels," in the novel's parlance) are a collective nonhuman actant, which the narrator explicitly compares to the effects of anthropogenic climate change: "The ocean [of the skels] had overtaken the streets, as if the news programs' global warming simulations had finally come to pass and the computer-generated swells mounted to drown the great metropolis" (2011, 302). Whitehead's figurative language establishes an intricate network of reciprocity: the skels are first compared to a nonhuman location, the ocean, while their invasion of the metropolis is assimilated to global warming (a phenomenon fueled by human activity), which in turn is seen through the lens of human technology (a computer simulation). Even as the skels may look like a fully nonhuman actant in the novel, the simulation simile conflates them with human societies and their impact on the natural environment, thus working toward a redistribution of agency across the human/nonhuman divide. At the same time, Whitehead's original contribution to the zombie genre is the invention of so-called "straggler" skels, who (unlike regular skels) are condemned to reenact a gesture or haunt a location that meant something to them before they became skels—a clear manifestation of the psychological cycles of trauma. An inkling of the skels' humanity is thus poignantly preserved. The figure of the straggler, along with the figurative blending of zombie invasion and climate change, steer clear of a sharp dichotomization between skels and humans and instead stress their reciprocal relation.

Beyond postapocalyptic fiction, another instance of human-nonhuman reciprocity in narrative form can be found in *A Tale for the Time Being*, a 2013 novel by American Canadian writer Ruth Ozeki. *A Tale for the Time Being* focuses on two protagonists located, respectively, in Japan and on a remote island off the coast of British Columbia. One is a Japanese teenager, Nao; the other is a Canadian writer, Ruth. The novel devotes a chapter to each character, in alternating order, but the characters themselves never meet. What brings them together is a material object: Nao's diary ends up in the Pacific Ocean, possibly as a result of the tsunami that struck Japan in 2011, and later washes up, miraculously unscathed, on Ruth's island. The Ruth-focalized chapters explore the emotional impact of reading this diary on the character's life. *A Tale for the Time Being* is, in the terminology introduced in chapter 1, an object-oriented narrative that unfolds against a global backdrop, connecting East Asian culture (particularly Buddhism) and the Western world. But, while the novel's main characters are human, the ocean—and particularly its currents, known as "gyres"—rises to prominence in the novel. Recuperating and reinterpreting a metaphor in use in oceanography, Ozeki suggests that the gyres have their own material "memory" made up of objects discarded or lost by humans, including Nao's diary: "The gyre's memory is all the stuff that we've forgotten" (2013, 114).[11] It is thanks to the inscrutable patterns of the ocean's memory that Nao and Ruth come into contact. If a prototypical example of reciprocal sentence is something like "Nao and Ruth met," *A Tale for the Time Being* shifts the emphasis from the human meeting to the ocean's participation in the meeting—not as a mere vehicle or even facilitator, but as a nonhuman actant entangled, diegetically and metaphorically, with the two characters' fate: "Nao, Ruth, and the ocean met."

PROMOTION OF PLACE TO CHARACTER

Ozeki's ocean is also an illustration of the next category of nonhuman actants, the equivalent of Goatly's "promotion of place to grammatical subject": stylistic and narrative strategies can push the space of the setting, which typically serves as a mere backdrop to human characters and events, toward an agentive position. This process can involve varying degrees of personification of nonhuman spaces.[12] There is a hint of anthropomorphism in Ozeki's attribution of memory to the ocean, but in other narratives the personification of place becomes much more overt. In an insightful ecostylistic reading of Amitav Ghosh's *The Hungry Tide* (2004), Elisabetta Zurru (2017) argues that the landscape of the Sundarbans on the Bay of Bengal is one of the main actants in Ghosh's novel, entering a reciprocal relationship with the human characters. Zurru's analysis shows that "the linguistic level turns 'the setting of the novel' into an active, major character in the story" (2017, 203–4) through, in particular, the personification of the river Matla, in sentences such as "The Matla laughed its mental laugh" or "The Matla took pity" on someone (quoted in Zurru 2017, 230).

A striking example of promotion of place to narrative actant that avoids straightforward personification is Area X in Jeff VanderMeer's Southern Reach trilogy (VanderMeer 2014a; 2014b; 2014c). Area X is a coastal region in North America where the ecosystem shows some serious, and inexplicable, anomalies. The US government dispatches a series of research teams to investigate, but these expeditions repeatedly (and dramatically) fail, suggesting that the anomalies run deeper than previously thought: the government's official version points to an environmental catastrophe, but there are strong indications that Area X was occupied by an alien life form that radically altered the landscape. Just like the Sundarbans in Ghosh's novel, Area X becomes an actant, but in a way that avoids direct personification, instead emphasizing Area X's nonhuman opacity and unreadability: "Nothing about language, about communication, could bridge the divide between human beings and Area X" (2014c, 311). When, in the course of the trilogy, Area X starts expanding and incorporating the rest of the world, there is little doubt that its behavior displays intentionality, but its exact motivations remain unclear and deeply perplexing; as one of the main characters reflects, she "felt that if she could make Area X react, then she would somehow throw it off course. Even though we didn't know what course it was on" (2014b, 262).

Ultimately, however, the physical expansion of Area X proves less unsettling than its capacity to shape and control the minds of those who come into contact with it. Consider the following passage: "That landscape was impinging on them now. The temperature dipped and rose violently. There were rumblings deep underground that manifested as slight tremors. The sun came to them with a 'greenish tinge' as if 'somehow the border were distorting our vision'" (2014a, 164). The idea is not just that the trilogy's spatial setting informs the characters' existential and material situation—which would be a simple inversion of the transitive subject-object structure—but that it becomes deeply implicated in their actions and psychological states. Through the actantial mediation of place, the nonhuman infiltrates both the storyworld and the characters' psychology. Far from being straightforwardly personified, the landscape of Area X ends up taking over and nonhumanizing the human.

NOMINALIZATION AND ABSTRACTION IN NARRATIVE PROGRESSION

Nominalization uses a noun to capture a process normally denoted by a verb, thus eliding the agents involved in that process. This is, fundamentally, an operation of linguistic abstraction, in two ways: the noun abstracts from a specific event ("the evaporation of water" is more general than "the water evaporates"), and the noun abstracts from the participants in that event (i.e., who or what caused the water to evaporate). How does this translate into narrative terms? A possible equivalent are narratives that foreground a spatiotemporal process beyond the human scale, which displaces human intentionality as the driving force of the plot.

As argued in chapter 2, plot tends to be both triggered and determined in its progression by the beliefs and desires of human (or human-like) characters. However, in a novel like Kurt Vonnegut's 1985 *Galápagos*, the narrative progression is governed by a long series of coincidences and unlikely outcomes that break with human intentionality. *Galápagos* imagines a future in which only a handful of humans survive a catastrophic virus outbreak, by finding shelter on one of the Galápagos islands. Thematically, natural selection is a major player in the novel: there are multiple references to Darwin and his theory of evolution, conveyed with such accuracy that Andrea

Bixler (2007) proposes using *Galápagos* in schools as an aid for teaching genetic drift in evolutionary processes. Vonnegut's engagement with natural selection is deeply grounded in form. The narrative is strewn with ironic counterfactual statements, which keep reminding the reader that humanity's survival is a mere stroke of luck: for instance, the narrator points out that if a certain soldier "had not burglarized that shop, there would almost certainly be no human beings on the face of the earth today. I mean it. Everybody alive today should thank God that this soldier was insane" (2011, 160).[13] If humanity survives a catastrophic virus outbreak, it is not due to the survivors' deliberate efforts but thanks to the unintended and surprising consequences of an action dictated by madness. In this way, Vonnegut's plot mirrors the haphazard, stochastic nature of natural evolution: just as natural selection is driven by random genetic mutations, the narrative proceeds by way of apparently random twists and turns. Evolution, as Porter Abbott (2003) argues in an insightful essay, cannot be narrativized directly, because the time frames it involves and its lack of teleology are incompatible with narrative representation. Vonnegut attempts to sidestep this limitation by capturing, through the formal logic of narrative sequence, the equally abstract logic of random mutations over large-scale time.[14] This strategy is the equivalent of nominalization as Goatly discusses it: in this reading of the novel, an abstract principle beyond the human scale is transformed into an actant, determining the characters' fate and putting the nonhuman in control of the narrative.

This chapter revisited Greimas's notion of "actant" from a perspective informed by the nonhuman turn and contemporary discussions on the Anthropocene. The structuralist approach to character, which Greimas systematized in his work, aimed to extricate character in narrative from a purely mimetic understanding. Thus, Greimas's actantial model promises to deanthropomorphize narrative agency and speaks to contemporary philosophical work that questions the metaphysical separation between human and nonhuman realities (as demonstrated by Latour's adoption of the term "actant" in his actor-network theory). However, from the perspective of what James (2015) calls an "econarratology"—a narratology attuned to human-nonhuman entanglements in narrative form—Greimas's operation falls short: his structuralist model rests on a syntactic system, transitivity, that is fundamentally dualistic and closely aligned with anthropocentric assumptions.

To remedy this problem, we need to think more carefully about linguistic devices that serve as sites of resistance to anthropocentrism and can potentially expose the enmeshment of human subjectivity and nonhuman realities. Goatly's work in the field of ecolinguistics offers helpful suggestions as to where to find these devices in the linguistic system. This chapter has attempted to scale up Goatly's devices to the level of whole narratives, tracing them in a corpus of contemporary novels that explicitly address the Anthropocenic interrelation of humans and nonhuman processes. This focus on contemporary fiction was determined pragmatically, but the five strategies discussed here are likely to be found in both nonfictional narrative genres (e.g., conversational storytelling) and in fiction that predates the current ecological crisis.

On a purely conceptual level, it is important to point out that this nonanthropocentric approach to character is anything but the systematic theory of narrative that Greimas sought to develop. Opening up the notion of character to nonhuman actants is, necessarily, an explorative and speculative project that strives to read between the lines of narrative's anthropocentric dominant: its bias toward the human scale. Conceptualizing actants in this way requires expanding our understanding of causality and agency (see Caracciolo 2018c): the modes of agency involved by nonhuman realities are, clearly, alternative to the psychological causation of human characters' beliefs and intentions—the traditional stuff of storytelling, as discussed in chapter 2.

It may be objected that there is a degree of metaphorical slippage in my overhaul of the concept of "actant." We have seen that tides and cranes and even an abstract scientific theory can become actants in narrative; isn't this "just" a metaphor? The challenge of developing a theory of narrative geared toward nonhuman realities lies precisely in learning to move beyond dichotomies of this kind, including dichotomies between the literal and the metaphorical use of concepts. Undoubtedly, attributing intentionality to nonhuman realities involves a metaphorical leap, because a powerful combination of cognitive predispositions and cultural factors (especially in a Western context) leads us to regard these realities as inert and passive.[15] Yet the metaphorical extension of human concepts such as agency and intentionality has great heuristic value, in that it can reveal the ways in which nonhuman realities *resist* anthropomorphic (and metaphorical) appropriation. Indeed, the main takeaway of chapters 6 and 7 is that metaphors, and particularly the creative metaphors that are deployed by literary narrative, participate in a process of discovery of human-nonhuman enmeshment. If we dismiss the notion of nonhuman actant as a "mere" metaphor, we have already closed the door on that possibility of discovery.

Before expanding on the role of metaphor, however, it is worth digging deeper into human-nonhuman enmeshment, exploring how narrative can embed the mesh in the consciousnesses of recognizably human characters. This is an alternative route for capturing interdependency: besides expanding the notion of actants to nonhuman entities (as highlighted by this chapter), narrative can plant the nonhuman into the subjective ground of the human.

CHAPTER 5

Minding the Anthropocene

In a 2012 study, two neuroscientists, Semir Zeki and Jonathan Stutters, asked sixteen participants to watch short video clips while their brain activity was being recorded in an FMRI scanner. The clips were exceedingly simple: they showed an array of white dots moving, in shifting configurations and along various trajectories of motion, against a black background. No human artist had drawn these images: as the researchers explain, the eight different patterns had been computer-generated using mathematical functions (2012, 2). The goals of the experiment were twofold: measuring the participants' preference for these patterns of motion and establishing whether their judgments went hand in hand with brain activation in the visual cortex. The study found that the participants favored the pattern shown on the left-hand side of figure 7; the pattern on the right-hand side, by contrast, received the lowest average rating.[1] The former pattern displays dot clusters traveling along different vectors, with one cluster occasionally intersecting another. The latter shows a grid of dots uniformly scrolling up and down and to the right. The FMRI part of the study highlighted a correlation between the participants' subjective preferences and brain activation in areas of the visual cortex known to be sensitive to the directionality of motion, particularly the V5 area, which is widely seen as playing a central role in motion perception.

Why are some of these patterns more visually attractive, and more stimulating for the brain, than others? Given that all these images are abstract, the participants' clear preference for certain patterns poses something of a puzzle. The explanation offered by the authors of the study points to the shaping influence of evolution, which tuned the human brain to respond to certain visual patterns. More specifically, for Zeki and Stutters the preferred patterns, while computer-generated, reflect "optical flow or biological motion" (2012, 5). This brief and vague phrase may pass unobserved in a cursory reading of the article, but anyone who has watched the video clips will know exactly what Zeki and Stutters mean. The patterns, which were mathematically programmed into a computer, are abstract and non-figurative. But the qualities of their motion are richly suggestive in a looser, metaphorical sense. The highly rated pattern in figure 7 strongly evokes the image of bird flocks crossing the sky, or leaves wafting through the air; another highly rated sequence combines a series of star-shaped patterns reminiscent of a flower or sea anemone. The least preferred pattern in figure 7, by contrast, displays a degree of uniformity and regularity of motion not commonly found in nature.

Read in this way, Zeki and Stutters's study illustrates the idea that our brains—and, by extension, our bodies—resonate deeply with the forms of nature. Evolution has steadily honed our perceptual system to apprehend natural patterns that were of significance to human survival. Our ancestors lived and passed on their genes through being able to observe the forms of nature, imitating them in their artifacts and manipulating them in their rituals and practices. Appreciation of nature is thus intimately related to its evolutionary value for human societies. Even in responding to stimuli as far from natural landscapes as the computer-generated, abstract images of Zeki and Stutters's neuroscientific study, we favor the patterns that most closely resemble natural phenomena.

Despite this body of evidence, philosophers working within the non-human turn have tended to push back against an understanding of reality that front-loads human experience and subjectivity. Bennett articulates this sidestepping of subjectivity in the preface to *Vibrant Matter*: "In what follows

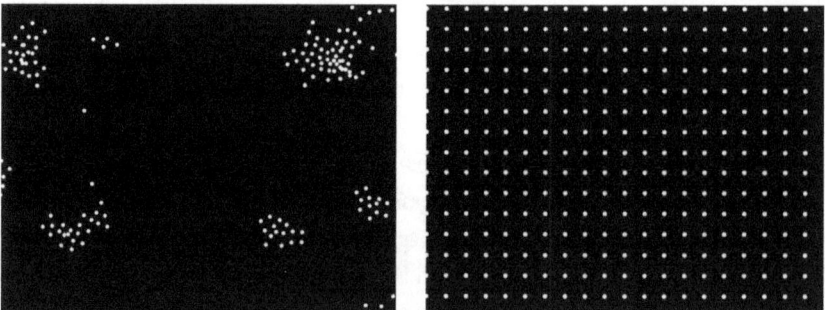

Figure 7. Two abstract dot patterns from Zeki and Stutters (2012). The one on the left (pattern 2 in the study) received considerably higher preference ratings than the one on the right (pattern 6 in the study). (Used with permission)

the otherwise important topic of subjectivity . . . gets short shrift so that I may focus on the task of developing a vocabulary and syntax for, and thus a better discernment of, the active powers issuing from nonsubjects" (2010, xi). The upshot of this line of argument is that, to fully grasp the materiality of the world and its entanglement with human societies, we need to leave the mind *behind*.[2] The overview of nonhuman actants in the previous chapter has adopted a similar approach, asking how we can reconceptualize character without treating it as a site of human or human-like subjectivity. The goal of that discussion was to create a level playing field for an understanding of human-nonhuman relations as fundamentally interdependent rather than hierarchical.

This chapter explores an alternative but complementary route to the interdependency of human and nonhuman subjects. It centers on the human mind's intrinsic attunement to nonhuman patterns, the kind of attunement brought into focus by Zeki and Stutters's study. Just like the geometric images used by the neuroscientists, narrative can deploy formal devices that capture human-nonhuman interdependency *from within the human mind*. Recent developments in the mind sciences suggest that, despite entrenched notions of dualistic separation from the material world, the human mind is "world-involving" at a fundamental level.[3] Work in embodied, enactivist, and extended approaches to cognition has developed a view of human-nonhuman interdependency that bears more than a superficial resemblance to the way in which interdependency has been theorized within the nonhuman turn. In short, embodied cognition foregrounds the body as underlying and shaping our cognitive skills, including conceptual abilities and language processing.[4] Enactivist accounts of the mind, such as Francisco Varela, Evan Thompson, and Eleanor Rosch's (1991), place a premium on the fundamental interaction between cognizing subjects and the external environment, seeing the mind as arising from its "structural coupling" with the world. Reality, from an enactivist perspective, does not preexist the mind but is enacted through embodied patterns of exploration based on the "affordances" (action possibilities) offered by the organism's surroundings.[5] The extended mind hypothesis, introduced by Andy Clark and David Chalmers (1998), argues that the mind is extended into the world through material artifacts, such as writing instruments or other tools, that play a causal role in cognition and form an integral part of our minds.

These theories are sometimes brought together under the heading of "e-approaches" to the mind (see Hutto 2012). They converge with discussions on the Anthropocene in two areas: first, they seek to overcome dualistic thinking, and, more specifically, dichotomies between subject and object, mind and embodied matter, human subjectivity and the world of inanimate (and supposedly inert) things; and, second, they critique representation insofar as it presupposes a subject autonomous from the external environment. "Minding the Anthropocene" is thus shorthand for an attempt to span or at least narrow the divide between the human mind and the nonhuman.

This chapter does not explore the interdisciplinary possibilities of this dialogue in purely theoretical terms, however. Rather, it uses fiction as a springboard for thinking through these issues. The convergence between the mind sciences and the nonhuman turn is foregrounded, via formal strategies, by three contemporary novels: *The Echo Maker* (2006) by Richard Powers (already discussed in passing in the previous chapter); *Atmospheric Disturbances* (2008) by Rivka Galchen, an American Canadian writer of Israeli descent; and *Qualcosa, là fuori* (Something, out there; 2016) by Bruno Arpaia, an Italian writer and journalist. These novels speak to questions about the Anthropocene and the current environmental crisis—straightforwardly in the case of Powers and Arpaia, more indirectly in the case of Galchen. To be more specific, these case studies hybridize Anthropocene-related anxieties with the "neuronovel," in Marco Roth's coinage (2009): a strand of contemporary fiction that engages with neuroscientific themes.[6] Thus, the protagonist of *Qualcosa, là fuori* is a neuroscientist, whereas *The Echo Maker* and *Atmospheric Disturbances* center on characters affected by the same psychiatric disorder, the Capgras syndrome. As Roth notes, neuronovels are defined by a materialist approach to the mind that explains "proximate causes of mental function in terms of neurochemistry, and ultimate causes in terms of evolution and heredity" (2009, n.p.). In this way, Roth argues that the neuronovel moves beyond previous—and less brain-based—frameworks for understanding the mind, such as psychoanalysis.[7]

Through this materialist view of mental processes Powers's, Galchen's, and Arpaia's works evoke and probe human-nonhuman enmeshment from within their characters' mental lives. These narratives thus displace the Anthropocene from the external world to the domain of inner, mental processes, and they expose—disturbingly—the power of geological or climatological realities to shape our minds at a fundamental level. This "shaping" is conveyed through formal strategies that can be effectively captured through the toolbox of contemporary narrative theory. The evocation of consciousness in narrative is a long-standing concern of narratology.[8] More recently, e-approaches have entered narratological discussions and shaped the understanding and analysis of the narrative evocation of characters' minds.[9] Narrative theory is thus in an ideal position to capitalize on the convergence between e-approaches to the mind and accounts of human-nonhuman entanglements. In *A Biocultural Approach to Literary Theory and Interpretation*, Nancy Easterlin has already taken a significant step in this direction, building on evolutionary psychology to raise the important point that "ecocritics [should] ground their field in knowledge of evolved human psychology in an effort to understand the species' relationship with the nonhuman natural world" (2012, 36). The discussion of mind and the nonhuman in this chapter shares many of Easterlin's assumptions, but it also moves beyond her focus on space and place as sites of encounter between the human mind and the nonhuman world. Rather, the chapter investigates how narrative can use the formal resources of internal focalization and first person narration to explore two key areas of overlap between e-approaches to cognition and contemporary thinking on the nonhuman: a rejection of dualistic thinking, and a critique of representation. Both conceptual stances, as we'll see, point to the interdependency of human subjects and nonhumans that this part of the book explores.

AGAINST DUALISMS

In introducing the nonhuman turn, Richard Grusin places the question of dualism front and center: "Each of these different elements of the nonhuman turn derives from theoretical movements that argue (in one way or another) against human exceptionalism, expressed most often in the form of conceptual or rhetorical dualisms that separate the human from the nonhuman" (2015a, x). The antidualistic commitments of the nonhuman turn flow from its denying clear-cut oppositions between human and nonhuman realities. The privative "non-" of the word "nonhuman" is in this sense rather misleading, because this category is not meant to be dualistically *opposed* to the human but constitutively intertwined with it. The Anthropocene reveals humankind's lasting impact on the climate and geological history of our planet but also shows how, in hindsight, human communities were always impacted by factors and forces beyond the human scale (from meteorological patterns to natural evolution and geological processes).

Eradicating simplistic dichotomies between the human and the nonhuman triggers a domino effect, toppling many other forms of dualisms.

Like scholars in material ecocriticism, Bennett takes aim at the idea of (human) agency as dualistically opposed to the world of inanimate, inert things: "Humanity and nonhumanity have always performed an intricate dance with each other. There was never a time when human agency was anything other than an interfolding network of humanity and nonhumanity; today this mingling has become harder to ignore" (2010, 31). Human/nonhuman and subject/object dualisms overlap to a large extent, because our understanding of subjectivity is based on *human* subjectivity, with animals occupying an uneasy, and often contested, position on the fringes of the subject. Emphasizing the "dance" of human and nonhuman agency, as Bennett does, thus means questioning the possibility of separating subjectivity from the world of "mere," insentient matter. Finally, the last dualism to be challenged by the nonhuman turn is that pitting nature against human culture: Iovino and Oppermann argue that "[instead] of nature and culture, we should . . . talk of 'natureculture,' and finally question the ontological boundaries set up by our cognitive practices" (2012, 454).

Iovino and Oppermann raise an important point toward the end of the quotation: dualistic thinking is the result of a basic cognitive propensity to distinguish between animate subjects and inanimate objects. This propensity has been observed in preverbal infants as young as seven months old.[10] Building on empirical findings from the mind sciences allows us to put culturally stratified forms of dualism (agent vs. passive object or culture vs. nature) on a continuum with a more elementary, and yet pervasive, tendency to categorize the world into animate and inanimate entities.

Not only do the mind sciences bring to light the developmental underpinnings of the binaries critiqued by the nonhuman turn, but they substantiate this critique. In their landmark *The Embodied Mind*, Varela, Thompson, and Rosch (1991, 151–57) take a decidedly antidualistic approach by arguing that a living organism and its environment arise simultaneously, in a structural coupling in which the features of the environment are defined by the organism's individual and collective (evolutionary) history of interactions with the world: in this sense, the environment does not preexist the organism but is cocreated by it. Likewise, the premise of the movement known as embodied cognition is that mind cannot be separated from our living bodies: even conceptual activities that seem distant from somatic modes of engagement with the world reflect our bodily makeup (see, e.g., Lakoff and Johnson 1999). From a different perspective, Clark and Chalmers's "extended mind hypothesis" suggests that material objects are actively involved in our thought processes, so that the mind does not end at the physical boundaries of our brains (or bodies) but embraces the material world as well. For Clark (1997), language and culture themselves are technologies that extend the human mind, playing an integral role in our cognitive processes rather than serving as mere external props. Clark draws an interesting analogy between culture and mangrove forests, which start with a seed floating on shallow water: once developed into a plant, the mangrove grows aerial roots that attract debris and, rather counterintuitively, "create" land all around the tree. In much the same way, language can "act like the aerial roots of the mangrove tree—the words would serve as fixed points capable of attracting and positioning additional intellectual matter, creating the islands of second-order thought so characteristic of the cognitive landscape of *Homo sapiens*" (1997, 209). This is what Clark terms the "mangrove effect." Thus, Clark contends that the mind incorporates the external, linguistic realities of culture in a way that flatly contradicts the dualistic tendency to segregate mental processes from material objects. What emerges, as in the nonhuman turn, is a sense of enmeshment and coconstitution between human subjectivity and nonhuman materiality.

BEYOND REPRESENTATION

A second theme shared by discussions on the nonhuman and e-approaches to cognition is their drawing attention to the limits of the concept of "representation." Emily Potter has addressed some of these conceptual difficulties in an article on climate change and its modeling in science and art. Representation, she argues, constrains thinking about climate change because it "is singular and undynamic. It instrumentalises relations between the assemblage of people, places, environments and emissions that it encompasses, excluding less calculable manifestations of impact and effect" (2009, 70). As Potter's argument unfolds, it becomes clear that the problem is not the representation of a given reality per se but the *assumptions* that inform representation, particularly its separating the subject from an environment seen as inert and pregiven.

Potter's solution to this impasse is to embrace "nonrepresentational" and "more-than-representational" thinking, which highlights "more-than-textual ways of knowing the world; knowledge emergent from embodied process and material practices" (2009, 72). Because the realization of our enmeshment with the nonhuman world is a deeply affective one, affect and bodily experience are instrumental in overcoming the strictures of representational thinking: affect destabilizes representation and questions dichotomies between human and nonhuman realities.[11] This does not mean that scientific and artistic practices can do without representation, of course, but reconceptualizing representation along more context-sensitive lines and foregrounding its affective dimension can go a long way toward addressing the issues raised by Potter.

This focus on more-than-representational modes of understanding reality ties in with the shift away from representation in the mind sciences. Traditional, artificial intelligence–inspired cognitive science saw the mind as a computational device turning perceptual input into symbolic, language-like representations.[12] Seen in this light, even something as biologically basic as perception involves the manipulation of representations that are fundamentally abstract and world-independent. Effectively, this move erects a representational barrier between the subject and the external world; e-approaches to cognition seek to eliminate this barrier. The most radical critique of representation can be found in the writings of "enactivist" thinkers such as the already mentioned Varela, Thompson, and Rosch (1991), Alva Noë (2004), or Daniel Hutto (Hutto and Myin 2012). The bottom line of this enactivist philosophy is that, at a basic level, reality is apprehended not through representational models but through patterns of sensory and affective engagement that weave together the organism and its environment.

These patterns are still present and active in conceptual or language-involving activities: readers' interaction with fictional characters, for instance, can take on a somatic dimension, and readers' understanding of spatial descriptions and even the temporal progression of narrative builds on embodied patterns (see chapter 2). Thus, e-approaches to cognition reveal the continuity between narrative representations and nonrepresentational thinking, which in turn speaks to the claims of theorists associated with the nonhuman turn. The next sections show how contemporary neuronovels by Powers, Galchen, and Arpaia integrate the critique of dualism and representationalism through a set of concrete stylistic and narrative strategies; these strategies are crucial to bringing together the novels' exploration of nonhuman realities with the workings of mind.

LIQUID MINDS IN *THE ECHO MAKER*

As seen briefly in the previous chapter, *The Echo Maker* is the story of a Midwestern man who suffers brain damage as a result of a car accident, developing a psychiatric condition known as "Capgras syndrome." The essence of this condition is that this character, Mark, thinks his sister, Karin, is a mere lookalike of his real sister. The plot focuses on Karin's emotional struggles as she takes care of someone who behaves as if she was an impostor, and it places her at the center of an intersubjective network formed by her brother and two other characters: Dr. Weber, a famous psychiatrist Karin turns to for medical advice, and Daniel, Karin's partner and a naturalist working at a nearby crane refuge. Most of the narrative takes place in Nebraska, by the banks of the Platte River, where hundreds of thousands of sandhill cranes congregate every spring.

The spectacle of the birds' migration is more than a backdrop to Karin's story, however. Powers weaves the nonhuman realities of the birds and river into the narrative at multiple levels: the birds are the sole witnesses to Mark's car accident, whose causes are surrounded by mystery; one of Mark's delusions is that the doctors who operated on him after his accident grafted parts of bird brain onto his brain; and Daniel is fighting a legal battle against a group of corporate investors who aim to turn a stretch of the Platte River into a tourist resort, endangering the cranes (and his own nature conservation efforts). By intertwining these plot strands, Powers's novel amplifies the thematic echoes between nonhuman realities (the birds and the space of the Platte River) and the characters' various attempts at explaining Mark's psychiatric condition (in medical terms) or coming to terms with it (in Karin's personal terms). Implicitly, this plot structure superimposes two dualisms (humanity vs. nature and mind vs. matter) and shows how they derive from the same fundamental mistake—namely, that of segregating human minds from their physical environment. At the end of the novel, Dr. Weber is flying out of Nebraska when he has an epiphany of our enmeshment with the nonhuman world:

> Everything is animate, green and encroaching. Dozens of millions of species seethe around him, few of them visible, even fewer named, ready to try anything once, every possible cheat and exploitation, just to keep being. He stares at his shaking hands, whole rain forests of bacteria. Insects burrow deep inside this plane's wiring. Seeds abide in the cargo hold. Fungus under

the cabin's vinyl lining. Outside his little window flap, frozen in the airless air, archaea, super-bugs, and extremophiles live on nothing, in darkness, below zero, simply copying. Every code that has stayed alive until now is more brilliant than his subtlest thought. And when his thoughts die, more brilliant still. (2006, 448–49)

Weber's imagination moves below human-scale experience, with its comfortably clear-cut boundary line between living creatures and the external world. The character's insight reveals spaces teeming with life forms where we would expect none (his hands are "whole rain forests of bacteria"). Equally striking is the implicit equation between Dr. Weber's thoughts and the genetic code that is being replicated by microorganisms outside the plane window: mental content is seen as inherently physical and subject to the same evolutionary constraints as DNA (which is the more "brilliant" the longer it can survive). The challenge to the living/lifeless binary extends to mind/matter dualism, suggesting that the conceptual polarities governing the human-scale world become unstable and unsustainable at other levels of reality.

The novel explicitly articulates and probes the problem of identifying a link between mind and matter, also known as "mind-body problem."[13] In a conversation with his wife, Dr. Weber remarks that "'everything's physical.' Chemical, electrical. Synapses" (2006, 354): the difficulty, as far as science is concerned, is understanding the exact ways in which physical processes cause Mark's delusion—his creating an imaginary world in which Karin is not his sister but an impostor caught in a web of conspiracy theories. At another level, the difficulty is reconciling Dr. Weber's interest in his patients' narratives, which are at the center of his books, and the experimental methods of neuroscience, which eschew storytelling in favor of physical brain events. The novel's focus on the Anthropocenic interrelation of humans and environment on the one hand and the staging of questions about the mind's bodily underpinnings on the other enter a reciprocal relation: Mark's mental illness—and the multiple reactions it triggers in the other characters—serve as a narrative and thematic prism, calling attention to the conceptual common ground between these dualistic tendencies.

As a consequence of physical damage to his brain, Mark comes to experience a deep connection with the cranes, a connection that escapes the other characters' more functional, but irretrievably dualistic, ways of thinking. Physical injury creates psychological delusion, which in turn reveals humans' embedding in a world that is physical *and* deeply nonhuman. Powers translates this intuition at the level of style and narrative technique through the strategic use of internal focalization. As Luc Herman and Bart Vervaeck observe in an insightful reading of *The Echo Maker,* "It seems hard to miss that the first representation of Mark's consciousness, while clearly focalized through Mark, is indebted to the narrator's external focalizations of the cranes elsewhere in the novel" (2009, 426).

In fact, the novel begins with—and is punctuated by—lyrical passages tracking the cranes' migration and describing, with the disorienting effect of a cinematic close-up, their bodies: "A neck stretches long; legs drape behind. Wings curl forward, the length of a man. Spread like fingers, primaries tip the bird into the wind's plane. The blood-red head bows and the wings sweep together, a cloaked priest giving benediction. Tail cups and belly buckles, surprised by the upsurge of ground. Legs kick out, their backward knees flapping like broken landing gear" (2006, 3). As Herman and Vervaeck point out, this rarefied prose is closely reminiscent of the internally focalized passages rendering Mark's mental experience during his coma: "A flock of birds, each one burning. Stars swoop down to bullets. Hot red specks take flesh, nest there, a body part, part body. Lasts forever: no change to measure. Flock of fiery cinders. When gray pain of them thins, then always water. Flattest width so slow it fails as liquid. Nothing in the end but flow. Nextless stream, lowest thing above knowing. A thing itself the cold and so can't feel it" (2006, 10). Both Powers's description and Mark's delirium dissolve reality into kinetic traces like the "stretching" of the birds' necks or the "swooping down" of the stars, language that is vague and yet at the same time deeply embodied. As such, this language is likely to resonate in readers' own bodies through a mechanism of embodied simulation: research in cognitive psychology and psycholinguistics shows that some of the same neural areas are involved in performing physical actions and in processing the verbal description of such actions.[14]

While narrative usually aligns these embodied resonances with the overt representation of characters' bodies, Powers's prose succeeds in uncoupling them: we find it difficult to visualize the cranes, or the contents of Mark's imagination, but we sense them through bodily patterns. In the process, human and animal bodies, animate and inanimate entities, are implicitly equated and thus brought together in readers' imagination. Further, because of its stylistic patterning and embodied materiality, this kind of prose is shot through with affect that cannot be "cashed out" in terms of representation. Commenting on the passage just quoted from *The Echo Maker*, Ridvan Askin raises this point: "In the passage's narrative discourse, this representational and experiential coherence is thoroughly shattered to the point of being barely recoverable" (2016, 25). Here is narrative striving to move beyond the realm of representation through poetic effects; the goal is that of closing the gap between mental states and the birds' material coupling with the Platte River.

This affective blending of mental and physical realities reemerges periodically in the novel, whenever the characters experience the "grip" of the nonhuman world: "Water wants something from [Karin]. Something only consciousness can deliver. She is nothing, as toxic as anything with an ego. A sham; a pretense. Nothing worth recognizing. But still, this river needs her, its liquid mind, its way of surviving" (2006, 408). Note how the river itself is endowed with mind: when narrative heightens its affective impact—that is, when it foregrounds its more-than-representational dimension—dualism collapses, and mind seeps into the material world.

METAPHORICAL CHALLENGES AND *ATMOSPHERIC DISTURBANCES*

If Powers fuses questions about mind with Anthropocenic concerns through focalization and careful plot orchestration, Rivka Galchen's approach in *Atmospheric Disturbances* is more character-driven. This is another novel about Capgras, but here the delusion inflects the mental processes of an unreliable first-person narrator, so that readers are locked into the protagonist's mental processes throughout the novel. The narrative begins on the day in which the narrator, Leo, suddenly fails to recognize his wife, Rema: he is convinced that this person is not the real Rema, but only a lookalike. Himself a psychiatrist, Leo had been treating a patient named Harvey, whose delusion "stemmed from a fixed magical belief that he had special skills for controlling weather phenomena, and that he was, consequently, employed as a secret agent for the Royal Academy of Meteorology. . . . According to Harvey, the Royal Academy dedicated itself to maintaining weather's elements of unpredictability and randomness" (2008, 12). Following Rema's suggestion, Leo had been going along with this fantasy in order to keep Harvey from disappearing and getting himself into trouble; he had pretended also being an agent for the Royal Academy and being in touch with a real meteorologist—and an agent of superior rank—named Tzvi Gal-Chen.

But with the onset of his Capgras delusion, Leo buys into this web of fabrications himself: he starts reading up on Tzvi Gal-Chen's scientific work, using it in often abstruse ways to shed light on his wife's "disappearance."[15] (The character Tzvi Gal-Chen is based on the author's father, who was a meteorologist.)

Thematically, the weather occupies the foreground of the novel's plot, while broader questions surrounding the climate (i.e., long-term atmospheric patterns and trends) are less prominent. This strategy may seem to shift the focus away from the Anthropocene, but we should not forget that this is a madman's delusion: confusing the climate with the daily experience of the weather and stressing the limitations of scientific knowledge or the failure of prediction are well-known tricks in the climate change denier's repertoire. Thus, Harvey's and Leo's strange ramblings about the Royal Academy of Meteorology and its efforts to maintain the weather's "unpredictability and randomness" function as a satire of climate change skepticism.

The novel prompts more than a satirical reading, however. It explores the personal relevance of meteorology and articulates what can be read as a displaced form of climate change anxiety.[16] The unreliable narrator's mindset is fundamentally paranoid in that he sees connections among events—and levels of reality—that would appear unrelated to a mentally healthy observer. Leo repeatedly compares himself to the butterfly of the butterfly effect (see chapter 2). Surely, this effect can explain meteorological anomalies, but the narrator extends the same logic to social and even psychological phenomena, in an antidualistic move that cuts across distinctions between physical causality and the intricacies of social interaction. For instance, the narrator applies the scientific theory of the Doppler effect to Rema's double, resulting in a bizarre thought experiment in which "a Rema look-alike emerges every second" (2008, 44) from a mysterious source. If one walks toward this source, the effect is that "there is now less spacing between the Remas, and therefore the wavelength has been affected, the perceived frequency of Remas has changed, has increased" (2008, 45). Behind the narrator's somewhat perplexing treatment of the "Dopplerganger effect," as he calls it, is a conflation of human selfhood and material phenomena, such as those studied by physics or meteorology.

Along similar lines, the narrative makes repeated use of metaphorical expressions that capture the narrator's phenomenology by way of a comparison with material processes.[17] Here is one of the many examples:

"Intrusive thoughts, rising as if carbonated, disturbed me from sleep" (2008, 29). This language works by bringing together the material reality of gas bubbles in a carbonated drink and the psychological reality of the narrator's mind. Later in the novel we read that the narrator "got caught within [a] syllogism, like in the still place inside of storms" (2008, 64). These metaphors and similes reflect a more general tendency to translate intangible realities—such as those of our mental life—into material scenarios that we can directly experience and share with other language users (the gas bubbles and the storm). Metaphorical language of this kind provides a crucial link between our conceptual apparatus and our bodily makeup, as stressed by cognitive scientists working in the wake of Lakoff and Johnson (1999). Such metaphorical mappings are common in everyday discourse, but Galchen's novel prompts a radical reading of metaphors and similes that use material, spatial processes to represent mind.[18] An expression such as "thoughts, rising as if carbonated" could easily be read as a *mere* simile when taken out of context. Put otherwise, it could be read as a simile that does not make any ontological claim as to the nature of our thought processes, and whether these are material or dualistically separate from the physical world. However, in the thick of Leo's narrative, metaphorical language of this kind functions as a symptom of the narrator's inability to truly distinguish between the physical and the mental—and, ultimately, of his tendency to conflate them.

For instance, the following passage moves nonchalantly from perceived temperature to the Doppler effect to interpersonal dynamics, as if these levels of reality could be collapsed into one another: "Is windchill analogous to Doppler effect, I philosophized in a feeble attempt to sound atmospherically savvy, but applied to the movement of heat rather than of light or sound? I thought about making a further analogy, to movements in human relationships, say, to interpersonal coldnesses that feel much colder than they actually are" (2008, 144–45). On paper, Leo claims to be aware that these are analogical leaps, but he seems to lose track of their metaphorical nature when he turns the weather into the guiding principle for his quest: the key to Rema's "disappearance" (a matter of psychology and, more specifically, psychiatric illness) lies in scientific theories about phenomena unfolding in physical space. For all its strangeness, the narrator's logic defamiliarizes the reader—and our understanding of similes such as "thoughts, rising as if carbonated"—by suggesting that there might be more in common between thoughts and carbonated drinks than we normally assume.

MINDING THE ANTHROPOCENE 129

In addition to challenging dualistic distinctions between mind and world, Leo's mental illness destabilizes the role of scientific representation. In an important episode, Leo reads into Tzvi Gal-Chen's highly technical prose clues about his situation. Of particular interest are Leo's comments on a graph (see fig. 8) appearing in an article by Gal-Chen. This graph is lifted from a scientific article coauthored by the *real* Tzvi Gal-Chen, the author's father (see Hane, Wilhelmson, and Gal-Chen 1981, 4); it was originally intended as the representation of wind speed and temperature inside a "model storm." But Leo turns it into something completely different: "I'm unable to reproduce the effect, the effect the image had on me, which was, well, uncanny, like those dolls whose eyes seem to follow you around a room. Like I was looking at a topographical map of a landscape I knew only from close up. Some sense of concordance, and meaning, of a pattern both inscrutable and yet, at some almost cellular level, detected" (2008, 59). This paranoid reading of the graph amplifies Potter's critique of representation:

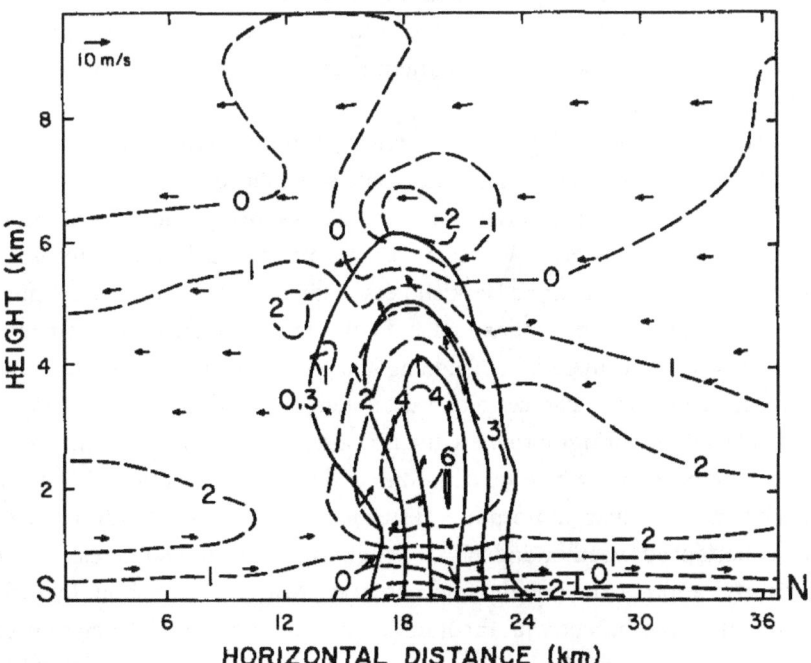

Figure 8. A cross section of a "model storm," from Hane, Wilhelmson, and Gal-Chen (1981, 4), reprinted in Galchen (2008, 59). (© American Meteorological Society; used with permission)

the narrator's remarks stress the affective nature of his engagement with the image, thus leveraging its emotional, personal relevance to unsettle, by way of humorous incongruity, the rigid scientific abstraction of the "model storm." Leo returns to this image in a later passage, in which the personification of the graph continues, but the affective tone shifts from humor to melancholic acknowledgement of the narrator's isolation: "In addition to reminding me of Rema, it also looked to me like a lonely man, in an alien landscape, glancing back over his shoulder as if to ask something of someone whom he was not sure was there" (2008, 120). Here the figure in the graph becomes a stand-in for the narrator's own existential condition—the "lonely man, in an alien landscape"—as he struggles with mental illness. The representation generates affect because the narrator reads (mistakenly, of course, but no less suggestively) a human body into an abstract graph. Just as material metaphors for mind point to the role of bodily experience in appropriating abstract or intangible phenomena, such as our thought processes, scientific knowledge implicates human embodiment and builds it into any attempt at understanding the nonhuman world. Thus, the diagram as a whole functions as a mirror of the structural coupling between humans and the environment that is foregrounded by enactivist philosophers.

By blending psychological and physical phenomena through metaphor, and by projecting affective significance onto scientific representation, psychiatric illness undermines notions of humankind's metaphysical segregation from the material world. We can all learn from this "delusion": our likely resistance to the narrator's "jerkish personality," as Roth (2009, n.p.) puts it, is a symptom of our individual and collective reluctance to fully come to terms with our material embedding in a more-than-human world—and with how our daily choices jeopardize such embedding. The narrator's unpredictability brings into view the precarity of humankind's Anthropocenic predicament, which he embodies and performs through his quirky behavior. The titular "atmospheric disturbances" are thus not only a matter of experienced weather, individual psychology, and mental illness, but a narrativization of the broader conceptual ruptures brought about by realizing our enmeshment with the nonhuman. The merit of Galchen's novel is that it shows this realization emerge from within the folds of a character's psychology, in a way that does not spell out climate change issues but still subtly implicates them, as an intrusive subtext to the narrator's delirium.

ANTHROPOCENIC PERCEPTION: *QUALCOSA, LÀ FUORI*

Of the novels discussed in this chapter, Bruno Arpaia's *Qualcosa, là fuori* (Something, out there) is the one most straightforwardly concerned with the Anthropocene at the level of subject matter: the premise is that climate change has turned most of Europe into a Sahara-like desert, with the rule of law becoming weaker by the day, crumbling infrastructure, and cities being torn apart by crime and violence. Only Scandinavian countries maintain acceptable living conditions, thanks to their mild climate and plentiful water and food supplies. In a clear commentary on the 2015 refugee crisis in Europe, the few rich Southern Europeans who can afford a trip to Scandinavia hire private mercenaries to escort them during the long, perilous trek toward the north. The novel's protagonist, Livio, is one of them. At first glance, there would seem to be little of neuroscientific or psychiatric relevance in this plot synopsis. But questions about mind are integrated into the plot through Livio's background as a neuroscientist working at Stanford.

Interspersed with the narrative of the protagonist's journey across a desertified Europe are a number of flashbacks, through which we learn about Livio's research and life in the United States. Livio's preoccupation with the environment and his interest in the human brain are directly juxtaposed: "Besides, by this time even the fate of the planet lashed by global warming did not interest him as much as the mechanisms of the human brain. Delving into those mysteries, exposing the intricate relations between neurons, entering unexplored paths in order to understand the workings of that marvelous 'future machine' hidden inside the skull, made up for any effort and almost any sacrifice" (Arpaia 2016, 25–26).[19] But that future-producing machine that is the human brain is now confronted with the specter of species-wide extinction—with the very real possibility that humankind may *not* have a future: "The day would come in which the mechanisms triggered by the rising temperatures, from the thawing of the tundra to the melting of ice caps, would spiral out of control and recreate the world without humanity's permission" (2016, 17). The key phrase here is "recreate the world": at one level, it refers to natural processes destabilized by humanity's Anthropocenic impact on the planet, and that threaten to erase humankind. At another level, the phrase resonates with the narrative's thematic focus on the ways in which the human brain can "create" reality. In the words of one of Livio's companions during the trek, Livio was "saying that there was something, out there, but that its structure is constructed by our neurons, which derive this structure from perception and then tell us about it in their own way . . ." (2016, 46; ellipsis in the original). As the author explains in the afterword, the inspiration for this idea came from the work of Italian physicist and historian of science Enrico Bellone, and particularly from his book titled—like Arpaia's novel—*Qualcosa, là fuori*. In this monograph, Bellone explores how the brain creates a reality on the basis of ambivalent external data: "Our neuronal networks are specialized in the unfaithful translation of stimuli originating from whatever is out there" (2011, xiii; my translation). Note that this "translation," when conceptualized along enactivist lines, does not deny the objective existence of something outside of the mind; the implication, rather, is that the exact "structure" of the encounter between the human mind and its surroundings is determined by our bodily makeup, evolutionary history, as well as culture and technology.

Humanity's mark on the Earth is thus a mirror image of the human brain's power to "enact" a world, as enactivist philosophers Varela, Thompson, and Rosch would put it: there is no fixed world that preexists the brain's attempts to create coherence, because humans are always caught up in a process of working out reality and what it means to them—in basic perception as well as in scientific theories about climate change.[20] Yet, tragically, enacting a world also involves altering it through patterns of individual and collective action that, in capitalist societies, have grown out of proportion, endangering the survival of our species as well as many other life forms. Arpaia's novel tracks the consequences of this dramatic realization as it emerges in Livio's consciousness after his departure from the United States. The mounting global crisis forces Livio to abandon his research career and make his way back to his hometown, Naples, from where he embarks on a journey toward Scandinavia. History would seem to obliterate Livio's neuroscientific pursuits, but in fact scientific knowledge keeps surfacing in the character's mind: with his intensifying involvement in the environmental catastrophe, Livio becomes more acutely aware of the neural mechanisms that his research had investigated through the safe distance of the laboratory. When one of Livio's travel companions places a comforting hand on his shoulder, he "felt another shiver, a pleasant thrill. How long ago had he learned that all sensations were due to dopamine, serotonin, and oxytocin? That those were only chemical and physical reactions in his brain?" (2016, 19). The barrenness—physical as well as affective—of the postapocalyptic landscape that surrounds Livio heightens his perception;

it reveals how mind is not, dualistically, an autonomous substance, but the result of physiological processes that are as material as the anthropogenic realities of climate change.

Thus, as in Galchen's novel, science is turned into a matter of experience and direct affective relevance. Facing up the realities of the Anthropocene involves a reevaluation of mental life and its neural underpinnings: invisible processes whose complexities mirror, with unexpected precision and poignancy, the unfolding of the environmental crisis. Arpaia's internally focalized prose is responsible for evoking a sense of resonance between the psychological and the material—and again embodiment looms large in the narrative, which leverages Livio's embodied perception and time consciousness as a bridge toward nonhuman realities.

Arpaia's style repeatedly attempts to capture Livio's perceptual field in its raw, undifferentiated, prerepresentational aspect, before distinct objects come into view. Consider, for example, the novel's beginning, in which Livio observes the desolate surroundings of his bivouac, early on in his journey: "Perhaps it was a fire, or a lantern, that reddish glimmer on top of the hill. Assuming that the dark mass that he sensed toward the east really was a hill, blacker than the darkness that surrounded it, muddy, dense, without nuances" (2016, 9). Note how, as the character fails to find perceptual purchase on this landscape, objects are dissolved into simple, geometrical patterns of light and shadow reminiscent of Zeki and Stutters's experiment. Later in the novel, a description of Livio's travel companions brings to the fore the affective component of this perceptual process: "Livio watched [Marta and Sara] walk away, among the backpacks, cots, carts, and dust, under the dogged light that fell down from the sky, livid like malicious radiation" (2016, 48). Here, as is often the case in Arpaia's novel, the light infuses the landscape and its inhabitants with a sense of threat and despair, which are communicated to readers via the use of mood-affecting spatial cues. In this respect, Arpaia's *Qualcosa, là fuori* resembles McCarthy's *The Road*, in which "the desolate landscape . . . and the characters' existential condition reinforce each other in a spiral that contributes significantly to readers' emotional and evaluative engagement with the novel" (Caracciolo 2013b, 426). Unlike *The Road*, Arpaia's novel pays particular attention to how the ecological catastrophe and the affect it elicits blend with Livio's neuroscientific knowledge, bringing him (and, possibly, the reader) closer to the prerepresentational "something, out there" that the human brain tends to slot into conceptual categories.

Livio's time consciousness is similarly heightened. If the brain is, as we've seen, a "future machine," the protagonist experiences humankind's lack of futurity in embodied terms: "The farther they went in that lunar landscape, the more time seemed to stagnate and come to a standstill, because the rise in body temperature slowed down the brain's perception of the passage of time" (2016, 124–25). The sentence blends together the physical motion of the travelers ("The farther they went"), Livio's embodied time consciousness, and scientific knowledge about the physiology of the human body. The "lunar landscape" is, of course, the result of a disastrous combination of human actions and geological and climatological forces. The Anthropocene thus directly taps into Livio's body and his lived experience of time, a connection that spells out what the novel as a whole implies: humans are physical organisms embedded in an equally physical world, and even the seemingly immaterial texture of their inner lives arises from physical patterns in the brain. The harshness of Livio's journey turns that scientific truth, with its claims to objectivity and impersonality, into an affective realization. At the end of the novel, as Livio faces death and—inevitably bound up with it—the specter of species-wide extinction, he is about to be "submerged" by "the last wave of time" (2016, 217): an image that summarizes the power of catastrophe to reveal—through heightened experience—the threads linking mind, body, and world. There is some consolation in this intensification of perception, just as there is consolation to be found in the stylistic form of Arpaia's language.

This chapter started by outlining two areas in which current discussions on the nonhuman overlap with embodied, enactivist, and extended approaches ("e-approaches") to cognition. Given that these frameworks stem from vastly different intellectual traditions (respectively, poststructuralist philosophy and scientific psychology), their confluence is in itself noteworthy. Both frameworks involve a critique of dualistic thinking, which builds on a cognitively basic (but illusory) dichotomy between conscious agents and the material world; moreover, both move beyond representation as a conceptual activity that presupposes a sharp demarcation between experiencing subjects and "external" reality. The notion of the Anthropocene discloses the fundamental entanglement of human-scale realities, including human societies, with nonhuman ones. E-approaches to cognition can contribute to our understanding of this entanglement by positioning mental processes in a continuous, and constitutive, dialogue with the material realities of our bodies, cultures, and environment. The metaphysical autonomy of mind can be unsettled from the outside, as Bennett and many other theorists within the nonhuman turn seek to do, but it can also be unsettled from the inside, by reflecting on the embodied, extended, and enactive nature of human minds.

Fully exploring this convergence is, of course, a task for philosophy. This chapter has undertaken the more modest task of charting the impact of that convergence on three contemporary novels that tackle the problems inherent in the scientific representation of reality. Not only do these novels belong to the subgenre of the neuronovel first identified by Marco Roth, but they engage with psychological themes in ways that are compatible with, and sometimes overtly indebted to, e-approaches to the mind. By probing questions about mind, these narratives are capable of raising broader Anthropocenic concerns: thematizing mind does not result in a dualistic separation of mind and world, but effectively questions that separation by bringing into view how mind fits into a material world marked by the consequences of human action. The chapter's case studies do so through different routes. Powers's *The Echo Maker* explores the consequences of the breakdown of subjectivity via Mark's Capgras syndrome; Mark's physical and emotional trauma forces him—and the characters that surround him—to renegotiate the divide between humans, animals (the cranes), and the material landscape of the river. The result is that mind is spread outward, in a psychophysical embrace between the river and its multispecies inhabitants. This embrace is signaled by the stylistic and thematic parallels between the passages focusing on the birds, the internally focalized rendering of Mark's coma, and the other characters' explicit reflections. Galchen's *Atmospheric Disturbances* builds on the unreliable narrator's paranoid tendency to sense connections between physical phenomena (such as the weather) and human subjectivity. Normally, these domains are only brought together metaphorically, but here metaphor is both literalized and turned into a global narrative strategy underlying the narrator's quest for his wife. In the process, the novel destabilizes human subjectivity and probes the affective relevance of scientific theories. Finally, Arpaia's *Qualcosa, là fuori* focuses on a neuroscientist's confrontation with the disastrous effects of climate change. It shows how environmental catastrophe can expose the phenomenology of perception, complementing and honing scientific knowledge. Through its rich rendering of Livio's embodied consciousness, Arpaia's style weaves together the intricacies of mind and the visceral affectivity of the postapocalyptic world that Livio finds himself navigating.

These novels perform, through the formal resources of consciousness evocation (i.e., focalization and first-person narration), the theoretical convergence articulated in the first part of the chapter: they show it at work in concrete and affectively charged contexts of human-world coupling that undercut dualism and representationalist assumptions. These narratives thus reveal the trickling down of human-nonhuman enmeshment and interdependency where we would least expect to find them—namely, in the midst of human psychology. We've seen that one of the formal strategies adopted by Galchen in *Atmospheric Disturbances* is based on regular patterns of metaphor usage. With its focus on multiscalarity, part 3 of this book takes a closer look at the role metaphorical language plays in bringing together human subjectivity and nonhuman materialities.

PART III

Multiscalarity

CHAPTER 6

Metaphorical Patterns in Anthropocene Fiction
With Andrei Ionescu and Ruben Fransoo

In a World Wildlife Fund campaign for climate change created by Belgian design studio BBDO, we see the familiar image of a wafer cone topped with melting ice cream. However, the scoop of ice cream has been digitally modified to look like the Earth, with clouds and a large swathe of the Asian continent clearly visible.[1] This is a striking visual metaphor for anthropogenic climate change, with the melting ice cream standing for the Earth's diminishing polar caps. In the visual as well as in the linguistic domain, the use of metaphorical language in climate change discourse is not surprising. The intangibility and multiscalarity of anthropogenic climate change (see the introduction) call for metaphorical language that is able to translate scientific models into concrete, affect-laden imagery. The vast majority of humans will never directly experience the melting of polar ice—although they may experience its devastating consequences. BBDO's visual metaphor offers a human-scale equivalent for the abstract causality involved in rising sea levels. In addition, the image takes on emotional connotations, as it evokes childhood memories of melting ice cream, which should be eaten before it goes to waste.

In the wake of George Lakoff and Mark Johnson's work (1980), cognitive metaphor theory is particularly well equipped to deal with a visual representation along these lines. Researchers in this area argue that, as a general tendency, humans understand abstract notions by comparing them metaphorically to more concrete actions and objects.[2] Thus, for instance, a concept can be "grasped"—a conventional metaphor mapping a physical operation of manipulating an object (source of the comparison) onto a mental operation (target of the comparison). This is precisely what happens in BBDO's visual metaphor, which brings together an abstract target (scientific models of climate change) and a directly perceptible, quotidian source (the melting ice cream), with the source being used to illuminate the target and make it more intelligible.³ Gerard Steen, another metaphor theorist, calls this the "perspective-changing" function of metaphor: how it can make "the addressee look at [the target of the comparison] from a different conceptual domain or space, which functions as a conceptual source" (2008, 222).

Scientific and societal discourse on climate change makes extensive use of metaphorical language for its power to encapsulate scientific theories and, potentially, shape people's views on the ecological crisis.⁴ Think about the phrase "greenhouse effect," for instance, which compares the Earth to a structure built by humans in order to retain heat and facilitate agriculture in cold climates. As has been frequently noted, the term is scientifically inaccurate insofar as the physical principles behind atmospheric greenhouse effect are completely different from the working of actual greenhouses.⁵ But, perhaps more important, the metaphor is problematic because it does not convey the urgency of the climate crisis: greenhouses are a helpful technology, one that does not endanger the survival of our species and many others. To communicate the severity of the environmental crisis, scientists and policy makers need more effective language—metaphors and similes that carry adequate emotional connotations and therefore maximize the perspective-changing value theorized by Steen. This is where the formal sophistication of literary language may offer a useful resource for climate change discourse more generally. Literature has long been associated with stylistic foregrounding—that is, the use of innovative rhetorical devices, including creative metaphor, that are capable of eliciting emotion and revitalizing the language of everyday discourse.⁶ Andrew Goatly's statistical survey (2011, 320–26) confirms that "active" (i.e., unconventional) metaphors are more frequent in literary genres such as novels and poems than in other discourse contexts. Arguably, these creative metaphors are particularly effective at exploiting the perspective-changing potential of metaphor in general (Caracciolo 2017). Because the combination of source and target domain is novel and emotionally impactful, readers' viewpoint on the target is more likely to be affected by literary metaphors than by conventional ones.

Taking these ideas as a point of departure, this chapter sees creative metaphor as the primary stylistic form through which narrative may realize multiscalarity, one of the main features of complex systems and of the human-nonhuman mesh. As already discussed in chapter 1 via Herman's account of allegory in animal-centered narratives (2018), the normally human-scale practice of narrative can reach beyond our species' lifeworld by way of analogical extensions based on metaphorical language, including metaphor proper, simile, and allegory. This chapter, which draws on collaborative work with Andrei Ionescu and Ruben Fransoo, seeks to deepen our understanding of how these devices enable multiscalarity. The combination of quantitative and qualitative methods sets this chapter apart—methodologically and, to some extent, stylistically—from the rest of the book. The discussion may prove less reader-friendly than the previous chapters, because our systematic analysis does involve some degree of abstraction. Technicalities aside, the payoff of our stylistic mapping is that it affords direct insight into the complexity and multidirectionality of metaphorical language in literary narrative—an idea that will be developed in a more theoretical vein in the book's final chapter. For now, the goal is to investigate metaphorical patterns in three novels that grapple with the specter of an ecological catastrophe: Margaret Atwood's *Oryx and Crake* (2003), Jeanette Winterson's *The Stone Gods* (2007), and Ian McEwan's *Solar* (2010).

These narratives offer striking perspectives on the interdependency of human experience and a wide gamut of nonhuman realities, such as the life of animals, the dynamics of ecosystems, or climatological and geological processes in the Anthropocene. This chapter demonstrates that metaphor is a uniquely powerful tool in revealing this interrelation. Thus, the visual metaphor of a melting Earth presents global warming as a process in which human agency (expressed by the familiar image of the ice cream) is inextricably bound up with the more-than-human (the planet). In the verbal domain, metaphor can challenge dualistic distinctions—for instance, between human agents and supposedly inert nonhuman objects—that are built into language itself. As Goatly puts it in the article that provided the theoretical framework for chapter 4, "Metaphor is, par excellence, the means of de/reconstructing common-sense ordinary language categories" (1996, 557).

Literary fiction holds particular promise in this respect, in that it can enhance the destabilizing power of metaphorical language by deploying clusters of semantically related metaphors. These "extended" metaphors are conceptually and affectively impactful in ways that would be difficult to achieve through a single metaphorical mapping. Put otherwise, metaphors in literary narrative can coalesce into what Gunther Martens and Benjamin Biebuyck (2013) call a metaphorical "paranarrative": a pattern of connected metaphors that complicate and extend the formal strands of narrative.[7] If Anthropocene fiction probes the divide between human societies and the nonhuman world, metaphorical paranarratives can modulate significantly the stakes and effects of the probing as it is performed by the "causal structuring" of the plot. Indeed, the import of metaphorical patterns can only be understood in the context of a narrative's broader strategies, which will be examined in the following pages through close engagement with the novels by Atwood, Winterson, and McEwan. Via, respectively, their irony, temporal and metaleptic loops, and exploration of grotesque embodiment, these novels serve as multiscalar blueprints for complexifying and deepening everyday discourse on climate change.

One of the central ideas of cognitive metaphor theory is that metaphorical language involves a specific "orientation," from a source to a target domain. The target is the focus of the metaphor—the person, object, or situation it seeks to shed light on—while the source is the person, object, or situation that is being used to reveal an aspect of the target. Potentially, this orientation implies a hierarchical, or at least an evaluative, relation: for instance, "That man is a dog" has vastly different connotations from "That dog is a man." The mapping from an animal (source) to a human (target) in the first sentence is demeaning and disempowering, while the mapping with the opposite orientation (human source, animal target) works toward collapsing the difference between human and animal life. This is an elementary example of how the orientation of metaphor influences meaning generation. The novels by Atwood, Winterson, and McEwan are much more sophisticated in their use of orientation, based on two factors: whether the human functions as source or target of the metaphor, and how each metaphorical mapping interacts with the larger context, including other metaphorical clusters (or "paranarratives").

PRELIMINARY MOVES

This chapter focuses on three significant works of Anthropocene fiction; all of them have received critical acclaim and been discussed from an ecocritical perspective.[8] The first instalment in the popular MaddAddam series, *Oryx and Crake* envisages a dystopian world in which humanity is wiped out by a mysterious epidemic. Readers soon learn that this virus was synthesized in a lab, the combined result of deranged science and corporate greed. The way in which the landscape is altered by human exploitation—and, later, by the disappearance of human beings—resonates with present-day anxieties about climate change: "The beach house her family had owned when she was little . . . got washed away with the rest of the beaches and quite a few of the eastern coastal cities when the sea-level rose so quickly" (2003, 71). Despite this postapocalyptic gloom, Atwood's narrative is highly readable and rich in irony as it traces the backstory of its protagonist, who appears to be the last human left on Earth.

Winterson's *The Stone Gods* eschews linearity and humor in favor of mythical overtones. Winterson's approach is also more self-consciously literary than Atwood's: for instance, the novel builds on a large number of intertextual references to Daniel Defoe's *Robinson Crusoe* as well as John Donne's poetry. *The Stone Gods* suggests that every civilization is bound to cause its own demise through the mindless exploitation of natural resources, in a loop that has been (and will be) repeated countless times in cosmic history. Billie, the narrator and protagonist, experiences this cyclicity firsthand as she is sent to a distant planet, known as Planet Blue, to recreate the civilization that is failing on Earth.

Finally, McEwan's *Solar* paints a largely satirical portrait of its protagonist, a Nobel Prize–winning physicist. The more-than-human scale of climate change here serves to throw into sharp relief the pettiness of a scientist more invested in women and junk food than in scientific problems. Yet the novel succeeds in conveying the deep interrelation between the climate, politics, and the personal lives of the scientists working to understand climate change.

These novels represent three different strands of Anthropocene fiction: first, work that grows out of speculative fiction and retains a clear connection to this genre (Atwood's *Oryx and Crake;* other examples include Paolo Bacigalupi's *The Windup Girl* and Kim Stanley Robinson's *Forty Signs of Rain*); second, work that reflects a mainstream "literary" novelist's engagement with science fiction and dystopian motifs (Winterson's *The Stone Gods;* other examples include Cormac McCarthy's *The Road* and Colson Whitehead's *Zone One,* both discussed in chapter 3); and, finally, work by major novelists that explores human-nonhuman entanglements in a realistic setting (McEwan's *Solar;* other examples include Barbara Kingsolver's *Flight Behavior* and Richard Powers's *The Echo Maker,* discussed in chapters 1 and 4–5, respectively). The three case studies thus demonstrate the complex positioning of Anthropocene fiction in the landscape of the contemporary novel.

In our approach to metaphor usage in these novels, we restricted our focus to a subset of metaphors: namely, metaphorical language that stages the entanglement of human life and nonhuman realities. Concretely, we identified three semantic domains that feed into the umbrella concept of the nonhuman: artificial or natural objects (to which we assigned the code O); living nonhuman creatures and biological processes in living creatures (coded as LN); and inanimate natural elements and processes (such as geological and geographical features of the landscape and meteorological phenomena, coded as W, for "world").[9] We proceeded to identify all metaphorical expressions in the novels that involve at least one of these categories. Metaphors proper as well as similes were taken into account, based on the assumption that they both rely on the same cognitive principle of "mapping," or comparison across semantic domains.[10] While similes were included in our identification task, conventional metaphors (e.g., "her voice was as bright as ever"; McEwan 2010, 11) were *not*, unless they interacted with the surrounding text in a way that significantly undercut their conventionality. The rationale for this choice was that, as explained above, due to their emotional impact creative metaphors hold particular potential for unsettling entrenched notions of human separation from the nonhuman world.

In a further step, we assigned the following tags to the metaphorical expressions, in addition to the already mentioned O, LN, and W: LH for the human body and biological processes occurring in the human body; A for abstract concepts such as those associated with social practices (e.g., religion or art) or institutions (e.g., politics or marriage); and P for psychological states (sensations and feelings, cognitive functions such as memory or the imagination). For instance, the sentence "[The women Jimmy encountered] were so emotionally starved even [he] avoided them as if they were quagmires," from *Oryx and Crake* (Atwood 2003, 292), was coded as LH and W on account of the final simile "as if they were quagmires," which compares human beings (LH) to a natural landscape (W). By contrast, the equally metaphorical expression "emotionally starved" was *not* tagged, because it only involves a comparison between biological processes in the human body (LH) and psychological experience (P) and thus does not address the nonhuman in any significant way. Table 1 offers an overview of the codes and the conceptual domains each of them covers.

The codes employed in this analysis fall on two different sliding scales. The first measures conceptual distance from the human world: LH, A, and P are central to this world, while LN and W point to a nonhuman alterity (in the form of other animal species, LN, or inanimate natural processes, W). Human-made objects (O) fall halfway between these conceptual poles, in that they occupy a more ambiguous position: they are closely bound

TABLE 1. AN OVERVIEW OF THE CODES USED IN THE ANALYSIS

Code abbreviation	Scope	Human or nonhuman?
W *(world)*	Cosmic, geological, climatological, or biophysical processes typically seen as a background to human action	Nonhuman
LN *(life-nonhuman)*	Nonhuman animals and their embodiment	Nonhuman
O *(objects)*	Human-scale objects, including naturally occurring ones (e.g., a rock) and human-made artifacts and structures	Treated as nonhuman in the quantitative analysis, but close to the human-scale world
LH *(life-human)*	People, human embodiment, biological processes occurring in the human body	Human
A *(abstract)*	Abstract concepts and social practices (e.g., religion, art, marriage)	Human
P *(psychology)*	Psychological processes (e.g., perception, emotion, reasoning) in the human mind	Human

up with human cultures, but they can also serve to destabilize anthropocentric worldviews, especially as far as advanced technology (e.g., artificial intelligence) is concerned. Posthumanist thinking, for instance, focuses on technological artifacts as a challenge to traditional humanism (see Hayles 2017; Wolfe 2010). This ambivalent role of human-made objects is reflected in our case studies, as we will see. Although we classified objects as "nonhuman" for the purposes of the quantitative analysis of metaphor usage, the close reading of the novels often reveals their uneasy proximity to the human world.

An alternative way of conceptualizing the relationship between these codes is via the "animacy hierarchy" (Croft 2002, 130) or "animacy scale" (Yamamoto 1999, 9–10), which ranks nouns on the basis of the degree of animacy (or sentience) they imply: LH and P involve a maximum of animacy; nonhuman animals (LN) display some degree of animacy; while objects, natural processes, and abstract concepts display none. Mutsumi Yamamoto notes that this scale is in itself "a product of anthropocentric human cognition" (1999, 9) as well as—one may add—of entrenched cultural assumptions in a Western context. Metaphorical language can unsettle these assumptions by ascribing animacy and even agency to objects and processes normally thought of as inanimate (an anthropomorphizing tendency discussed in the next chapter).

For each of the relevant metaphorical expressions, a target and a source domain were identified, and the orientation of the metaphorical mapping was thus established (in the case of "as if they were quagmires," this mapping was represented as "W → LH," meaning that W is the source of the metaphor, LH the target domain). The main limitation of this approach is that it forces metaphorical expressions into a target-source grid, without accounting for ambiguity or additional meanings created by the context. For instance, a passage in *The Stone Gods* reads as follows: "Had I lordship of the Universe I should roll men like marbles in the pan of space" (Winterson 2009, 100). "Roll men like marbles" is a simile of the form O ("marbles") → LH ("men"), while "pan of space" is a metaphor O ("pan") → W (cosmic "space"). However, this tagging does not reflect the fact that, in the reader's experience, the references to the universe and space confer a cosmic quality to the "men as marbles" simile as well. While such ambiguities fall through the cracks of the coding and counting of the metaphors, they come to the fore fully in our interpretive engagement with the novels.

OVERVIEW OF METAPHOR USAGE

Tables 2 and 3 present the absolute and relative frequency of the main metaphorical types across the three novels, and the relative frequency of each type per novel.[11] This means that, for instance, O → LH metaphors occur 145 times in the corpus, representing 13.44 percent of the total metaphor usage across the novels. O → LH mappings amount to 15.22 percent of the metaphors we identified in *Oryx and Crake,* 12.80 percent of the metaphors in *The Stone Gods,* and 12.20 percent of the metaphors in *Solar.* As pointed out in the previous section, only mappings that involve nonhuman objects (O), animals, plants, and organic processes (LN), or natural elements (W) are listed. Table 2 presents the mappings with human-related targets (LH, A, and P), while table 3 focuses on nonhuman-related targets (W, LN, and O).

TABLE 2. MAIN METAPHORICAL TYPES ACROSS THE THREE NOVELS, HUMAN AS TARGET DOMAIN

Metaphorical types: human as target			Absolute frequency across novels	Relative frequency (percent)			
				Across novels	Oryx and Crake	The Stone Gods	Solar
O	→	LH	145	13.44	15.22	12.80	12.20
LN	→	LH	131	12.14	19.02	9.60	7.44
O	→	A	101	9.36	8.15	5.60	14.88
O	→	P	86	7.97	13.59	1.60	8.93
W	→	LH	53	4.91	2.17	8.27	4.17
W	→	P	40	3.71	4.08	1.87	5.36
W	→	A	35	3.24	1.90	2.13	5.95
LN	→	P	24	2.22	4.62	1.07	0.89
LN	→	A	18	1.67	1.63	0.80	2.68
Total			633	58.66	70.38	43.74	62.50

In the following sections, we use these quantitative results to trace the broader metaphorical paranarratives at play in the novels, analyzing how metaphorical clusters interact with the plot and other stylistic and narrative strategies.

OBJECTIFICATION AND IRONY IN *ORYX AND CRAKE*

The four most frequent mappings in *Oryx and Crake* (LN → LH, O → LH, O → P, and O → A) have LH, P, or A as a target domain, alone making up more than 50 percent of the metaphors we identified in the novel. Because, as argued above, these categories are closely aligned with human subjectivity and culture, this is a strong indication that in this novel the human gravitates toward the target position. This impression is confirmed if we look at *The Stone Gods* and *Solar*, where the human also tends to take the target position, but less significantly than in *Oryx and Crake* (with a relative frequency of 70.38 percent vs. 62.50 percent in *Solar*; *The Stone Gods* has 43.74 percent). Thus, among the most common mappings (relative frequency higher than 7 percent) in Winterson's and McEwan's novels there

TABLE 3. MAIN METAPHORICAL TYPES ACROSS THE THREE NOVELS, NONHUMAN AS TARGET DOMAIN

Metaphorical types: nonhuman as target	Absolute frequency across novels	Relative frequency (percent)			
		Across novels	Oryx and Crake	The Stone Gods	Solar
O → W	71	6.58	3.53	8.53	7.74
O → O	47	4.36	5.16	4.53	3.27
LN → W	42	3.89	0.82	8.27	2.38
O → LN	40	3.71	5.16	5.07	0.60
LH → W	37	3.43	1.09	5.33	3.87
LH → O	29	2.69	1.36	2.67	4.17
LN → O	26	2.41	1.36	2.93	2.98
W → O	19	1.76	2.45	1.33	1.49
LN → LN	17	1.58	3.26	1.33	0.00
A → W	16	1.48	0.00	3.73	0.60
P → W	15	1.39	0.00	3.20	0.89
P → O	11	1.02	0.00	0.80	2.38
Total	370	34.30	24.19	47.72	30.37

is at least one type in which the target is W (O → W and LH → W in *The Stone Gods*, O → W in *Solar*). On the other hand, in both *Oryx and Crake* and *Solar* the most frequent mappings have either O or LN as a source domain, with LN ranking first in Atwood's novel.

Here are some examples from *Oryx and Crake*, one for each of the top four mappings: "Snowman, please tell us—what is that moss growing out of your face?" (LN → LH; Atwood 2003, 9); "what she reminded him of at such times was a porcelain sink: clear, shining, hard" (O → LH; 2003, 36); "another baffling item on the cryptic report card his mother toted around in some mental pocket" (O → P; 2003, 80); "the vital arts and their irresistible reserved seat in the big red-velvet amphitheatre of the beating human heart" (O → A; 2003, 219). The human body, mind ("mental pocket"), and even a core component of human culture (the arts), are objectified. But, as these examples suggest, Atwood's mappings work differently from a common use of objectification, whereby humans belonging to a minority group are relegated to a subordinate role and thus denied autonomy and subjectivity (see, e.g., Papadaki 2010). In fact, the salient feature of virtually all these mappings is that they "demote" humans by comparing them to things and objects that rank lower on the animacy scale (such as "moss," a "porcelain sink," a "pocket," or a "seat"). The effect of this demotion is distinctly ironic.[12] Atwood's metaphors take the perspective of someone equating human subjectivity and culture to inanimate objects, which is evidently an ironic point of view insofar as it clashes with ingrained ideas of human exceptionalism and mastery. The incongruity generated by this conceptual clash is at the root of Atwood's irony, which performs what we may think of self-deprecating humor on a species level: via the objectifying paranarrative, a human author mocks the presumed metaphysical primacy of humankind for the benefit of the human audience.

Perhaps the clearest manifestation of this strategy is a pervasive metaphorical cluster comparing human beings to food, which suggests a loss of animacy. In the final pages of the novel, the protagonist, Snowman, makes a desperate attempt at scavenging the research facility in which the deadly virus was first synthesized. The reason for this risky foray is that Snowman is running out of food, which creates an archetypical narrative situation: in the terminology of Algirdas Julien Greimas's actantial theory (1966; see chapter 4), food becomes the "object" of Snowman's (the subject's) quest. However, the metaphorical paranarrative reverses this situation, since the human body is repeatedly turned into the *target* of metaphorical mappings that use food as the source. For instance, Snowman thinks: "[Like] a horse, his life now depends on [his ability to use his feet to walk]. If he can't walk, he's rat food" (2003, 270). Noteworthy here is the metaphorical progression from LN → LH ("like a horse") to O → LH ("he's rat food"), which performs a two-step "demotion" of the narrative's human protagonist along the animacy scale: from human being to animate nonhuman creature to inanimate substance. Later, we read that the vultures were "waiting for him to be meat" (2003, 416), or—in a more elaborate variation, with an element of P—that "his foot feels like a gigantic boiled wiener stuffed with hot, masticated flesh, boneless and about to burst" (2003, 389). These metaphorical mappings serve the ironic purpose of destabilizing the distinction between human flesh and animal meat, thus feeding into the novel's broader critique of anthropocentrism. Furthermore, the metaphors dislodge the human from the agentive subject position that it still retains in the plot, in which Snowman, a new Robinson Crusoe in a postapocalyptic wasteland, scavenges for food in order to survive. Importantly, the irony implicit in these metaphors is not just the result of a narratorial stance, but a reflection of the protagonist's self-deprecating humor, so that Snowman serves as a diegetic embodiment of the antianthropocentric worldview articulated by the novel as a whole.[13]

Nowhere does this metaphorical critique become more evident than in the novel's ending. Here Snowman manages to escape from the research facility in which his childhood friend Crake concocted the virus that caused humanity's demise. Crake died in the facility, and his bones are still there, "mingled and in disarray, like a giant jigsaw puzzle" (with an O → LH mapping; 2003, 391). Snowman makes his way back to the village inhabited by "Crakers," the new human species genetically engineered by Crake to be immortal and immune to the deadly epidemic (but also simple-minded and incapable of sophisticated cultural expression). Upon Snowman's return, the Crakers ask him whether they can meet their creator, whom Snowman has been depicting so far (quite accurately, at least as far as the Crakers are concerned) as a divine figure. That of the creature meeting its maker is a classic science fiction trope, which can be traced back at least to Mary Shelley's *Frankenstein*. Atwood gives it an ironic twist by having Snowman remember Crake's bones and remark that the Crakers are not allowed to meet him, because he has "turned himself into a plant." To which one of the Crakers, who eat a vegetarian diet, responds: "Why would Crake become food?" (2003, 421).

Crake, the scientist who embodies a dream (soon turned into a nightmare) of technological mastery over the nonhuman world, is literally metamorphosed into unrecognizable bones, and symbolically into a plant and mere "food." This exchange between Snowman and the Crakers marks the emergence into the novel's plot of the metaphorical paranarrative that questions the distinction between human beings and food, and—more generally—the divide between humans, other life forms, and inanimate objects: Crake himself thus becomes the target of Atwood's ironic narration, just as humankind had been the regular target of the narrator's metaphorical mappings. Unlike Crake, Snowman becomes poignantly aware of the thin line that separates our species from nonhuman realities: remember the simile that captures the experience of his aching foot by comparing it to a "gigantic boiled wiener"—in itself an image rich in humorous overtones.[14] Through the persona of the likable, irony-prone protagonist, Atwood's novel offers readers the chance to develop a similar awareness of the continuum between human and nonhuman realities.

METAPHORICAL LOOPS IN *THE STONE GODS*

As we observed in the previous section, metaphorical mappings in *The Stone Gods* present a less linear picture than in *Oryx and Crake*, where 70.38 percent of the metaphors have the human as a target domain. In Winterson's novel, by contrast, that percentage is much lower (43.74 percent). Indeed, three of the most frequent types (O → W, LN → W, and LH → W) place inanimate natural processes in the target position, making up over 20 percent of the total mappings. Here are some examples for each of these types: "The sky exploded in grenades of colour" (O → W; Winterson 2009, 192); "one star just visible like the bud of a horn" (LN → W; 2009, 120); "strands of rock, splintered out from the surface like thick plaits of hair" (LH → W; 2009, 50). These passages inscribe visual forms associated with the human body (hair), technology (grenades), and animals (a horn) into astronomical or geological phenomena. This strategy goes hand in hand with the explicit anthropomorphization of the nonhuman, in common mappings such as A → W and P → W: for instance, "There must be planets that are their own mistakes—stories that began and faltered" (A → W; 2009, 87), where the abstract notions "mistakes" and "stories" are projected onto planets. A similar case is the ascription of psychological qualities onto inanimate landscapes: "The petrified forest is there—carbonized tree remains, held in the heat, we don't know how, like a memory" (P → W; 2009, 53), and "the Pennines that held the towns like a memory" (P → W; 2009, 129). A → W and P → W mappings are absent in *Oryx and Crake* and extremely infrequent (< 1 percent) in *Solar*, highlighting the distinctiveness of Winterson's approach to metaphor. In contrast to *Oryx and Crake,* in which the metaphorical paranarrative tends to collapse the human into nonhuman elements, *The Stone Gods* makes extensive use of metaphors that "promote" the nonhuman to a higher position on the animacy scale—that of a minded agent.

One of the most self-conscious uses of this anthropomorphizing strategy builds on a line from John Donne's poem "The Sun Rising," which recurs, like a leitmotif, throughout the novel. The line reads: "She is all States, all Princes I." Donne's conceit is to compare his lover to "all States" (i.e., all countries on Earth), and himself to "all Princes," suggesting that their romantic union is as complete and metaphysically sovereign as the planet itself. In terms of the coding system adopted in this chapter, Donne's metaphor could be construed as W → LH, since the image of the Earth is leveraged to shed light on the poet's feelings toward his lover. However,

Winterson puts a vastly different spin on this metaphor, employing it to characterize not a human lover but an actual planet, known as "Planet Blue," a promised land in which humanity could rebuild civilization from the ashes of the Earth's environmental depletion. In the following scene, for instance, the narrator is on a spaceship, hurtling toward Planet Blue with a handful of settlers: "'To Planet Blue,' [the captain] said, raising his glass, and there on the diode screen was the picture of our new world, and underneath: *She is all States, all Princes I*" (2009, 48; italics in the original). The planet is thus endowed with human-like qualities, which make it worthy of the poet's (and the captain's) love. But this personification is caught in a sophisticated intertextual dance, in which the lover and the planet swap metaphorical positions (W → LH in Donne, LH → W in Winterson), evoking a sense of circularity between the human and the nonhuman.

In fact, this impression of circularity is consistent with Winterson's metaphor usage in *The Stone Gods,* where the mappings tend to travel in both directions, from the human to a nonhuman target (47.72 percent of the metaphors) and back from the nonhuman to a human target (43.74 percent). We have been emphasizing mappings where W takes the target position so far, but types such as LN → LH or W → LH are also present in the novel, and statistically even more frequent. In some cases these mappings objectify the human body, introducing an ironic distance comparable to the humor of Atwood's novel: "All men are hung like whales. All women are tight as clams below" (LN → LH; 2009, 19). But far more significant are metaphors in which—just like in Donne's poem—astronomical or geological references serve to transfigure and enchant the human body: "These are men glamorous as comets, trailing fame in firetails" (W → LH; 2009, 6). Even psychological processes are portrayed as astronomical entities: "We see the boxed-up miseries and fears, orbiting two miles up, outside our little world" (W → P; 2009, 199). W → LH mappings are far more frequent in *The Stone Gods* (8.27 percent) than in Atwood's and McEwan's novels (2.17 and 4.17 percent, respectively). Winterson's metaphors appear to seek a balance between the human as source and the human as target. The result is that the embodied self and the material world meet halfway in the metaphorical paranarrative, as suggested by the symmetry of this passage, where the metaphorical target (the human mouth) and the nonhuman source (the cave) become fully interchangeable: "Kiss me. Your mouth is a cave. This cave is your mouth" (2009, 92).

Crucially, this loop-like logic extends far beyond the novel's metaphor usage: as in two of the examples examined in chapter 1 (the short stories by Cortázar and Chiang), the "loop" image schema recurs repeatedly in the narrative. *The Stone Gods* embraces a philosophy of history reminiscent of Mircea Eliade's eternal return (2005), or the cyclical account of the rise and fall of civilizations offered in the early eighteenth century by Italian thinker Giambattista Vico (1999). In Winterson's novel, the cyclical end of civilizations is determined by the exhaustion of natural resources and—ultimately—by human greed. This circularity is formally built into the narrative, in that similar situations and even passages (such as the Donne quotation) recur at different moments in the novel's chronology. In what Hofstadter (1999) would call a "strange loop," the novel even contains a version of itself, in the form of a manuscript titled *The Stone Gods*. This mise en abyme is made even more puzzling by the fact that the narrator first claims to have found the manuscript on a train, and later adds that she left it there herself: "'What's that?' Spike asked. 'It's what I told you about, today, yesterday, when, I don't know when, it seems a lifetime ago. *The Stone Gods*.' 'I wonder who left it there?' 'It was me.' 'Why, Billie?' A message in a bottle. A signal. But then I saw it was still there . . . round and round on the Circle Line. A repeating world" (2009, 203; ellipsis in the original). The image of the circle pervades the novel at multiple levels: diegetic, temporal, and thematic. But only the metaphorical paranarrative reveals the deep significance of this circularity: it holds a mirror up to Winterson's fluidly circular metaphysics, in which the human, embodied subject seeps into, and is at the same time shaped by, the nonhuman realities of geology and the cosmos.

CLIMATE CHANGE, THE BODY, AND SATIRE IN *SOLAR*

The most frequent mapping in *Solar* is O → A, which is present in the other novels as well, but much less common (14.88 percent vs. 8.15 and 5.60 percent). Table 2 reveals that 23.51 percent of the novel's total mappings have abstract ideas as a target domain, a considerably higher percentage than in either *Oryx and Crake* (11.68 percent) or *The Stone Gods* (8.53 percent). This tendency clearly goes hand in hand with the fact that the novel's protagonist is a scientist who tends to think in abstract terms. As Elena Semino and Kate Swindlehurst argue in a seminal article (1996), recurrent metaphorical mappings contribute to the textual evocation of a character's mind. Superficially, this would seem to be the case for McEwan's portrait of Michael Beard, the Nobel Prize–winning physicist who occupies the foreground of *Solar*. Yet, if we take a closer look at the metaphors deployed by McEwan, it is sometimes hard to tell where the character's bias toward abstract concepts ends and where the narrator's satire begins. Consider, for instance, the following extended metaphor of the O → A type: "Theoretical physics was a village, and on its green, by the village pump, Beard still had influence" (2010, 97). This comparison conflates an abstract target (the academic field of theoretical physics) with the human-scale—and in that sense object-like—structure of the village. The passage reflects Beard's belief that he retains some leverage over his colleagues, despite having made extremely limited contributions to science after the discovery that led to his receiving the Nobel Prize. However, the use of the village as a source domain is hardly flattering and unlikely to originate in the character's thought processes. In fact, the quotation suggests that theoretical physics, for all its high-flown ambitions, is a parochial world; the metaphor thus develops McEwan's critique of scientific institutions and their inability to influence the public debate on the ecological crisis—one of the novel's main thematic concerns.

Many of McEwan's metaphors belong to this ambivalent no-man's-land between mind style and satire. Another example foregrounds Beard's uneasy personal life: "Weren't marriages, his marriages, tidal, with one rolling out just before another rolled in? But this one was different" (2010, 3). Here the target is an abstract idea (Beard's attitude toward marriage, A), the source a natural phenomenon (the tides, W). This metaphorical mapping is far more frequent in *Solar* (5.95 percent) than in *Oryx and Crake* (1.90 percent) and *The Stone Gods* (2.13 percent). In this particular instance, the "tidal" metaphor would seem to express Beard's jaded understanding of his romantic life on the basis of an analogy with the nonhuman world, and yet the overall effect is mostly humorous, in that it contradicts expectations of long-term stability and commitment associated with marriage. McEwan's satire is thus quite different from the self-deprecating irony of Snowman in *Oryx and Crake*: while Snowman's ironic comparisons between the human body and food play into Atwood's antianthropocentric project, so that the protagonist and the novel appear to be on the same wavelength, McEwan's satire operates to a large extent against the grain of the protagonist. As readers, we have to work out McEwan's engagement with climate change while juggling the protagonist's perspective with the novel's satirical overtones.

As scholars such as Greg Garrard (2013) have argued in detail, McEwan articulates a critique of scientific institutions, which appear unable to deal with or communicate adequately the scale of anthropogenic climate change. Beard becomes the prime target of this satirical attack. Yet—and herein lies the novel's main complexity—McEwan also assigns his protagonist a more positive role, by using his somatic experience as a probe into the nonhuman realities of the climate. The implication is that the body might be capable of addressing the shortcomings of scientific thinking and establishing a connection between humans and the environment. Once again, this work of bridge-building is performed by the metaphorical language that runs through *Solar* and complicates the narrative of Beard's personal as well as professional life.

Quantitatively, mappings that involve the human body (LH) as either a source or a target are not more frequent in *Solar* than in our other case studies. But they take on extra interpretive significance as the novel explores Beard's grotesque embodiment. In fact, just as his marriages are "tidal," his experience of the body is governed by forces that the novel portrays through a set of W → LH mappings. Consider this passage, for instance: "He went home to his flat and lay brooding in the scum-rimmed bath, gazing through steam clouds at the archipelago of his disrupted selfhood—mountainous paunch, penis tip, unruly toes—scattered in a line across a soapy gray sea" (2010, 164). Beard's body is here compared to a landscape, whose jagged features mirror—with a further W → P mapping—his mental state of dejection and confusion. It is unclear whether this analogy should be attributed to the character or to the narrator, but, as readers hesitate between Beard's mental perspective and the narrator's possibly satirical intentions, the body itself gains prominence and becomes a focus of attention in its own right. In this way, the novel's ambivalence brings to the fore an embodied channel of communication, perhaps even of communion, with the nonhuman world.

One pivotal scene highlights this embodied connection between Beard and the environment. He is about to deliver a keynote speech at a conference in London, addressing an audience of "institutional investors, pension-fund managers, solid types who would not easily be persuaded that the world, their world, was in danger" (2010, 129). Suddenly, Beard feels sick: "[As Beard] took his place behind the lectern, gripping tightly its edges in both hands, he felt an oily nausea at something monstrous and rotten from the sea stranded on the tidal mudflats of a stagnant estuary, decaying gaseously in his gut and welling up, contaminating his breath, his words, and suddenly his thoughts. 'The planet,' he said, surprising himself, 'is sick'" (2010, 170–71).

The passage builds on an LN → P metaphor in which Beard's queasiness is compared to decaying organic matter emerging from the sea, a parallel further extended into the mapping between the recesses of his body and a natural landscape (W → LH). Two words, "oily" and "contaminated," denote Beard's experience, inevitably linking this landscape to the exploitation of natural resources ("oil," a word that Beard will use to refer to petroleum a few lines below) and environmental contamination. This complex metaphorical strategy establishes a multiscalar connection between natural processes and bodily experience, which Beard himself explicitly acknowledges by declaring the planet "sick" in his opening remark. Here the key phrase is "surprising himself": the embodied route to the nonhuman bypasses Beard's conscious appraisal of the ecological crisis (which, the novel implies, he never felt strongly about, jumping on the environmentalist bandwagon only out of narcissistic self-interest).

The link between the planet's metaphorical sickness and Beard's embodiment emerges again in the novel's ending, in which he discovers that the "reddish brown blotch" (2010, 276) on his wrist is a potentially life-threatening melanoma, described through another W → LH mapping ("a map of unknown territory"; 2010, 276). Through this plot device and the metaphorical patterns that accompany it, the parallel between Beard's body and the ecological crisis comes into the open. This conclusion suggests that Beard is more than a satirical butt in McEwan's critique of the scientific community's shortcomings. The protagonist becomes an unlikely, and to a large extent unsuspecting, embodiment of climate change—where the word "embodiment" refers to Beard's actual body, not to a merely conceptual or symbolic connection with the environment. By developing a metaphorical paranarrative through the character's somatic experience, McEwan gestures toward an understanding of human-nonhuman entanglements based not on conceptual models, but on affective and embodied resonances across scalar levels.

This chapter examined metaphorical patterns in three contemporary novels that engage with the current ecological crisis: Margaret Atwood's *Oryx and Crake*, Jeanette Winterson's *The Stone Gods*, and Ian McEwan's *Solar*. As argued by Martens and Biebuyck (2013), literary narratives tend to deploy clusters of semantically related metaphors, or "paranarratives," that enrich—conceptually and affectively—the meanings emerging from the plot. Assemblages of metaphors and similes create formal patterns in their own right, intersecting with other narrative strategies and contributing to a story's overall impact. The combined quantitative and qualitative analysis in this chapter sought to bring out these patterns in a systematic way, demonstrating their multiplicity as well as their interactions with other components of a narrative. Our findings strengthen the idea that metaphor is an extremely powerful tool in bridging human embodied experience with the large-scale processes modeled by science (e.g., the dynamics of ecosystems, climatological and geological realities). Metaphorical language enables narrative to recreate the multiscalarity of complex systems—and thus capture the complexity of the Anthropocenic enmeshment of human and nonhuman phenomena.

In the case of Atwood's novel, the human gravitates to a central position (by being the target of 70.38 percent of the metaphors), but it is ironically devalued and undermined by being continuously compared to objects (including, most poignantly, food). Thus, even though at the level of the novel's plot the human maintains its centrality, the underlying paranarrative stages an antianthropocentric worldview, questioning clear-cut distinctions between the human species and nonhuman realities. Winterson's novel, on the other hand, appears to seek a balance between the human as source and the human as target in its metaphors, staging a circular metaphysics in which human subjectivity both infiltrates nonhuman realities such as geology or the cosmos (an aspect revealed by metaphorical clusters in which the nonhuman is anthropomorphized) and is inherently shaped by them (in metaphors where astronomical and geological references are used to enchant and transfigure the human body). Finally, in McEwan's *Solar*, the protagonist's grotesque embodiment is satirically employed as a channel of communication with the nonhuman realities of climate change. By using metaphorical paranarratives that conceptualize Beard's body in terms of the increasing (anthropogenic) decay of our planet, McEwan builds a powerful satire on the limitations of scientific institutions (and perhaps of humanity at large) in dealing with the ecological crisis.

As these close readings make clear, the methodology employed in this chapter can systematize the study of metaphorical patterns in narrative by allowing for more precise, statistically grounded comparisons between thematically related texts. Yet the quantitative analysis of the novels has not served to discount interpretive forms of engagement, but to extend the foothold of interpretation and narratological discussion, through a productive back-and-forth between the identification of quantifiable patterns and the close reading of the broader context in which those patterns occur. One of the tenets of conceptual metaphor theory is that metaphorical language tends to collapse the abstract and intangible into human-scale, embodied interactions with the environment (see, e.g., Turner 1996). In broad strokes, this is confirmed in this chapter's case studies by the high frequency of mappings such as O → A or O → P, which use human-scale objects as the source domain and more abstract concepts as the target domain. Yet our findings show that this tendency can be partly reversed by literary language through mappings that leave the human on the sidelines (LN → W), use the nonhuman as a source domain (W → LH), or project the human onto the nonhuman world (LH → W).

These formal mappings challenge the anthropocentric setup of everyday language—as reflected in the animacy scale, for instance—and make a key contribution to the broader critique of anthropocentrism performed by much Anthropocene fiction. In this way, creative metaphors afford an opportunity for rethinking our imagination of the nonhuman outside of literary fiction as well. A fuller awareness of the potential of creative metaphor could benefit media discourse and science communication (see, e.g., Dahlstrom 2014), both of which need more sophisticated and emotionally impactful narratives to convey humanity's precarious position vis-à-vis the nonhuman world. The promise as well as the challenges inherent in using metaphor to achieve narrative multiscalarity will be the focus of the final chapter of this book.

CHAPTER 7

Metaphor, Scale, and the Value of Conceptual Trouble

In a seminal psychological study, Fritz Heider and Marianne Simmel (1944) showed participants an animation film containing four geometric shapes: one circle, two triangles, and one large rectangle with a side that opens and closes like a door. The shapes move against a white background, approaching one another and parting ways in short bursts that suggest deliberate interaction, not random movement. The study found that viewers of the film readily interpreted these abstract shapes and movements in terms of human intentions and psychological traits. Crucially, participants offered these interpretations by constructing narratives about the moving images. This is an excerpt from one of the participants' statements: "A man has planned to meet a girl and the girl comes along with another man. The first man tells the second to go; the second tells the first, and he shakes his head. Then the two men have a fight, and the girl starts to go into the room to get out of the way and hesitates and finally goes in. She apparently does not want to be with the first man" (1944, 246–47). As this excerpt shows, the animation film strongly cues viewers to draw on the basic skills for understanding mind that philosophers call "folk psychology": beliefs, intentions, and other mental states are ascribed as abstract shapes are transfigured into human characters.[1] This anthropomorphization is all the more surprising because these geometric figures are not in any obvious way human-like. Heider and Simmel's film thus raises the question—central to this book—of whether anthropomorphism is a useful resource for narratives that engage with human-nonhuman entanglement.

The previous chapter has shown, through textual exploration and empirical analysis, how creative metaphors in the context of fictional narrative may blur the dividing line between human subjects and nonhuman creatures, objects, and processes. Clearly, anthropomorphism bears a close resemblance to metaphorical projections that use the human as the source and the nonhuman as a target domain. There is something to be said for such projections: anthropomorphism may help narrative achieve multiscalarity by describing the nonhuman world in ways that resonate with our human emotions and assumptions. This is the argument proposed by Bennett in an oft-cited passage of *Vibrant Matter*: "We need to cultivate a bit of anthropomorphism—the idea that human agency has some echoes in nonhuman nature—to counter the narcissism of humans in charge of the world" (2010, xvi).

Likewise, in *How Things Shape the Mind*, a contribution to the growing field of cognitive archeology, Lambros Malafouris argues that anthropomorphic interpretations can be uncoupled from anthropocentrism. Malafouris seeks to develop an account of agency inspired by Bruno Latour's actor-network theory (2005): from this perspective, agency is not an exclusively human quality but can be shared between human minds and material objects such as tools. Anthropomorphic readings of the nonhuman are central to this antianthropocentric project. Building on Arjun Appadurai's work (1986, 5), Malafouris calls this anthropomorphizing approach "methodological fetishism." Malafouris defines it as follows: "If the social and cognitive life of things is the phenomenon you seek to understand, then, methodologically speaking, it is more sensible and productive to treat material things as agents (and be wrong) than to deny their agency (and be wrong)" (2013, 134). Methodological fetishism is a close correlate of the "strategic anthropomorphism" advocated by Iovino in the field of material ecocriticism. An example discussed in detail by Iovino is Italo Calvino's use of anthropomorphism in the short story collection *Cosmicomics*, in which, "despite the anthropomorphism of the narrative, the human comes out flattened, but is also restructured as a compound individual" (Iovino 2014, 132; my translation).

The strategic use of anthropomorphism aims to create a level playing field for human-nonhuman encounters, a goal that distinguishes it from the naïve anthropomorphic appropriation of nonhuman entities and processes.[2] Malafouris himself warns his readers that "when we are approaching the agency of things we should be extremely cautious not to transform the 'symmetry' [between humans and nonhuman things] into a mere isomorphic projection" (2013, 135). Isomorphic projection is thus a perspective on the nonhuman that collapses it into the human by presupposing their isomorphism or equivalence—a problematic assumption, especially when it comes to developing an ethics of human-nonhuman relations. By contrast, when there is genuine symmetry between humans and the nonhuman, we acknowledge that their entanglement can go both ways, and that anthropomorphic readings may reveal, paradoxically, how the "agency" of things (i.e., their causal efficacy) can both differ from and undercut established notions of human agency. In other words, we acknowledge that the nonhumanness of the nonhuman matters. In that respect, the stance encouraged by Heider and Simmel's film falls closer to isomorphic projection than to symmetry: viewers ascribe human qualities to geometric figures, in coordination with the human researchers who conceived the film, but in doing so viewers are unlikely to go beyond the mere anthropomorphic appropriation of the geometric figures. There is no conceptual pushback, no moment of epistemological or ethical hesitation as we apply our folk psychology to abstract shapes; on the contrary, viewers are likely to be aware that their engagement with the film is fully inscribed within the human practice of scientific psychology.

Contrast this dynamic with the narrator's anthropomorphizing description of a meteorological model in *Atmospheric Disturbances* by Rivka Galchen (see chapter 5); just as the viewers of Heider and Simmel's film interpret geometric figures as human characters, Galchen's narrator reads—or, rather, spectacularly *mis*reads—a human body into the abstract shape of a graph. But the audience of *Atmospheric Disturbances* is familiar with both the source from which the graph was lifted (a scientific journal) and the more-than-human reality it was originally meant to represent (meteorological patterns). Because of this context, the narrator's anthropomorphizing reading is more than isomorphic projection: it is an implicit recognition of the scalar discrepancy between the source and the target of his comments. There can be no isomorphism across these levels, and no symmetry, even, in the sense of one-to-one correspondence; the narrator's misreading is significant because it reveals the constitutive differences between the human body and the more abstract realities that the diagram represents. In this way, anthropomorphism is employed—behind the narrator's back—to expose what Derek Woods calls "scale variance": the fact that "the observation and the operation of systems are subject to different constraints at different scales due to real discontinuities" (2014, 133). Woods argues that scale variance should be a primary concern of ecocriticism as it addresses climate change and the Anthropocene.[3]

This final chapter explores the stakes and significance of scalar discontinuities as they are brought out by metaphorical language in narrative, including anthropomorphizing metaphors (the "personification" of the nonhuman). A key element of narrative multiscalarity is that metaphors—and creative metaphors in particular—generate semantic and affective "feedback" via their mapping of source and target domains. Metaphorical language has the potential for triggering far more than a linear, unidirectional transfer of meanings from source to target; it can offer new insights into *both* the source and the target domain. This is precisely the bidirectional flow from source to target domain, and back, that the mere counting of metaphorical expressions in the previous chapter could not account for fully; close reading proved necessary to make up for that methodological limitation. The bidirectionality of metaphor is amplified by the nonlinear nature of the mappings discussed in the previous chapter: in the novels by Atwood, Winterson, and McEwan, the "paranarrative" was not a single overarching metaphor but rather a meshwork of mappings that straddle the boundary between human and nonhuman realities. Consider the passage from McEwan's *Solar* in which Beard feels sick while delivering a high-profile lecture on climate change. An effective example of bidirectional transfer is the way in which the character's phenomenological experience of nausea blends into the sickness of the planet: it is difficult to establish whether the main mapping is LN → P (a natural landscape, the "tidal mudflats of a stagnant estuary," is used to characterize Beard's experience) or LH → W (the human experience of sickness is projected onto the planet). Both mappings take place at the same time, generating a metaphorical transaction of remarkable complexity.

This idea of bidirectional flow plays a central role in Gilles Fauconnier and Mark Turner's "blending theory" model of metaphor (2002): in this account, metaphorical language can integrate source and target domains in a third mental space, which Fauconnier and Turner call the "blend." New meanings arise when features of the metaphorical source and target are selectively picked out and combined within the blend.[4] In the passage from *Solar*, for instance, Beard as a physical embodiment of the planet is the emergent meaning brought out by my analysis; it results from a conceptual integration of two semantic domains—sickness as a lived experience in the character's human body, and the anthropogenic activity that is destabilizing the Earth's ecosystems (i.e., our planet's metaphorical "sickness"). These emergent meanings are responsible for a bidirectional transfer: because Beard's nausea allows us to think about the ecological crisis in experiential (rather than conceptual or statistical) terms, not only is the planet anthropomorphized, but our understanding of physical sickness is Earthmorphized.[5] Put otherwise, the bidirectionality of the metaphorical transfer generates feedback *from the target of the metaphor to the source*. Also in the narratives that will be investigated in this chapter, conceptual and affective feedback is created as the text attempts to bridge across scalar levels by blending distinct semantic domains—for instance, by applying notions of agency and subjectivity beyond the human. These case studies are a novel by Jonathan Lethem, *As She Climbed across the Table* (1997), and a short story by Ursula K. Le Guin, "Vaster than Empires and More Slow" (1971).

The discussion is structured around two metaphorical projections that create rich emergent meanings. Lethem's novel builds on the ascription of human-like qualities to the nonhuman world (broadly speaking, LH → W); by contrast, Le Guin's short story develops a scenario in which a complex physical system is seen either as a superorganism or as a brain-like structure (corresponding to LN → W). In both cases there is feedback traveling in the direction opposite to the projection: anthropomorphizing an inanimate entity, or seeing it as a living, sentient system, puts extreme pressure on anthropocentric assumptions and on our understanding of sentience. We'll see that the narratives by Lethem and Le Guin exploit, strategically, the incongruous nature of multiscalar projections, using emergent meanings to highlight "real discontinuities" across scales (to again borrow Woods's words) but also bringing out the formal nature of human-nonhuman encounters. The result ties in with one of the key ideas advanced by this book: it is by cultivating an imagination of abstract pattern that narrative can move beyond isomorphic projection, or naïvely anthropomorphic accounts of the nonhuman.

FALLING IN LOVE WITH A BLACK HOLE

Chapter 4 discussed five ways in which nonhumans can become actants in narrative, achieving a degree of agential parity with human characters. What was not discussed there is how these irruptions of the nonhuman into narrative agency can wreak havoc on human characters' lives. We—meaning both characters and readers—inevitably attempt to anthropomorphize, but such attempts create unsettling and potentially unpredictable effects that destabilize the very notion of the human: here lies the bidirectionality of metaphorical projections of the LH → W type. The pitfalls of anthropomorphization are explored by contemporary novels that draw direct inspiration from posthumanist discourse, such as Jeff VanderMeer's *Borne*, which centers on a strange creature, "dark purple and about the size of my fist, . . . like a half-closed stranded sea anemone. I found him only because, beacon-like, he strobed emerald green across the purple every half minute or so" (2017, 3). Like a posthuman descendant of Gregor Samsa in Franz Kafka's *The Metamorphosis*, Borne is a profoundly ambiguous, shape-shifting creature that defies attempts at visualization, yet Borne is also able to speak, aspires to personhood, and professes his love for the narrator. It is hard not to anthropomorphize Borne, but one must live with the disturbing consequences of this expansion of concepts of personhood and agency to the nonhuman.

In *As She Climbed across the Table*, Lethem stages the incongruity of this conceptual transaction in an even more spectacular (and spectacularly incongruous) way. "What could be more nonhuman than a blackhole?" asks Morton in *Humankind* (2017, 160); in Lethem's novel, what looks like a black hole takes center stage in the narrative. The premise of the plot is that a team of physicists at an American university are able to stabilize in a lab "a big nothingness" that could "detach and grow into a universe tangential to ours" (1998, 3). The narrator's wife, Alice, is one of these physicists.

With a foregrounding of spatial scale, the black hole becomes a stand-in for astronomical realities that can normally be studied only from an enormous distance, and through various layers of technological and statistical mediation.[6] Instead, this mini–black hole sits on a table in a university lab and can be examined at leisure. The narrator, who is an anthropologist, observes with great interest the scientists' frantic attempts to understand this entity: "I was liking the way it defied theory, the way it had the physicists scrambling. Breach, gap, gulf, hub—the lack was obviously an explosion of metaphor into a literal world. I felt a secret kinship with it" (1998, 26). The perplexing nature of the black hole registers in the competing spatial metaphors with which the scientists attempt to describe it, projecting various kinds of familiar image schemata onto this spatial anomaly: "Portal or breach? There seems to be some blurriness," the narrator tells Alice (1998, 17). More at ease with the permeable conceptual boundaries of metaphor than the literal-minded physicists are, the anthropologist initially develops a sense of kinship with the black hole.

Paradoxically, however, this kinship becomes more and more problematic as the black hole is anthropomorphized. First, it receives a nickname, "Lack," and even a gender, "he." The scientists also begin to realize that Lack shows a marked preference for certain things; when they start placing objects inside Lack, they find out that he will reject certain "offerings" such as "curly lasagne, a twist of macaroni, a strand of nonskid spaghetti" (1998, 50) and accept others, including a copy of *The Hunting of the Snark* by Lewis Carroll. The only conclusion is that Lack, far from being an inert physical anomaly, displays intelligence that the novel's characters cannot but interpret anthropomorphically—that is, in terms of agency, personality, and subjective preferences. If this wasn't strange enough, Lethem's narrative employs as its main conceit an even more radical form of anthropomorphization, one that converts the analogy (Lack as human-like) into a bizarre, but literal, feeling of attachment. Much to the narrator's disbelief, his wife, Alice, falls in love with Lack: "'You're in love with someone else,' I heard myself say. 'Yes.' A change came over me, a phase transition. A flush rose through my chest and neck. 'You're in love with Lack,' I said. 'Yes'" (1998, 68).

Alice tries to enter Lack, in what is obviously a sexually charged gesture, but she is repeatedly rejected. Still, she insists: she must be one with Lack. The narrator's distress at the collapse of his marriage registers the conceptual trouble with nonhuman agency in profoundly personal terms. A perplexing nonhuman entity breaks into the normally human-scale configuration of narrative and alters—dramatically but also, of course, ironically—the intersubjective space of marriage. The narrator describes his shock as follows: "I stood rooted to the lawn. I felt stiff but bent, off-center, like a plank warped by storage in a mildewy cellar" (1998, 27). Noteworthy here is that the irruption of a nonhuman actant into narrative generates a parallel movement within the human subject—a shift stylistically encoded in Lethem's metaphorical language. The narrator's affective landscape is objectified through scientific jargon (emotion as a "phase transition"), just as his proprioceptive experience of the body is equated with a nonhuman, inanimate object (the "plank warped by storage"). The nonhuman infiltrates the narrator's phenomenology, similar to what happens in the case studies of chapter 5. We're now in a better position to appreciate how this strategy inverts the directionality of the personifying metaphor through which Lack is seen in the narrative: the anthropomorphizing mapping (with human ideas of agency, intentionality, personality as source, and a nonhuman entity, Lack, as target) abruptly changes direction; the nonhuman becomes the *source* of the metaphor, while the human mind (the narrator's emotion) serves as the target.

This is only a local feedback effect of the personification, of course. Less local effects can be detected at the level of the novel's emphasis on geometric patterns and at the level of readers' experience. As the nonhuman disrupts the human-scale world of the narrative, form comes to the fore and transfigures the characters' interactions. Some of these forms are superimposed on the narrator's relationship with Alice. Desire itself is depicted, humorously, through the formal language of geometry: "'I feel an initial singularity,' I whispered. 'Pressed against your spherical symmetry.' Nothing. She was deaf to me. 'I want to adhere my Schwarzshild [sic] space to your De Sitter space,' I said" (1998, 4). Later in the novel, an embrace between the narrator and Alice is described as follows: "I put my arms around her shoulders, my face in her hair. We cried together. Our bodies made one perfect thing, a topological whole, immutable, complete, hollows turned to each other, hollows in alliance. We made a system, a universe" (1998, 86). Via metaphorical language, embodied interaction is defamiliarized into abstract, geometric shapes and concepts: "Spherical symmetry," the "topological whole," the "hollows." In the novel's final scene, the narrator enters Lack in pursuit of Alice; he finds himself in a version of the college campus where the novel is set, but the landscape is greatly simplified—abstracted, one could say: "Ahead was the administration building, but it looked wrong. The building had been robbed of its color, texture, vitality. It looked like it had been reproduced in chewing gum" (1998, 175). This denial of visual detail is the first symptom of a complete breakdown of spatial awareness, which marks the narrator's experience inside Lack. The coordinates of human experience—from embodied intersubjectivity to basic perception—are pared away and transformed into geometric properties.

A parallel with Heider and Simmel's animation film, discussed in the previous section, will help bring into focus Lethem's artistic method. The film displays geometric figures but encourages viewers to impose an anthropomorphic reading on the spatiality of the images: anthropomorphism trumps the visual abstraction of the images, which leaves only a hint of incongruity behind as viewers realize that these are "just" geometric shapes. But, in Lethem's novel, the anthropomorphic reading of Lack does not completely occlude the abstract spatiality that the black hole brings into the narrative. On the contrary, the spatial abstraction appears to expand, taking up more and more of the narrator's experiential reality. Finally, when the narrator enters Lack he is admitted to an unfamiliar world of pure sensory pattern: "My clothes were a collage of weights and textures, and I felt tiny impacts of pollen or pollution on my face. My ears were two echo chambers, reading soundscapes that warped madly if I turned my head even a fraction" (1998, 180). No more a mere metaphor that transfigures, ironically, embodied interactions, abstraction seeps into the texture of the narrator's perception. Just as an abstract, nonhuman entity is anthropomorphized, the world of human experience is refracted through a kaleidoscope-like lens that brings out its patterned nature. Through this formal flattening of the human/nonhuman distinction, Lethem's novel thus establishes metaphysical parity, far more than Heider and Simmel's experiment.

But an account of Lethem's stylistic and spatial abstraction in *As She Climbed across the Table* cannot be complete without a discussion of how abstraction infiltrates the formal organization of the narrative. As Alice falls in love with Lack, a woman named Cynthia Jalter makes sexual advances to the narrator. Still in love with Alice, the narrator cannot reciprocate, just as Lack appears to reject Alice. The plot thus results in a markedly geometric arrangement, which the narrator captures with the spatial image of a chain: "I was numb to Cynthia Jalter the way Alice was numb to me, the way Lack was numb to Alice. Were we links in a chain?" (1998, 107). The form of the chain—and the image schema of linkage that it implies—is another abstract formal pattern foregrounded by the novel (see fig. 9 for a visualization).

A chain is a form that creates connection, but also one that transmits movement (as in a bicycle chain or in a chain reaction): in Lethem's novel, the connection is between a deeply nonhuman entity and the narrator's marriage, while the movement is the dynamic that subtends the narrative progression. The chain is also different from the linear model of plot critiqued in chapter 2 in that it involves a series of gaps, or scalar leaps,

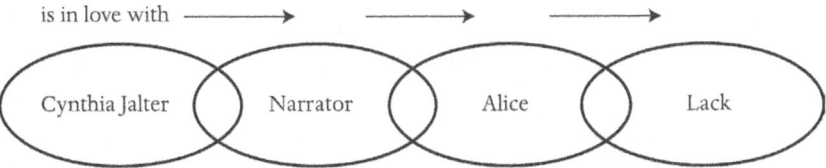

Figure 9. The chain-like narrative organization of *As She Climbed across the Table*. (Image created by the author)

reminiscent of Pendell's discontinuous plotting in *The Great Bay*. The narrator draws attention to these spatial discontinuities through a jigsaw simile: "Could Cynthia Jalter simply uncouple me like a jigsaw-puzzle section and move me into her frame?" (1998, 105). The answer, it turns out, is in the negative: the characters remain stuck in a chain. Thus highlighted by the narrator, the chain serves as a direct narrative equivalent of the abstract forms that define the novel's account of embodied intersubjectivity and space.

How are we to interpret this emergence of abstract patterns? Simply put, the abstraction is a feedback effect of the projection of human qualities onto Lack—an emergent meaning of Alice's anthropomorphizing reading of an entity that remains inaccessible in its nonhumanness. In that respect, there can't be any doubt that the abstraction amplifies the affective incongruity of the narrative: as we read Lethem's novel, our experience of amused puzzlement—but also of genuine sympathy for the narrator's predicament—mirrors the conceptual trouble that the plot creates as it blurs the boundary between spatial scales and pushes an astronomical reality into the familiar world of a college campus—and, even more pointedly, of marital attachment. At the same time, the emergence of abstract patterns eases the work of multiscalarity by highlighting the similarities between the quasi-geometric configuration of bodies in space (and of characters in a narrative) and the abstract, mathematical models through which entities like Lack are normally conceptualized by scientists. The multiscalarity does not imply "scale invariance" (in Woods's terminology) or perfect isomorphism, because readers are aware, precisely through the incongruity of the spatial and narrative abstraction, that the plot involves scalar as well as epistemological leaps. The foregrounding of abstract patterns becomes a narrative means of thinking about scale variance and its disturbing effects on the human-scale world.

ONE BIG GREEN THOUGHT?

If Lethem's novel builds on an anthropomorphic mapping of the LH → W type, "Vaster than Empires and More Slow," a science fiction short story by Ursula K. Le Guin, stages the conceptual tensions created by projecting notions of life and sentience onto an entire planet (LN → W). In *Sense of Place and Sense of Planet,* Heise (2008, 19–20) reads Le Guin's short story alongside theories of ecological interconnectedness that emerged in the 1970s, particularly the "Gaia hypothesis," which sees our own planet as a vast, self-sustaining system whose atmosphere has been progressively shaped by living organisms. The parallel with Le Guin's short story is, as we'll see, suggestive and striking, but Heise doesn't develop it beyond a passing mention. Before turning to Le Guin, it is worth examining the Gaia hypothesis in some detail, because it will allow us to better appreciate the stakes of the story.

First elaborated by British scientist and inventor James Lovelock while working at NASA in the 1960s, the Gaia hypothesis was further developed by Lovelock in collaboration with biologist Lynn Margulis in the course of the following decade (Lovelock and Margulis 1974). More recently, Lovelock has defended the hypothesis in a series of publications for a popular audience (e.g., 2007), where he also argues for the relevance of Gaia to the contemporary climate change debate. Thanks to these efforts, Lovelock has become an influential figure in the environmentalist movement. His theory has been reappraised and expanded by Bruno Latour in a series of lectures published under the title *Facing Gaia* (2017; we'll come back to Latour's version of Gaia in a moment). However, the Gaia hypothesis has also proved remarkably controversial—in large part because of its extremely broad-ranging scope, which doesn't sit well with the cautious and data-driven mentality of most scientists. But Lovelock's ambivalent metaphors for Gaia also played an important role, as he himself admits: "Occasionally it is difficult, without excessive circumlocution, to avoid talking of Gaia as if she were known to be sentient. This is meant no more seriously than is the appellation 'she' when given to a ship by those who sail in her, as a recognition that even pieces of wood and metal when specifically designed and assembled may achieve a composite identity with its own characteristic signature, as distinct from being the mere sum of its parts" (2000a, x).

It is no coincidence that, as Lovelock mentions in his autobiography (2000b, 255), the name for Gaia was suggested to him by the author of *The Lord of the Flies,* William Golding. The reference to the Greek mythological figure is fundamentally a literary device inscribing Lovelock's theory in a long tradition of personifications of nature—a rhetorical trick that Darwin himself adopted in *On the Origin of Species* even as he was delivering a crippling blow to a teleological view of natural processes based on a personal God.[7] Lovelock's metaphorical language, like Darwin's, lends itself to misrepresentation: the Gaia hypothesis can be seen to ascribe intentionality and autonomous agency to the Earth system. At other times, Lovelock is careful to avoid the language of intentionality, but still resorts to the term "superorganism," which is—arguably—in itself a metaphor scaling up the concept of organism to an entire planet.[8]

As Bruce Clarke (2012) reconstructs in detail, Lovelock's collaborator Margulis fiercely opposed metaphorical presentations of the hypothesis, which could easily slide into an animistic view of the Earth. Instead, Margulis favors the more abstract language of systems theory.[9] Lovelock and Margulis's intuition was that the relatively stable atmospheric balance that makes life on Earth possible is not a mere cosmic fluke, but rather a condition that living organisms themselves contributed to creating in the course of evolutionary history. This process, with its circular, self-sustaining logic, bears the hallmark of complex systems.[10] Although Latour resists systems-theoretical readings of Lovelock's hypothesis, his restatement of Lovelock's central problem—"how to speak about the Earth without taking it to be an already composed whole, without adding to it a coherence that it lacks" (2017, 86)—strongly resonates with complex systems theory. As chapter 1 indicated, a complex system is one in which there is no plan, no design for the functioning of the whole: order and coherence emerge, spontaneously, through interlocking cycles of activity across the system's components. If we understand systems in a nondeterministic and nonmechanistic way, there is more scope for thinking about Gaia as a system than Latour admits.[11]

Trying to wrest Lovelock's hypothesis from a holistic reading—one in which there is a preordained Earth system that precedes life, not a dynamically emergent one—Latour asks: "If it isn't a goddess, why call it Gaia? And what difference is there, for a 'superorganism,' between the status of 'sentient being' and that of 'self-regulated system'? This is to place a heavy burden on the poor little conjunction *as,* charged all by itself with preventing us from *really taking* Gaia to be a Whole" (2017, 95; emphasis in the original). But "as," besides being a "poor little conjunction," is also an explicit marker of cross-domain mapping—that is, of a metaphorical connection between Lovelock's view of the Earth and a sentient being, superorganism, or self-regulating system.

The problem with Gaia, it appears, is a problem with metaphor and how to deal with its conceptual instability. Metaphorical linkage affords unique cognitive and creative possibilities, as psychologists have long recognized, and yet the ambivalence of metaphor carries a high risk of conceptual slippage.[12] It is precisely this double-edged potential of metaphor that Le Guin explores, well before the Gaia debate arose, in "Vaster than Empires and

More Slow." Originally published in 1971 and titled after a line from Andrew Marvell's poem "To His Coy Mistress," the story centers on a team of explorers tasked with reconnoitering a remote planet. One of them, Osden, is a man with extraordinary empathetic skills: he experiences the full force of other people's feelings directly, without having to interpret their verbal statements, facial expressions, and body language more generally.[13] Osden's talent, the narrator tells us, "wasn't species-specific; he could pick up emotion or sentience from anything that felt. He could share lust with a white rat, pain with a squashed cockroach, and phototropy with a moth. On an alien world, the Authority had decided, it would be useful to know if anything nearby is sentient, and if so, what its feelings towards you are" (1983, 499). When the explorers land on the planet, Osden does not pick up any signal. They are surrounded by a vast number of plants, but there is nothing that would seem to bear the mark of consciousness: in the narrator's words, this is a "warm, sad world, sad and serene" (1983, 502).

Suddenly, however, the serenity of this world is disrupted. Osden goes missing, then is found senseless in the middle of a forest, the back of his head covered with blood. He has been struck from behind, but he is still alive. Osden reports having experienced intense fear as he was lying on the forest floor: it was, he remarks, "[as] if they'd finally known I was there, lying on them there, under them, among them, the thing they feared, and yet part of their fear itself" (1983, 513). But Osden is unable to identify the "they" and deeply puzzled by the empathetic feeling he experienced because, he assures his companions, "there was no creature to emit [feelings of fear]" (1983, 516). Then one of the explorers confesses to having assaulted Osden; he justifies himself by saying that Osden's extraordinary empathy is a destabilizing factor for the mission. But, strangely, even after the mystery of Osden's attacker is resolved, the fear lingers. Osden detects it in the forest where he was assaulted, but also miles away; it envelops the planet.

As the characters begin to realize, the plants that cover the surface of the planet are a vast collective—and conscious—entity: "It's all one . . . One big green thought," Osden suggests (1983, 520). "Thought" is, of course, a rhetorical figure, though not quite metaphorical yet: it is a metonymy that substitutes the thinking thing—the forest—with the cognitive activity it contains. The underlying metaphorical expression is that of the forest as an organism on a planetary scale. But the Lovelockian idea is instantly met with resistance, à la Margulis:

> "It doesn't think. It isn't thinking," Harfex said, lifelessly. "It's merely a network of processes. The branches, the epiphytic growths, the roots with those nodal junctures between individuals: they must all be capable of transmitting electrochemical impulses. There are no individual plants, then, properly speaking. Even the pollen is part of the linkage, no doubt, a sort of windborne sentience, connecting overseas. But it is not conceivable. That all the biosphere of a planet should be one network of communications, sensitive, irrational, immortal, isolated." (1983, 520)

Harfex resorts to abstract, computational language ("merely a network of processes") that denies cognitive activity even as it admits the possibility of deep interconnection between the "plants." Yet, with the image of the "windborne sentience," the cognitive reading of the assemblage seems to slip into Harfex's reasoning, to the point that the character has to take it back, abruptly, adding that "it is not conceivable." The inconceivability of Osden's hypothesis has to do with the scale variance involved in the upward movement from human-scale organism (the implied source of the metaphor) to planet-scale superorganism (the forest as the metaphorical target). Planetary sentience cannot be thought of because it is unlikely to be isomorphic to organismic sentience, even if the forest does show signs of emotional experience (the fear detected by Osden). If the characters are finally able to overcome this conceptual impasse, it is by complementing the "forest as superorganism" metaphor with another metaphor, that of the "forest as brain." Here the metaphorical connection travels in an opposite, downward direction, reducing the forest to microscopic brain activity instead of magnifying it to the scale of a planetary superorganism: "[Let's] just suppose, most improbably, that you knew nothing of animal brain-structure. And you were given one axon, or one detached glial cell, to examine. Would you be likely to discover what it was? Would you see that the cell was capable of sentience?" (1983, 516). Specifying this idea, another character, Mannon, adds that "sentience or intelligence isn't a thing, you can't find it in, or analyze it out from, the cells of a brain. It's a function of the connected cells. It is, in a sense, the connection: the connectedness" (1983, 517). The same applies, analogically, but on a far larger scale, to the plants that make up the planet's vegetable mind: sentience is not something that can be pinned down at the level of a single cell or plant, but an emergent property of a complex system.[14] Once again, scale makes a significant difference, and certain key properties—in this case, sentience—manifest themselves only at a higher scalar level than the individual components of the system.

The exchange between Osden, Harfex, and Mannon captures well the trouble with metaphor: how mapping the forest onto a "superorganism" makes it possible to consider sentience on a planetary scale, but also changes—drastically—our understanding of cognition. Far from being a mental substance dualistically separated from matter, consciousness is a property of physical matter when organized in sufficiently complex ways. Seen at the confluence of distinct metaphors ("forest as superorganism" and "forest as brain"), the forest can finally take on the role of a nonhuman actant in Le Guin's story. But acknowledging its narrative efficacy requires a considerable amount of time and intellectual effort, as the characters' intersubjective tensions demonstrate. The most likely explanation for Osden's empathetic feeling of fear is that the planet's vegetable serenity was shattered by the intruders' arrival: confronted with otherness for the first time, the forest could only broadcast back the human anxieties and conflicts the explorers brought with them to the alien planet.

Let us go back for a moment to Latour's interpretation of Lovelock's Gaia hypothesis: "The whole originality—and it's true, I recognize it—the whole difficulty—of Lovelock's enterprise is that he plunges head first into an impossible question: how to obtain effects of connection among agencies without relying on an untenable conception of the whole" (2017, 97). Le Guin's story suggests that creative metaphor is at least part of the solution to this difficulty: metaphorical language is the formal *and* cognitive tool that enables us to think about multiscalar "effects of connection" without introducing the presumption of a stable, teleologically oriented whole. But for this to happen metaphor has to be embraced in its dynamic multiplicity. This polyphonic nature of metaphor is neatly captured in Le Guin's story by the competing conceptualizations of the forest (superorganism or brain?).[15] The previous chapter illustrated this polyphony empirically by exploring the numerous strands of metaphors that, traveling in different and sometimes conflicting directions, make up a text's "paranarratives." Embracing the ambivalence that comes from this multiplicity isn't easy. In that sense, Le Guin's planet is a testament to the conceptual trouble engendered by metaphorical apprehensions of the nonhuman. Just as the explorers ultimately have to accept the consciousness of the forest's vegetable assemblage, this conceptual destabilization is something that we must learn to welcome if we want to rise to the challenges of the Anthropocene, with its inherent "bumpiness," in William Connolly's terminology (2017). Donna Haraway (2016) makes a compelling case for this need to "stay with the trouble," in her words, adopting an ethical practice of instability as a premise for a radical reappraisal of humankind's embedding in a more-than-human world. The ambivalence of metaphorical blends in narrative can play a role in teaching us how to cope with an unstable reality that largely eludes our human grasp—and yet, paradoxically, is the result of human-caused disruption. Appreciating the nonlinear play of literary metaphor offers insight and ethical guidance in grasping the tangle of ethical responsibilities and material reliance that ties human communities to nonhuman animals and ecosystems.

Le Guin's short story thus wrestles with the difficulty encountered by Lovelock (and lucidly identified by Latour) as Lovelock tried to develop a language for interconnectedness on a planetary scale. But Le Guin's solution is conceptually more satisfying, because it is grounded in deeper awareness of the formal nature of the problem of multiscalarity. Welcoming the ambivalence of creative metaphor—which is another way of saying its *complexity*—presupposes the ability to appreciate formal patterns. Le Guin's prose is highly attuned to the entangled forms and visual regularities of the alien planet: "There's a hypnotic quality in the colors and spacing of the stems and branches, especially the helically-arranged ones; and the spore-throwers grow so regularly spaced that it seems unnatural" (1983, 506). With an even stronger emphasis on the haptic texture of the alien forest, we read that the "boles stood well apart, almost regularly, almost alike; they were soft-skinned, some appearing smooth and others spongy, grey or greenish-brown or brown, twined with cable-like creepers and festooned with epiphytes, extending rigid, entangled armfuls of big, saucer-shaped, dark leaves that formed a roof-layer twenty to thirty meters thick" (1983, 507). It is perhaps not a coincidence that Osden's own body flaunts the formal configuration of his circulatory system: "His skin was unnaturally white and thin, showing the channels of his blood like a faded road map in red and blue" (1983, 497). The transparency of Osden's body mirrors the transparency with which he perceives other minds, as if the affective form of their thinking was available to him without any cognitive mediation. Therefore, Osden's empathic abilities may be an aspect of the more general sensitivity to form that comes to the fore in the story's ending.

In a desperate gesture, Osden attempts to dispel the planetary fear he had experienced by taking it on himself, in an apparent mental fusion with the sentient forest. Mannon observes that the "scale is wrong. What can a single human brain achieve against something so vast?" (1983, 522), to which another of the explorers, Tomiko, replies that a "single human brain can perceive pattern on the scale of stars and galaxies . . . and interpret it as Love" (1983, 522). Abstract pattern emerges in its tight coupling with affect. Indeed, by fusing with the planet, Osden—a controversial and disagreeable character—redeems himself and affirms a utopian vision of cosmic unity. It is the abstraction of form, in itself a result of metaphorical, multiscalar linkage, that makes this vision possible. By staging and probing the conceptual trouble of metaphor, Le Guin's story brings into view its remarkable potential to reduce the separation between mental processes and the physical world—a separation that is central to modern Western thinking.

Le Guin's story revolves around the structural as well as visual analogy between an apparently sentient forest and synaptic networks in a brain. It suggests that the imagination can span the gap between these realities by becoming attuned to formal, abstract patterns "on the scale of stars and galaxies." This recognition of similarity, driven by metaphor, contributes to the conceptual meshwork of Le Guin's short story, which is in my reading a manifestation of human-nonhuman enmeshment more generally.

Le Guin is not alone in foregrounding the similarity between brain structure and patterns at other levels of physical reality. Literary scholar Stephan Besser has offered a highly perceptive account of this "disposition to detect and construct meaningful similarities in terms of form and shape between the human brain and the extracerebral world on the basis of principles of analogy and morphological congruity" (2017, 419). Besser terms this disposition "isomorphic imagination," arguing that it is highly productive in contemporary culture, from literary fiction to animation film (his example is James Cameron's *Avatar*) and philosophical accounts of body-world interaction.[16] For Besser, the isomorphic imagination is facilitated and fueled by three factors, all of which are widely represented in contemporary discourse: the "fascination with patterns as material interfaces between the brain and the world" (2017, 437); an emphasis on "neuroplasticity," or the idea that the brain is not a stable structure, but a dynamically adaptive and evolving one; and, finally, the aesthetic significance of form as a focus of affective, embodied experience, which leads to the privileging of similarities over significant scalar and contextual differences.[17]

The isomorphic imagination thus promises to bring the brain—and the subjective experiences that brain and body make possible—back into the fold of the material world, advancing and strengthening a critique of dualistic thinking. By paying attention to form, bridges are created between the mind, the materiality of the brain structures that underlie the mind, and the multiple configurations of the world that surrounds the experiencing subject. Nor are these neural correspondences only to be found in living organisms and natural landscapes: as Hayles argues in *Unthought* (2017), various kinds of technological assemblages, from cities to computer networks, also display brain-like structure and functioning. There is much to be said for the heuristic value of the imagination when it is attuned to such patterns: by projecting our brain anatomy onto the nonhuman world we learn to appreciate the visible traces of the evolutionary history that we share, largely, with other living species; we become more fully aware of the Gaia-like structural coupling between life on Earth and the geological, atmospheric, and climatological conditions of our planet; we realize that the configurations of human life, including those of advanced industrial societies, are anything but exceptional in the natural order, in that they reflect constraints and possibilities operating across the gamut of reality. As physicist Geoffrey West argues in an authoritative treatment of scale, these isomorphic patterns are not a mere illusion but reflect "remarkable [statistical] regularities" across the nature-culture divide. The upshot, West continues, is the existence of "a common conceptual framework underlying all of these very different highly complex phenomena and that the dynamics, growth, and organization of animals, plants, human social behavior, cities, and companies are, in fact, subject to similar generic 'laws'" (2017, 4).

But there are also limits to the discourse of isomorphism, as both Le Guin's short story and Lethem's novel, in different ways, attest. The analogy between the human and the nonhuman should not be allowed to flatten multiscalarity; it should not insist on stable and absolute isomorphism, because these analogical practices carry a high risk of anthropocentric appropriation—of projecting the human in a way that erases the distinctiveness of the nonhuman as well as the nonlinearity of their entanglement. Instead, the bridge between human experience and the nonhuman, in its manifold instantiations, should remain malleable and open to dynamic input in both directions. This is the openness that both Le Guin and Lethem achieve through a combination of metaphorical mappings that eschew linearity in favor of bidirectionality and complexity: not only are conceptual categories extended beyond the human, but the human characters' experience and familiar life world are reciprocally shaped by perplexing nonhuman entities. Thus, in Lethem's novel, the narrator's marriage is deeply (and of course humorously) destabilized by his wife's falling in love with a black hole. Le Guin's short story explores the interpersonal tensions generated by a forest that challenges human notions of sentience. These conceptual instabilities are exciting opportunities for narrative—a practice driven by patterns that are simultaneously formal (image schemata, in the language of chapter 1) and affective (the characters' attempts to cope with a disruptive event).[18] The patterning of verbal narrative can build on the isomorphic imagination without being bound to visual isomorphism and its rigid structures. This observation goes a long way toward explaining narrative's extraordinary capacity to move beyond anthropocentrism, uncoupling plot from characters' goal-oriented, intentional behavior. Arguably, this capacity is not unique to modern genres such as the novel but shared with earlier forms of storytelling (e.g., in the epic tradition). In both contemporary and historical narrative practices, it is the complexity of formal resources that enables stories to stage the dynamic instability of human-nonhuman enmeshments.

Creative metaphor is the formal device that best captures a challenge to an isomorphic model of human-nonhuman relations, as the stylistic analysis in the previous chapter, with its centrifugal and unruly trajectories of metaphorical mapping, has demonstrated. But the power of metaphor is significantly augmented by the other formal strategies examined in this book: nonlinear plot structures that mirror the discontinuous, "freak" temporality of the Anthropocene, or the circular capture of the human in a nonhuman world; and the foregrounding of nonhuman entities as narrative actants and even in the thick of characters' mental experience. There is remarkable complexity in the interaction between these narrative strategies, a complexity that—better than perfect isomorphic analogy—approximates the variable and unstable feedback loops of the Anthropocene and offers ethical tools for understanding humankind's position within such loops.

Coda
Thinking beyond Literary Form

Growing cultural awareness of the impact of industrial activities is raising unprecedented challenges for the human imagination, challenges that are simultaneously conceptual, technological, and sociopolitical. The ramifications of this crisis are exceedingly vast, as we know far too well by now, and are bound to shape the future of our species as well as that of innumerable other species on Earth. My hope is that narrative, with the formal means specific to it, will be recognized as an essential—if certainly partial—springboard for renegotiating human societies' position vis-à-vis the natural world. There is great value in the training in complexity that the identification and appreciation of narrative forms can bring. Exposure to formally sophisticated narratives could foster argumentative, ethical, and (in a broad sense) attentional skills that heighten our awareness of human-nonhuman connection and its underlying complexity. As this book has attempted to show, complexity involves nonlinearity, interdependency, and multiscalarity—all features of the Anthropocenic condition that can be encapsulated and channeled by way of narrative form. A prerequisite for the success of that operation is the creative use of the resources of storytelling, so as to overcome the anthropocentric tendencies inherent in narrative practices, and particularly in established Western genres such as the (realist) novel.

Gaining insight into the Anthropocene through narrative is a preliminary step toward embracing the ecological ethics articulated by anthropologist Deborah Bird Rose in *Wild Dog Dreaming* (2011): an ethics founded on respectful reciprocity in our transactions with the nonhuman, but also on the realization that there are no "morally unambiguous or pure sites to occupy" (2011, 142). No matter our personal convictions and choices, individuals living in Western or Westernized societies are always implicated in a network of environmental exploitation, which reaches down to the very hierarchical structures of our thinking and language. Appreciating the complex, nonlinear patterning of story may contribute to reshuffling these structures and embracing the enmeshment of human communities and the nonhuman world at large. Stories, and particularly literary stories, don't shy away from contradictions and ambiguities—unstable affective forms that vary, complicate, and sometimes undercut the linearity of the telling, presenting a concrete alternative to hierarchical and teleological thinking that front-loads human subjectivity. When framed and understood in ecological terms, these complex stories can invite us to take responsibility and acknowledge the moral messiness (and profound meshiness) of our position vis-à-vis a nonhuman world that is already, in so many ways, dramatically marked by human activity.

However, it should be stressed that the link between narrative and conceptual form and ethical responsibility is in itself highly nonlinear. Welcoming the complexity of form—through the patterns traced by literary metaphor or plot structures, for instance—is a morally empowering stance, but it can offer no guarantee of ethical action in our dealings with the effects of climate change or catastrophic species extinction. Action is always profoundly mediated by social structures and political institutions that have, no doubt, enormous impact on our responses to the ecological crisis; it would be delusional to see literary form as a "solution" to the crisis. What can form do, then? From the perspective I have developed in this book, form can attune our minds to the nonhuman and allow us to experience it with an affective and imaginative intensity that is in short supply in the Western world. This qualitative intensity is at least a seed of a new awareness of the responsibilities that we bear toward both future human generations and the nonhuman species we have coevolved with, because human-nonhuman relations are always caught in a form—vertical or circular, centralized or distributed. The form of literary narrative does not *lead* to action, but it puts us in a position to better grasp conceptually, affectively, and ethically the intricacies of our historical and material predicament, as well as the tragic consequences of inaction.

While this book has focused on the possibilities of narrative within the practice of literary fiction, there is no reason to think that such complexity is intrinsic to literature. It is, on the contrary, a possibility inherent in a narrative repertoire that straddles various media, from film to video games to oral storytelling. These media have much to learn from the formal sophistication of literary fiction, and literary fiction—no doubt—has much to learn from them. This is fertile ground for an exchange that can demonstrate the continuing relevance of literary techniques, no matter how challenging and experimental, in today's world. Likewise, contemporary fiction should draw inspiration from premodern and non-Western storytelling traditions to augment its engagement with the nonhuman and overcome the entrenched dualism of Western thinking about nature, with its devastating consequences. Becoming attuned to the patterns of literary form—in dialogue with both current and past storytelling practices—can sharpen and complexify our imagination of the human-nonhuman mesh as it is implicated in the conversational and mediatized narratives that make up our everyday reality.

A final example can perhaps make this point more concrete; it comes from an interview conducted by Susannah Crockford as part of NARMESH, the European Research Council–funded project from which this book stems. The NARMESH interviews aimed to elicit stories about the nonhuman in the English-speaking world, stories in which political and religious attitudes toward nature and the environmental crisis are embedded in concrete contexts of personal interaction. In an important contribution to the field of phenomenological psychology, Howard Pollio, Tracy Henley, and Craig Thompson (1997) used qualitative methods to outline what they call a "phenomenology of everyday life," which presents thick descriptions of widely shared experiences such as loneliness, love, separation, and grief. The goal of the NARMESH team was to paint an equally nuanced picture of people's experiences of the nonhuman world in light of current discussions on the Anthropocene. We decided to address three target groups that occupy a key position in these debates: climate scientists, climate change deniers, and individuals affiliated with the environmentalist movement. While a fuller analysis of the collected narratives will have to wait for another occasion, an interview from the third group will demonstrate the possibilities of the formal imagination when trained upon nonfictional discourse.

The interviewee (I will call him "Stephen") is a writer and journalist involved in a network of environmentally engaged artists. In the course of an hour-long interview, the idea of "deep time"—the large-scale temporality of geological and evolutionary history—emerges in relation to two different topics, the physical landscape of Sweden and the experience of parenthood.[1] Deep time raises the question that this book has addressed under the rubric of "multiscalarity": how to bring together geological or natural processes and the world of human interaction without collapsing their fundamental differences in magnitude and shaping forces (the "blind" physical causality of natural history vs. human agency and social structures). Here is how Stephen narrates the experience of relocating from his native England to Sweden:

> I grew up in the north Pennines, it was a particular kind of English landscape which has got lots of ups and downs to it, and Sweden is like very kind of gently rising from the sea to the mountains so kind of unsatisfying in its lack of hills for me, but the place where I started to feel like I was tuning in to the landscape after several years of living in Sweden and feeling like the landscape was kind of out of focus for me, is a couple of miles from our house, you head just out of the town, you come to this thing called an ås, um, the English word would be esker, which comes from Irish because they don't really happen in the English landscape.

Stephen's estrangement from the Swedish landscape is expressed with a visual metaphor: it "was kind of out of focus for me." By contrast, the process of becoming adjusted to the new natural environment is described with a metaphor that recalls radio or TV technology: "I started to feel like I was tuning in to the landscape." This metaphorical discrepancy suggests a change in perspective, as if becoming adapted to the new surroundings did not just require a response in the visual mode ("bringing it into focus") but an entirely new conceptual strategy. Stephen explicates this point by elaborating on the reference to the esker:

> It's essentially the ghost of a, um, subglacial river, it's the detritus of a massive river running under a mile of ice, that then when the ice went you have sometimes thirty sometimes sixty meter high ridges curving and following the course of a river that existed ten thousand years ago across the landscape, and walking along there and getting to know it in different seasons, was the beginning for me of feeling a way of being connected to the landscape in the country that I've ended up living in rather than the landscape that felt like home from my growing up, so and it's a landscape—so on the one hand, you know, it's a fairly awesome thing to think about that you're walking on this oh a skeleton of a river or whatever you want to call it, and you know how much change is represented in that but it's also tangled up with the way that people and other nonhuman inhabitants of that part of the world, um, navigate because after the ice went away these kind of raised river-like structures that stretched for hundreds of miles

across the landscape were the first parts of roads used by humans for journeys through this landscape, um, and that was the case until about a thousand years ago, when the increase of trade meant that rivers became useful because you could be carrying more than you could carry yourselves with a pony which was about the limit of what you could take as you were following these eskers across the landscape, but also even today migratory birds follow the lines of this, you can see the geese coming south, navigating by this line of—this structure in the landscape, so to me being in nature and being in the landscape is very much about time as well as place and that's— I think that's why that—I gravitated to that part of the, um, surroundings.

Again, the metaphorical choices stand out. The esker is first seen as a "ghost" of an ancient river, a metaphor suggesting that geological history "haunts" the landscape, like a trace of deep time. Paradoxically, the trace is as material as it is ghostly—a negated presence reminiscent of the negative strategies we have seen at work in chapter 3. It is this ambiguous presence-absence of deep time, combined with the semipersonified and mythical nature of the "ghost," that opens up the possibility of Stephen's connection with the Swedish landscape. But metaphors become unstable, and the following figurative reference to the esker—"this oh a skeleton of a river or whatever you want to call it"—reinforces the materiality of the "ghost" by calling attention to the physical structure of the ancient river. Even more clearly personified, the esker is compared to human remains strewn across the landscape.

Suddenly, however, the scale of Stephen's account changes, and the ghost-skeleton is presented, from a bird's eye perspective, as infrastructure, an abstract feature of the landscape that serves human as well as nonhuman purposes: a thoroughfare for people and goods, and a landmark for migratory birds. Here personification is almost entirely absent, and human-nonhuman parity is foregrounded. The "line" or "structure in the landscape" are the most abstract metaphors that the passage deploys for this geological feature, but they are also in some ways an extension of the "ghostliness" and "skeletal" nature of the first metaphorical references: metaphor bridges between scales by foregrounding abstract pattern, as we've seen in the foregoing chapter, and it is precisely the increasing abstraction of Stephen's language, together with his skillfulness in using and combining metaphors, that suggests he has fully interiorized the landscape.[2] The visual metaphor Stephen had adopted in the previous passage ("out of focus") is enriched by a cluster of metaphorical expressions that resist the visual model, until vision emerges again in the "structure in the landscape," with its suggestion of an aerial perspective. These metaphorical shifts convey a particularly complex impression of the landscape that incorporates its geological history and at the same time captures the affective patterning of Stephen's interactions with it. The final metaphor—"gravitating" toward the esker—presents Stephen's own embodied person as a cosmic object attracted to the temporal depth of the landscape: the initial personification, the esker as "ghost," is thus turned on its head; the human, as we have seen many times in this book, is nonhumanized.

Embodiment plays an equally important role when deep time surfaces again in the interview—here not in geological terms, but in biological ones. When asked if he ever felt connected to something larger than himself, Stephen hints at the experience of parenthood, of "being one link in a chain of generations" that extends not just across human history but into evolutionary history as well: "Some of those activities that are very deep in terms of the number of generations are not just human deep, they're mammal deep." This depth that blurs the human/animal binary is captured by way of a metaphorical expression—the chain—that, as we saw in the previous chapter, underlies the narrative pattern of Lethem's novel. This chain evolves in Stephen's language, morphing into two new figurative expressions:

> I think that lots of the things that we try to achieve through very individualistically framed searches for meaning and fulfilment and so on are much more there to be found if we take the pressure off, um, the idea that it needs to be found at the level of this kind of individual possessed of a set of rights, and creating a narrative that is stretched over 70, 80, whatever number of years of this lifetime, and instead oh put ourselves into the fabric of, um, yeah, something that is just obviously larger than ourselves. Talking to children about belly buttons uhh [*laugh*] is one route into deep time and into the interconnectedness [*laugh*] of ourselves.

What is suggested here is that the expanse of human generations in biological deep time offers more stable ground for ethical action than "individualistically framed searches" based on the cultivation of life narratives ("creating a narrative that is stretched over 70, 80, whatever number of years of this lifetime"). That insight is channeled through two variations on the "chain" image. The first is "fabric," which resonates with Morton's equally textural mesh and temporarily increases the abstraction of the chain of generations (note how Stephen adds "of" but then fails to name the strands that make up the fabric).³ The second image abruptly returns us to the domain of physical, embodied experience: the belly button inscribes biological deep time into the intimacy of our bodies ("Yeah, and then you have to ask your mummy about her belly button and then we're in this set of chains," Stephen adds). The umbilical linkage between mothers' and children's bodies is directly implicated in the sequence of human generations—a quintessentially metonymic relation of cause-effect substitution. But the scalar leap between the personal experience of motherhood and evolutionary time is such that "belly button" can also be read metaphorically. From this perspective, "belly button" joins motherhood and the procession of human generations by evoking an abstract "linkage" image schema, not by way of cause-effect sequentiality (as metonymy would): the umbilical connection thus offers a metaphorical "route into deep time and into the interconnectedness of ourselves."

The result is more conceptual instability—not just through the multiplication of metaphors, but also through the exploration, suspended between metonymy and metaphor, of Stephen's embodied awareness of deep time. The unstable forms of the chain-fabric-belly button, just as those of the ghost-skeleton-structure discussed above, are of course affective through and through, and interwoven with Stephen's identity as it is performed by his answers.⁴ But, crucially, the instability is not paralyzing: on the contrary, it empowers Stephen to talk about patterns of human-nonhuman enmeshment that transcend the individual, even as they have their roots in personal encounters with more-than-human phenomena (as seen here through the lens of the Scandinavian landscape, or the imagination of evolutionary history). Just as important, Stephen's answers, through their elaborate (if largely spontaneous) formal structures, stress the nonlinearity of the mesh and the fragility of our moral implication within it. These qualities are steeped in affective values ranging from the sublime ("it's a fairly awesome thing to think about that you're walking on this oh a skeleton of a river") to the humorous, childlike humility of a "belly button."

If Stephen, a writer and former environmental activist, is well versed in the art of human-nonhuman connection, it is largely because of his mastery of forms that are, in the same breath, linguistic, narrative, conceptual, and ethical. Literature can train readers to conceptualize with nuance their position with respect to more-than-human realities: if we could find ways to maximize the effects of this training on the collective imagination of the nonhuman in schools and other public contexts (a big "if," of course), we would have a powerful case for the ecological value of literary form. This analysis of the interview thus begins to show how the distinctions developed in this book are relevant beyond literary studies, and even beyond the practice of literary reading or writing. More empirical work is necessary to examine how the mesh appears in everyday interactions and how its imagination can be fostered through various kinds of cultural interventions. This book's ambition was to offer conceptual categories that can serve as a—perhaps ghostly and skeletal—template for future investigation. Becoming more attuned to the human-nonhuman mesh involves embracing nonlinear explanations, a vision of interdependency, and multiscalar patterns; in short, it involves deepening the imagination of form.

Notes

INTRODUCTION

1. Abram continues: "For these other shapes and species have coevolved, like ourselves, with the rest of the shifting earth; their rhythms and forms are composed of layers upon layers of earlier rhythms, and in engaging them our senses are led into an inexhaustible depth that echoes that of our own flesh. The patterns on the stream's surface as it ripples over the rocks, or on the bark of an elm tree, or in a cluster of weeds, are all composed of repetitive figures that never exactly repeat themselves, of iterated shapes to which our senses may attune themselves even while the gradual drift and metamorphosis of those shapes draws our awareness in unexpected and unpredictable directions" (1997, 63–64).

2. The label "postclassical narratology" was introduced by Herman (1997).

3. As Dissanayake explains, in baby talk "visual, vocal, and gestural signals of affinity are exaggerated (e.g., made larger, held longer) and repeated, often with dynamic variation and elaboration (louder, softer, faster, slower, larger, smaller)" (2011, 59).

4. See also Hogan's earlier *The Mind and Its Stories* (2003), which correlates three widespread plot types—the romantic, the heroic, and the sacrificial—with universal emotional routines.

5. Thus, commenting on *Hamlet* as an outlier in the genre, Hogan argues that "part of our understanding of and response to *Hamlet* is connected with our understanding of revenge plots and the way *Hamlet* both fits into the revenge category and deviates from its standard [emotional] routines" (2011, 8).

6. Of course, this is a generalization that only captures large-scale shifts in the practice of literary studies. See Levinson: with "remarkable regularity, one reads that New Criticism was more historical and more activist in its notions of form than reputation has it and that new historicism's notion of form was both more formalist and more agential in its working ideas of form than current practice suggests. In other words, the sharp antithesis between the two isms falsifies them both" (2007, 563).

7. "The form that best captures the experience of colliding forms is narrative. . . . What narrative form affords is a careful attention to the ways in which forms come together, and to what happens when and after they meet" (Levine 2015, 19).

8. See also Berlant's claim that genre is "an aesthetic structure of affective expectation" (2008, 4). Berlant articulates, perhaps more clearly than other (new) formalist

scholars, the link between affect and form that underlies my argument: "Affect is formalism *avant la lettre*" (2008, 268).

9. A similar corporeal turn is advocated by Böhme, an ecological philosopher in the German tradition. Like Abram, Böhme draws attention to the divide between the experience of nature and scientific knowledge (Böhme 2016; see also Rigby 2011).

10. See, e.g., Chakrabarty (2009; 2014) and Cohen, Colebrook, and Hillis Miller (2016). Crist (2013) offers a pointed, and highly influential, critique of Anthropocene discourse.

11. See Smith and Zeder (2013) for a helpful overview of current proposals on the onset of the Anthropocene.

12. For an insightful discussion of the controversies surrounding the naming of the Anthropocene, see Vermeulen (2020, 1–19).

13. In Abram's words: "Oblivious to the quality-laden life-world upon which they themselves depend for their own meaning and existence, the Western sciences, and the technologies that accompany them, were beginning to blindly overrun the experiential world—even, in their errancy, threatening to obliterate the world-of-life entirely" (1997, 41).

14. See Ryan (2001) and Kuzmičová (2012) for phenomenologically inspired accounts of immersion as sensory "presence" within a fictive domain or "storyworld."

15. For Nersessian, these breakdowns of analogy are a driver of conceptual change in science: realizing that a given analogy is imperfect prompts scientists to adjust their theories. This process bears a close resemblance to the "feedback" of metaphorical mappings that will be discussed in chapter 7.

16. See "I Think," *Darwin* exhibition, American Natural History Museum, New York, November 19, 2005–August 20, 2006, https://www.amnh.org/exhibitions/darwin/the-idea-takes-shape/i-think/ (accessed June 28, 2020).

17. By foregrounding the link between bodily form, environment, and "conditions of existence," Haeckel's theory anticipates the concept of *Umwelt* introduced by another naturalist writing in German more than half a century later, Uexküll (1957).

18. Frank's concept of "spatial form" (1945) comes to mind here: Frank used it to describe the tendency toward spatial juxtapositions in modernist literature, which (Frank claims) favored spatial pattern over the temporal organization of narrative. See also Bruhn (2015) for a recent reappraisal of Frank's concept in a cognitivist vein.

19. My argument here builds on, and extends, the ideas I introduced in Caracciolo (2019a).

20. In *How Forests Think*, Kohn (2013, 20) also discusses the emergence of form in terms influenced by Terrence Deacon's account of complexity science. Deacon's work plays an important role in chapter 1 as well.

21. For an overview of recent developments in narrative theory, see the collections edited by Alber and Fludernik (2010) and Dinnen and Warhol (2018).

22. See also an anthology and a special issue of *English Studies*, both coedited by James and Morel (2018; 2020) in an econarratological vein.

23. This is true for both "first-wave" and "second-wave" ecocriticism, to draw on Buell's influential distinction (2005, 21–22). The former focuses on literary

explorations of nature as opposed to environments shaped by human activity; the latter, by contrast, looks beyond the wildernesses of nature writing and centers on human-nonhuman interactions in, for instance, literary representations of cities or environmental pollution. In both cases, the thematic dimension of literature tends to take center stage.

24. For discussion of how narrative form can convey ideological positions via specific "templates," see Herman and Vervaeck's account of narrative negotiation (2017).

25. Likewise, a number of recent ecocritical studies turn to affect in exploring human-nonhuman interactions (see, e.g., Houser 2014), but they do not foreground the link between scientific models, affect, and narrative form that inspires my discussion.

26. For more on the idea of "cognitive form" from a perspective that productively combines new formalism and cognitive literary studies, see Kukkonen (2013).

27. See the "network model" of narrative experientiality I develop in Caracciolo (2014b, chapter 2).

28. In a similar vein, philosopher Hutto (2008) has argued for the narrative basis of folk psychology.

29. See Watt (1957) for the eighteenth century and also Childers for the Victorian period: "A neat separation of industrialism and the novel is nearly impossible in the years between 1832 and 1867" (Childers 2001, 77–78).

30. See also McGurl's seminal discussion of the "posthuman comedy" in the contemporary novel (2011; 2012) and Vermeulen's focus on the fluidity of genre (2020, 60–63), which opposes Ghosh's rigid concept of "serious fiction."

31. Ulstein (2017) reads the new weird in connection to contemporary debates on climate change and the Anthropocene. See also Hegglund (2020) for a perceptive reading of VanderMeer's novel *Annihilation* within an econarratological framework.

32. McLaughlin (2004) and Armstrong (2014) have written insightfully on the centrality of ethical questioning and affective involvement in contemporary fiction. I refer to Boxall (2013) for a comprehensive and astute discussion of twenty-first-century literature.

1. COMPLEX NARRATIVE IN THE ANTHROPOCENE

1. In the humanities, complexity science has been discussed by influential commentators such as Hayles (1990) and Clarke (2014).

2. See, for instance, Pier (2017), Walsh and Stepney (2018), and Grishakova and Poulaki (2019). It is important to stress that not all narrative theorists agree that narrative can convey complexity in the sense of systems theory. For Walsh (2018, 17), in particular, narrative relies on an inherently "linear logic" that is unable to represent the nonlinear behavior of complex systems. A great deal hinges on what is meant by "representation," though. My discussion throughout this book does not assume that narrative in general can serve as a model of complex systems, which appears to be

Walsh's standard for "representation." Rather, I am interested in how *particular narratives* are able to evoke, analogically and of course partially, the structural features of complex systems (nonlinearity, interdependency, and multiscalarity).

3. On narrative's emotional impact, see Tan (1996) and Hogan (2011).

4. Marlow's embedded tale in Conrad's novella is a highly sophisticated narrative strategy, as Conrad scholars have long recognized. For more on narrative complexity in contemporary film—with *Memento* as a prototypical example—see Buckland (2009).

5. Here is Baranger's more technical definition of emergence: a "certain behavior, observed at a certain scale, is said to be emergent if it cannot be understood when you study, separately and one by one, every constituent of this scale, each of which may also be a complex system made up of finer scales" (2000, 9–10).

6. The metaphor of language and culture as a "scaffold" for human mental processes comes from work in the philosophy of mind, particularly Clark's theory of extended cognition, which will be discussed more at length in chapter 5 (1997, 45–47).

7. Morton lifts the phrase "strange loop" from Hofstadter's influential *Gödel, Escher, Bach* (1999), where it refers to the self-referential nature of conscious experience.

8. On loops and metalepsis in postmodernist fiction, see also Malina's study (2002).

9. For more on the challenge of developing a genuinely "transmedial" narratology, see Ryan and Thon (2014).

10. Note that this doesn't mean that linearity can be eliminated completely. Nonlinearity is a matter of degree: McGuire's *Here* (discussed below) is clearly more nonlinear than Forster's example of plot, but certain aspects of the comic strip can still be construed as linear.

11. This circular shape will be discussed in chapter 2 under the rubric of "image schema," which comes from cognitive linguistics.

12. McGuire released a longer version of this strip in 2014, with a substantially different aesthetics, but I'll restrict my focus to the original text. Hegglund (2019) focuses on the "convergence of planetary and domestic concerns" (2019, 186) in the 2014 album. See also Caracciolo (2016a) for a fuller analysis (in Italian) of both versions of *Here*.

13. The term "do it yourself story" is lifted from Ryan (2006, 671).

14. "Films with network narratives follow [a] complex systemic logic. By increasing the number of agents they also increase the relational range and complexity of the network that these relations form" (Poulaki 2014, 388).

15. See Wohlleben (2017) for a popular-science account of mycorrhizal networks that dovetails with Patricia's work in *The Overstory*. See also Lambert (forthcoming) for a more sustained reading of the novel in light of the science of mycorrhizal networks.

16. Scale is a major concept in recent ecocritical discussions, see at least Woods (2014) and Clark (2015). We'll return to Woods's "scale variance" in chapter 7.

17. On cross-domain mappings, see Kövecses (2010, 7–10). Chapter 6 discusses the cognitive basis of metaphor in more detail; Ortony (1979) collects a number of influential essays on the relation between metaphor, analogy, and human cognition.

18. The quotation "proverbial good science-fiction movie" comes from a letter of Kubrick's to Arthur C. Clarke. See Clarke (1972).

19. For more on film and embodied cognition see Gallese and Guerra (2012).

20. See also Keen's important observation that reading fiction "alone (without accompanying discussion, writing, or teacherly direction) may not produce the same results as the enhanced reading that involves the subsequent discussion" (2007, 92). For more on this point, see the discussion in Caracciolo and Van Duuren (2015).

2. THE FORM OF THE BUTTERFLY

1. For more on the story vs. discourse distinction, see at least Chatman (1978).

2. Despite Lorenz's scientific contribution to the study of long-term climate patterns, chaos theory is often invoked by climate change deniers and skeptics to overthrow the idea of anthropogenic climate change (see M. Barnard 2018).

3. Connolly (2017) discusses these unpredictable events under the rubric of "bumpy temporality," which denotes the nonlinear, emergent nature of the material and sociopolitical processes that have led to the current ecological crisis.

4. The term "folk psychology"—the skills we use to interpret other people's mental states—was introduced by Churchland (1991).

5. "Narrative may function as a virtual reality, enabling humans to acquire knowledge useful to the pursuit of fitness without undertaking the risks and costs of first-hand experience" (Scalise Sugiyama 2001, 223–24).

6. The concept of "tellability" has been extensively discussed in narrative theory; see Baroni (2013).

7. Zunshine (2006) offers an influential discussion of how characters' engagement with mental states ("mind reading") plays a central role in narrative.

8. One of the implications of this scalar account is that linearity can never be eliminated completely, because of our strong cognitive bias toward linear thinking. Put otherwise, it is always possible to establish some degree of narrative linearity in temporal or thematic terms, but the kind of stories I call "nonlinear" greatly complicate this process.

9. For further discussion on image schemata, see the collection edited by Hampe and Grady (2005).

10. For more on narrative and temporality, see the bibliography in Fludernik (2005).

11. On the embodied approach to language and narrative, see Bergen (2012) and Caracciolo and Kukkonen (forthcoming).

12. One of the core ideas of embodied approaches to cognition is that our mental makeup is closely integrated with external objects and practices, including language and culture (see Menary 2010; Caracciolo 2014a).

13. See Eliade's magisterial study of cyclical time from the 1950s (2005).

14. In a brief narratological reading of "Story of Your Life," McHale also draws attention to these temporal anomalies, but then argues that "temporal dislocation in 'Story of Your Life' occurs at the level of the storyworld rather than the level of discourse" (2018, 321). McHale's conclusion is debatable: the temporal anomalies certainly originate at the diegetic level but appear to deeply influence Chiang's organization of discourse, leading to the juxtaposition of the two plotlines and the circularity implicit in the ending.

15. I am grateful to Mahlu Mertens for bringing Pendell's book to my attention and for her comments on this section.

16. Like Chiang's narrator, I struggle with the verb tense here, and I settle for the present "decimates" because it sits between the future of prediction—this is fiction and not a forecast, after all, although it seems remarkably prescient during the Covid-19 pandemic—and the past of the narrative's own retrospective stance toward these events. For the "future anterior" as the verb tense that captures the peculiar narrative situation of climate change fiction, see Craps (2017).

17. See also what Ryan (2006, 671) describes as "do it yourself" stories.

18. Note that these forms are ideal types, not templates that can be neatly superimposed onto the verbal medium of narrative, where the involvement of image schemata is always mediated by readers' imaginative activity and personal inclinations.

3. NEGATIVE STRATEGIES AND NONLINEAR TEMPORALITY IN POSTAPOCALYPTIC FICTION

1. The term "storyworld" was introduced by Herman to refer to psychological "models built up on the basis of cues contained in narrative discourse" (2002, 20). In a broader sense, the storyworld denotes the spatial macrodomain constructed by narrative and filtered through the reader's imagination. See the discussion in Caracciolo (2019b), which critiques and reconceptualizes the "story as world" metaphor.

2. Underlying Vermeulen's discussion is Rob Nixon's influential claim on the "slow violence" of environmental devastation in the developing world (2011).

3. See Kohlmann (2014) for a detailed discussion of the Cold War's influence on the postapocalyptic imaginary and early intimations of the posthuman in Anglophone literature.

4. Trexler (2015, 87–91) discusses Ballard's novel from an ecocritical perspective.

5. Richardson defines denarration as "a kind of narrative negation in which a narrator denies significant aspects of her narrative that had earlier been presented as given" (2001, 168).

6. See Scarry (2001), Caracciolo (2011), Kuzmičová (2012), and Caracciolo and Kukkonen (forthcoming, chapter 1).

7. See also Vermeulen's concept of the "litany," "a key component of some kinds of critical engagement with the Anthropocene world, which evoke the multiplicity and excess of that world through long enumerations" (2020, 176).

8. For a more comprehensive analysis of internet commentaries on narrative space in *The Road* and its affective significance, see Caracciolo (2013b, 431–32).

9. Formal closure is, of course, an important concern in Woolf's modernist aesthetics (see Caracciolo 2010).

10. Schechtman, for instance, writes that "we constitute ourselves as persons by forming a narrative self-conception according to which we experience and organize our lives. . . . What this means more specifically is that we experience the present in the context of a larger life-narrative" (2007, 162).

11. See Cohen, Colebrook, and Miller: "Humanity as global anthropos comes into being with the Anthropocene, with the declaration that there is a unity to the species, and that this unity lies in its power to mark the planet" (2016, 8).

12. Rigby argues along these lines, drawing attention to "the entanglement—material, but potentially also moral—of human and nonhuman actors and factors in the etiology, unfolding, and aftermath of catastrophes that turn out to straddle the dubious nature-culture divide" (2013, 214).

4. FIVE WAYS OF LOOKING AT NONHUMAN ACTANTS

1. See Wolfe (2010, 118–26) for discussion of this category of subjectivity and its roots in the liberal humanist tradition.

2. Chatman summarizes the structuralist theory of character as follows: "The structuralists wish to base their analyses strictly on what characters *do* in a story, not what they *are*—by some outside psychological measure" (1972, 57; italics in the original).

3. While my analysis privileges contemporary narrative, as noted in the introduction I don't claim that this destabilization of dualism is unique to present-day engagements with the nonhuman.

4. As Latour explicitly acknowledges, actor-network theory "uses the technical word actant that comes from the study of literature" (2005, 54).

5. Davidse and Geyskens put this point more formally, taking the sentence "He spread the bread" as an example: "The causal model encoded by transitive [sentences] is one of *directedness* . . . , in which an Actor directs action onto a Goal. We have a *unilateral* model of causality here in the sense that all the energy involved in the causal event comes from the Actor, viz. the bread butterer. The Goal, *the bread*, undergoes this causal event in a fully passive, inert manner" (1998, 158).

6. In Goatly's article, and certainly in my use of his model, this point does not imply that dualism is entirely *created* by linguistic structure, as a strong version of the Sapir-Whorf hypothesis would have it. Language does not necessarily determine the subject/object divide but plays a central role in reinforcing it, via the interrelation of culture and cognition discussed in chapter 2.

7. Herman (2002, 28–50) offers a detailed overview of verb semantics, focusing on the link between verbs and various types of events in narrative.

8. In Davidse and Geyskens's words: "The causal model encoded by ergative [sentences] is not one of directing action onto a goal, but one of *instigating* a process involving the second participant" (1998, 158–59).

9. For more on collective actants in narrative, including a close reading of Powers's novel in this light, see Caracciolo (2020b).

10. By contrast, Fludernik's discussion of these texts hinges on the reader's *projection* of subjectivity into the empty deictic center: "Just as, in figural narrative, the reader is invited to see the fictional world through the eyes of a reflector character, in the present text the reader also reads through a text-internal consciousness, but since no character is available to whom one could attribute such consciousness, the reader directly identifies with a story-internal position" (1996, 150). The reading strategy I am advocating here *resists* such projection of anthropomorphic subjectivity.

11. In oceanography, the term "ocean memory" refers to the way in which large bodies of water can retain traces of past climatological trends: for instance, scientists Old and Haines explain that the "persistence of volume (heat) anomalies is equivalent to the ocean's memory of warming or cooling climatic events" (2006, 1144). See also Caracciolo (2019a) for a fuller discussion of Ozeki's novel that focuses on the intersection of narrative form and scientific models.

12. Personification and anthropomorphism will be discussed more at length in chapter 7.

13. In narratologist Prince's terminology, these counterfactual statements are "disnarrated": in Prince's definition, disnarrated events "do not happen but, nonetheless, are referred to (in a negative or hypothetical mode) by the narrative text" (1988, 2).

14. See Caracciolo (2018b) for a more in-depth reading of Vonnegut's novel.

15. As Slingerland puts it in his cognitive account of religion: "The dualism advocated by Plato and Descartes was not a historical or philosophical accident, but rather a development of an intuition that comes naturally to us, as bearers of theory of mind: agents are different from things. Agents actively think, choose, and move themselves; things can only be passively moved" (2008, 394).

5. MINDING THE ANTHROPOCENE

1. The original video files are available at the University College of London Laboraty of Neurobiology website: http://www.vislab.ucl.ac.uk/kinetic_beauty _movies/ (accessed June 30, 2020).

2. There are some notable exceptions to this tendency within the nonhuman turn. While working within intellectual coordinates close to Bennett's vital materialism, Shaviro and Hayles engage in a critique of human exceptionalism by turning *toward* subjectivity, not away from it. In *Discognition* (2015), Shaviro explores how science fiction can endow computers, aliens, and even mold with consciousness so as to undermine an anthropocentric understanding of subjectivity. Hayles's argument in *Unthought* (2017) works along similar lines, probing the cognitive powers of various

kinds of nonhuman (computational) assemblages, from high-frequency trading to the "Automated Traffic Surveillance and Control" system in Los Angeles. Both projects converge with my argument in this chapter.

3. The phrase "world-involving" comes from the work of Hutto (2012), one of the main proponents of the "enactivist" approach to the mind discussed in this chapter.

4. See Gibbs's overview of the embodied cognition movement (2005).

5. The term "affordance" was introduced by Gibson (1986) in his ecological psychology, which anticipates enactivist thinking about the mind.

6. This reflects the generic hybridity of Anthropocene fiction: in Trexler's words, "novels about the Anthropocene cannot be easily placed into discrete generic pigeonholes" (2015, 14). For more on the neuronovel and contemporary fiction's engagement with neuroscience, see Burn (2015).

7. Roth offers a critical reading of the neuronovel, seeing the adoption of scientific models of the mind as a symptom of literature's decreasing relevance in society: "The neuronovel tends to become a variety of meta-novel, allegorizing the novelist's fear of his isolation and meaninglessness, and the alleged capacity of science to explain him better than he can explain himself" (2009, n.p.). This is an uncharitable reading at best: many neuronovels, and certainly those explored in this chapter, perform a critique of science and its many blind spots in representing reality.

8. See seminal work by Cohn (1978) and Leech and Short (1981), among others.

9. Palmer (2004), for instance, argues for an "externalist" account of fictional minds on the basis of what he calls the "thought-action" continuum: namely, the way in which characters' physical actions are directly expressive of cognitive activity, even when the narrator does not spell out their mental states. Also building on e-approaches, Bernaerts (2014) distinguishes between different forms of "coupling" between characters' minds and the external, material environment. For my part, I have drawn on work in embodied and enactive cognition to bring out the dynamics of readers' engagement with fictional consciousnesses, including the somatic involvement that fiction can elicit (see Caracciolo 2014b; 2018a; Caracciolo and Kukkonen forthcoming).

10. According to psychologists Woodward, Phillips, and Spelke, "Current findings support the conclusion that by 7 months, infants differentiate between people and objects in their reasoning about simple causal sequences" (1993, 1090).

11. Affect theory à la Massumi (2002) has repeatedly made this point. However, it seems problematic to completely uncouple affect from emotional experience or from a sentient subject; from the perspective of embodied cognition, affect, emotion, and subjectivity fall on a continuum from purely somatic ways of engaging with the world to more conceptually mediated ones. Brinkema (2014) links affect to artistic form (as I do in this book), but then dichotomizes—problematically, in my view—the affect inherent in form and the audience's experience of art: "Affective experience is an utterly different approach from a reading that lingers with the many questions posed by textual form itself" (2014, 36). For an effective critique of strong versions of affect theory that regard affect as existing beyond human experience, see Leys (2011).

12. In the words of philosopher Ramsey, "One of the most distinguishing (and to some degree defining) hallmarks of cognitivism has been a strong commitment to internal representations as an explanatory posit" (2007, 223).

13. See, e.g., Maxwell (2000).

14. See, for instance, Pulvermüller's review of neuroscientific evidence (2005) and work by Glenberg and Kaschak (2002) in the field of psycholinguistics. Embodied simulation has been discussed extensively by scholars affiliated with cognitive approaches to narrative (Esrock 2004; Wojciehowski and Gallese 2011; Caracciolo 2013a).

15. *Atmospheric Disturbances* is thus an example of what Bernaerts (2009) terms "narrative delirium": an unreliable narrative driven by the narrating character's mental illness.

16. For more on affective responses to the climate crisis in the Anthropocene, see Head (2016) and Bladow and Ladino (2018).

17. Note that I am not making a distinction between metaphor and simile here: both rhetorical figures imply what cognitive linguists call a "cross-domain mapping"—a link between distinct semantic domains (see also the next chapter). For more on phenomenological metaphors and similes, see Caracciolo (2013c) and, with a specific focus on the nonhuman, Caracciolo (2018c).

18. Barnden (1997) offers an overview of such metaphors and similes.

19. In the absence of a published translation, all translations from Arpaia's novel are mine.

20. For an application of this enactivist idea to narrative theory, see Caracciolo (2019b).

6. METAPHORICAL PATTERNS IN ANTHROPOCENE FICTION

1. See "WWF–Ice Cream," Adforum, https://www.adforum.com/creative-work/ad/player/49872/ice-cream/wwf (accessed June 30, 2020).

2. As Semino puts it: "Cognitive metaphor theorists emphasize that target domains typically correspond to areas of experience that are relatively abstract, complex, unfamiliar, subjective or poorly delineated, such as time, emotion, life or death. In contrast, source domains typically correspond to concrete, simple, familiar, physical and well-delineated experiences, such as motion, bodily phenomena, physical objects and so on" (2008, 6). See also Grady (2007).

3. "Source" and "target" are technical descriptors used in cognitive linguistics to talk about the "vehicle" and the "tenor" of a metaphor, in Richards's terminology (1936).

4. For more on metaphor and the climate crisis, see Nerlich and Jaspal (2012) and Skinnemoen (2009).

5. For a detailed discussion of the history of the term "greenhouse effect," see a blog post by Easterbrook (2015).

6. Influential discussions of foregrounding can be found in Miall and Kuiken (1994) and Short (1996, 9–13).

7. Likewise, in a comprehensive discussion of metaphor and narrative, Popova argues that metaphor can make "specific contributions to the causal structuring of a story" (2015, 113). The term "paranarrative" was first introduced by Pimentel (1990) in the context of a discussion of metaphor in Marcel Proust's *À la recherche du temps perdu*.

8. See Garrard (2013), Ionescu (2017), Merola (2014), Snyder (2011), and Zemanek (2012).

9. The choice of these codes was influenced by the USAS semantic tag set developed by researchers at Lancaster University; see Lancaster University's University Center for Computer Corpus Research website: http://ucrel.lancs.ac.uk/usas/ (accessed June 30, 2020). However, the metaphors were identified and tagged manually in order to bring into focus the most salient semantic domains, which would have been difficult to extrapolate from the complex results of an automated analysis (see Koller et al. 2008). Further, the identification was performed at sentence level, not at lexical level: if semantically related metaphors occurred in the same sentence, they were considered as one metaphorical unit in order to avoid excessive fragmentation of the data.

10. See Michael, Harding, and Tobin (2005). Note that this point about the shared underpinnings of metaphor and simile does *not* mean that the explicitness of the comparison in similes makes no difference, and that metaphors and similes are completely interchangeable. They are not (see Harding 2017, 12–38), but for the purposes of the discussion in this and the following chapter, it is the underlying conceptual mapping that matters most.

11. More specifically, by "main metaphorical types" we mean mappings whose relative frequency across the corpus is higher than 1 percent of the total metaphor usage. We identified 1079 relevant metaphors across the novels: 368 in *Oryx and Crake*, 375 in *The Stone Gods*, and 336 in *Solar*. We used these figures to calculate the relative frequency of the metaphorical types in each novel.

12. See, for instance, Currie's theory of irony as a form of perspective-taking: "[The] ironist's utterance [is] an indication that he or she is pretending to have a limited or otherwise defective perspective, point of view, or stance F, and in doing so puts us in mind of some perspective, point of view, or stance (which may be identical to F or merely resemble it) which is the target of the ironic comment" (2010, 157). See also Hutcheon (1994) for a discussion of irony as a strongly evaluative form of perspective-taking.

13. Szerszynski (2007) and Seymour (2018) explore the link between irony and environmentalism in a way that dovetails with Atwood's approach in this novel.

14. For more on this phenomenological use of metaphor, see Caracciolo (2013c).

7. METAPHOR, SCALE, AND THE VALUE OF CONCEPTUAL TROUBLE

1. For further discussion of this study from the perspective of folk psychology, see McGeer (2007, 137–38).

2. See also Weik von Mossner's treatment of anthropomorphism and its strategic role in producing audience involvement in *Affective Ecologies* (2017, 130–32).

3. These dramatic discontinuities in scale are also at the core of Clark's discussion of "scale framing" in *Ecocriticism on the Edge* (2015, 71–87).

4. For more on blending theory and its application to the study of narrative, see the collection edited by Schneider and Hartner (2012).

5. See Morton: "When you hear the wind, you hear the wind in the trees—the trees dendromorphize the wind. You hear the wind in the door: the door doormorphizes the wind" (2013, 120).

6. In Caracciolo (2020a) I discuss how such cosmic entities can enter a tension with embodied experience in a corpus of twentieth-century fiction.

7. On Darwin's literary strategies, see Beer's seminal study (2000).

8. For example: "Gaia is the superorganism composed of all life tightly coupled with the air, the oceans, and the surface rocks" (Lovelock 2000a, xii).

9. Thus, for Clarke, "Margulis points to the scientific details of Lovelock's developed presentation of the theory in order to tether the metaphorics back to the science of Gaia. It is not an organism; rather, Gaia is a system, a metabiotic system within which organisms are elements" (B. Clarke 2012, 35).

10. In a related vein, Clarke (2014, 139–82) examines the Gaia hypothesis—in Margulis's version—in light of Maturana and Varela's theory of autopoiesis.

11. On Latour's rejection of systems language, see his provocative questions: "'System'? What weird animal is that? A Titan? A Cyclops? Some twisted divinity?" (2017, 85).

12. For an interesting empirical demonstration of the creative potential of metaphor, from the perspective of embodied cognition, see Leung et al. (2012).

13. Osden's talent is also a striking example of how fictional narrative may deviate from standard folk-psychological assumptions. See Caracciolo (2016b) for more on the interplay between fiction and folk psychology, with particular emphasis on mentally deviant first-person narrators.

14. In the article discussed in chapter 1, Deacon offers a similar account of how human consciousness emerges from multiple feedback loops of biology and culture: "Human consciousness—with its features of autonomous causal locus, self-origination, and implicit 'aboutness'—epitomises the logic of emergence in its very form" (2006, 149). Of course, invoking the concept of emergence is only the beginning of an explanation, as Deacon acknowledges: the "hard problem of consciousness" (Chalmers 1995)—that is, the problem of how consciousness arises from physical processes—does not go away easily, not even with the language of emergence and complex systems. However, fictional narratives like Le Guin's can get away

more easily with this epistemological trick than scientific accounts of consciousness; see Caracciolo (2016c).

15. Bakhtin (1984) is the *locus classicus* on polyphony in the novel. For a recent reappraisal of Bakhtin's theory, see Delazari (2019).

16. See also Clarke (2014, 158–77) for a related discussion of *Avatar* from the perspective of neocybernetics.

17. Hutto, Peeters, and Segundo-Ortin (2017) offer a radical account of neuroplasticity.

18. See also Vermeulen's discussion of scale in Anthropocene literature: "Critical theory's nonhuman turn needs to be complemented with a consideration of discontinuities and tensions that cannot be neutralized in flat ontologies or in fantasies of benign interconnectedness" (2020, 100).

CODA

1. For more on deep time, see a collection edited by Shryock and Smail (2011), as well as McGurl (2011).

2. Stephen's discussion of a "line" or "structure in the landscape," and the association with a "ghost," also recall Tim Ingold's "anthropological archeology" of lines as structures that hover between the physical and the abstract: "Whether however a line is real or a ghost—whether, in other words, it is a phenomenon of experience or an apparition—cannot always be unequivocally determined, and I have to confess that the distinction is decidedly problematic" (2007, 50).

3. See Morton's comment in *The Ecological Thought:* "'Mesh' can mean the holes in a network and threading between them. It suggests both hardness and delicacy. It has uses in biology, mathematics, and engineering and in weaving and computing—think stockings and graphic design, metals and fabrics" (2010, 28).

4. On identity as performed by "small stories" emerging in oral interaction, see an influential article by Bamberg (2004).

Works Cited

Abbott, H. Porter. 2003. "Unnarratable Knowledge: The Difficulty of Understanding Evolution by Natural Selection." In *Narrative Theory and the Cognitive Sciences*, edited by David Herman, 143–62. Stanford, CA: CSLI.
Abram, David. 1997. *The Spell of the Sensuous: Perception and Language in a More-Than-Human World*. New York: Vintage.
Alber, Jan. 2016. *Unnatural Narrative: Impossible Worlds in Fiction and Drama*. Lincoln: University of Nebraska Press.
Alber, Jan, and Monika Fludernik, eds. 2010. *Postclassical Narratology: Approaches and Analyses*. Columbus: Ohio State University Press.
Anders, Charlie Jane. 2011. "Colson Whitehead's *Zone One* Shatters Your Post-Apocalyptic Fantasies." Gizmodo, December 29, 2011. https://io9.gizmodo.com/colson-whiteheads-zone-one-shatters-your-post-apocalypt-30794719.
Appadurai, Arjun, ed. 1986. "Introduction: Commodities and the Politics of Value." In *The Social Life of Things: Commodities in Cultural Perspective*, 3–63. Cambridge: Cambridge University Press.
Armstrong, Nancy. 2014. "The Affective Turn in Contemporary Fiction." *Contemporary Literature* 55 (3): 441–65.
Arpaia, Bruno. 2016. *Qualcosa, là fuori*. Milan: Guanda.
Askin, Ridvan. 2016. *Narrative and Becoming*. Edinburgh: Edinburgh University Press.
Atwood, Margaret. 2003. *Oryx and Crake*. New York: Random House.
Baillargeon, Renée. 2004. "Infants' Physical World." *Current Directions in Psychological Science* 13 (3): 89–94.
Bakhtin, Mikhail. 1984. *Problems of Dostoevsky's Poetics*. Translated by Caryl Emerson. Minneapolis: University of Minnesota Press.
Bamberg, Michael. 2004. "Talk, Small Stories, and Adolescent Identities." *Human Development* 47 (6): 366–69.
Banfield, Ann. 1987. "Describing the Unobserved: Events Grouped Around an Empty Center." In *The Linguistics of Writing: Arguments Between Language and Literature*, edited by Nigel Fabb, Colin MacCabe, Derek Attridge, and Alan Durant, 265–85. Manchester: Manchester University Press.

Baranger, Michel. 2000. "Chaos, Complexity, and Entropy: A Physics Talk for Non-Physicists." New England Complex Systems. Accessed July 1, 2020. http://necsi.edu/projects/baranger/cce.pdf.

Barnard, Michael. 2018. "Chaos Theory Does Not Invalidate or Explain Global Warming." CleanTechnica, August 23, 2018. https://cleantechnica.com/2018/08/23/chaos-theory-does-not-invalidate-or-explain-global-warming/.

Barnard, Rita. 2009. "Fictions of the Global." *Novel* 42 (2): 207–15.

Barnden, John A. 1997. "Consciousness and Common-Sense Metaphors of Mind." In *Two Sciences of Mind: Readings in Cognitive Science and Consciousness*, edited by Seán Ó Nualláin, Paul Mc Kevitt, and Eoghan Mac Aogáin, 311–40. Amsterdam: John Benjamins.

Baroni, Raphaël. 2013. "Tellability." In *The Living Handbook of Narratology*, edited by Peter Hühn. Hamburg: Hamburg University Press. Accessed July 6, 2020. http://www.lhn.uni-hamburg.de/article/tellability.

Barthes, Roland. 1975. "An Introduction to the Structural Analysis of Narrative." Translated by Lionel Duisit. *New Literary History* 6 (2): 237–72.

Beer, Gillian. 2000. *Darwin's Plots: Evolutionary Narrative in Darwin, George Eliot, and Nineteenth-Century Fiction*. Cambridge: Cambridge University Press.

Bellone, Enrico. 2011. *Qualcosa, là fuori: Come il cervello crea la realtà*. Turin: Codice Edizioni.

Bennett, Jane. 2010. *Vibrant Matter: A Political Ecology of Things*. Durham, NC: Duke University Press.

Bergen, Benjamin K. 2012. *Louder Than Words: The New Science of How the Mind Makes Meaning*. New York: Basic Books.

Berger, James. 1999. *After the End: Representations of Post-Apocalypse*. Minneapolis: University of Minnesota Press.

Berlant, Lauren. 2008. *The Female Complaint: The Unfinished Business of Sentimentality in American Culture*. Durham, NC: Duke University Press.

Bernaerts, Lars. 2009. "*Fight Club* and the Embedding of Delirium in Narrative." *Style* 43 (3): 373–87.

———. 2014. "Minds at Play: Narrative Games and Fictional Minds in B. S. Johnson's *House Mother Normal*." *Style* 48 (3): 294–312.

———, Marco Caracciolo, Luc Herman, and Bart Vervaeck. 2014. "The Storied Lives of Non-Human Narrators." *Narrative* 22 (1): 68–93.

Besser, Stephan. 2017. "How Patterns Meet: Tracing the Isomorphic Imagination in Contemporary Neuroculture." *Configurations* 25 (4): 415–45.

Bixler, Andrea. 2007. "Teaching Evolution with the Aid of Science Fiction." *American Biology Teacher* 69 (6): 337–40.

Bladow, Kyle, and Jennifer Ladino, eds. 2018. *Affective Ecocriticism: Emotion, Embodiment, Environment*. Lincoln: University of Nebraska Press.

Blanchot, Maurice. 1986. *The Writing of the Disaster*. Translated by Ann Smock. Lincoln: University of Nebraska Press.

Böhme, Gernot. 2016. *The Aesthetics of Atmospheres*. Edited by Jean-Paul Thibaud. London: Routledge.

Bordwell, David. 2008. *Poetics of Cinema*. New York: Routledge.
Boroditsky, Lera. 2000. "Metaphoric Structuring: Understanding Time through Spatial Metaphors." *Cognition* 75 (1): 1–28.
———. 2010. "Lost in Translation." *Wall Street Journal*, July 23, 2010. http://www.wsj.com/articles/SB10001424052748703467304575383131592767868.
Boxall, Peter. 2013. *Twenty-First-Century Fiction: A Critical Introduction*. Cambridge: Cambridge University Press.
Bracke, Astrid. 2018. *Climate Crisis and the 21st-Century British Novel*. London: Bloomsbury.
Bradbury, Ray. 2004. "A Sound of Thunder." In *The Best Time Travel Stories of the 20th Century*, edited by Harry Turtledove and Martin H. Greenberg, 75–86. New York: Ballantine.
Brinkema, Eugenie. 2014. *The Forms of the Affects*. Durham, NC: Duke University Press.
Brockmeier, Jens, and Donal Carbaugh, eds. 2001. *Narrative and Identity: Studies in Autobiography, Self and Culture*. Philadelphia: John Benjamins.
Brooks, Peter. 1984. *Reading for the Plot: Design and Intention in Narrative*. New York: Knopf.
Bruhn, Mark J. 2015. "Time as Space in the Structure of (Literary) Experience." In *The Oxford Handbook of Cognitive Literary Studies*, edited by Lisa Zunshine, 593–612. New York: Oxford University Press.
Bruner, Jerome. 1991. "The Narrative Construction of Reality." *Critical Inquiry* 18 (1): 1–21.
Buckland, Warren, ed. 2009. *Puzzle Films: Complex Storytelling in Contemporary Cinema*. Chichester: Wiley-Blackwell.
Buell, Lawrence. 2005. *The Future of Environmental Criticism: Environmental Crisis and Literary Imagination*. Malden, MA: Blackwell.
Burn, Stephen J. 2015. "Neuroscience and Modern Fiction." *Modern Fiction Studies* 61 (2): 209–25.
Caracciolo, Marco. 2010. "Leaping into Space: The Two Aesthetics of *To the Lighthouse*." *Poetics Today* 31 (2): 251–84.
———. 2011. "The Reader's Virtual Body: Narrative Space and Its Reconstruction." *Storyworlds* 3: 117–38.
———. 2013a. "Blind Reading: Toward an Enactivist Theory of the Reader's Imagination." In *Stories and Minds: Cognitive Approaches to Literary Narrative*, edited by Lars Bernaerts, Dirk De Geest, Luc Herman, and Bart Vervaeck, 81–106. Lincoln: University of Nebraska Press.
———. 2013b. "Narrative Space and Readers' Responses to Stories: A Phenomenological Account." *Style* 47 (4): 425–44.
———. 2013c. "Phenomenological Metaphors in Readers' Engagement with Characters: The Case of Ian McEwan's *Saturday*." *Language and Literature* 22 (1): 60–76.
———. 2014a. "Interpretation for the Bodies: Bridging the Gap." *Style* 48 (3): 385–403.
———. 2014b. *The Experientiality of Narrative: An Enactivist Approach*. Berlin: De Gruyter.

———. 2016a. "Qui e allora: Narrazione e temporalità cosmica in *Here* di Richard McGuire." In *Bande à part: Graphic novel, fumetto e letteratura*, edited by Sara Colaone and Lucia Quaquarelli, 177–91. Milan: Morellini.

———. 2016b. *Strange Narrators in Contemporary Fiction: Explorations in Readers' Engagement with Characters*. Lincoln: University of Nebraska Press.

———. 2016c. "'The Bagatelle of Particle Waves': Facing the Hard Problem of Consciousness in Houellebecq's *Les Particules Élémentaires* and Mitchell's *Ghostwritten*." *Critique: Studies in Contemporary Fiction* 57 (5): 487–501.

———. 2017. "Creative Metaphor in Literature." In *Routledge Handbook of Metaphor and Language*, edited by Elena Semino and Zsófia Demjén, 206–18. London: Routledge.

———. 2018a. "Degrees of Embodiment in Literary Reading: Notes for a Theoretical Model, with *American Psycho* as a Case Study." In *Expressive Minds and Artistic Creations: Studies in Cognitive Poetics*, edited by Szilvia Csábi. Oxford: Oxford University Press.

———. 2018b. "Posthuman Narration as a Test Bed for Experientiality: The Case of Kurt Vonnegut's *Galápagos*." *Partial Answers* 16 (2): 303–14.

———. 2018c. "The Nonhuman in Mind: Narrative Challenges to Folk Psychology." In *The Edinburgh Companion to Contemporary Narrative Theories*, edited by Zara Dinnen and Robyn Warhol, 30–42. Edinburgh: Edinburgh University Press.

———. 2019a. "Form, Science, and Narrative in the Anthropocene." *Narrative* 27 (3): 270–89.

———. 2019b. "Ungrounding Fictional Worlds: An Enactivist Perspective on the 'Worldlikeness' of Fiction." In *Possible Worlds Theory and Contemporary Narratology*, edited by Alice Bell and Marie-Laure Ryan, 113–31. Lincoln: University of Nebraska Press.

———. 2020a. *Embodiment and the Cosmic Perspective in Twentieth-Century Fiction*. New York: Routledge.

———. 2020b. "Flocking Together: Collective Animal Minds in Contemporary Fiction." *PMLA* 135 (2): 239–53.

———. 2020c. "Object-Oriented Plotting and Nonhuman Realities in DeLillo's *Underworld* and Iñárritu's *Babel*." In *Environment and Narrative: New Directions in Econarratology*, edited by Erin James and Eric Morel, 45–64. Columbus: Ohio State University Press.

Caracciolo, Marco, and Thom van Duuren. 2015. "Changed by Literature? A Critical Review of Psychological Research on the Effects of Reading Fiction." *Interdisciplinary Literary Studies* 17 (4): 517–39.

Caracciolo, Marco, and Karin Kukkonen. Forthcoming. *With Bodies: Narrative Theory and Embodied Cognition*. Columbus: Ohio State University Press.

Chakrabarty, Dipesh. 2009. "The Climate of History: Four Theses." *Critical Inquiry* 35 (2): 197–222.

———. 2014. "Climate and Capital: On Conjoined Histories." *Critical Inquiry* 41 (1): 1–23.

Chalmers, David J. 1995. "Facing Up to the Problem of Consciousness." *Journal of Consciousness Studies* 2 (3): 200–219.
Chatman, Seymour. 1972. "On the Formalist-Structuralist Theory of Character." *Journal of Literary Semantics* 1 (1): 57–79.
———. 1978. *Story and Discourse*. Ithaca, NY: Cornell University Press.
Chiang, Ted. 2016. "Story of Your Life." In *Stories of Your Life and Others*, 91–146. New York: Vintage.
Childers, Joseph W. 2001. "Industrial Culture and the Victorian Novel." In *The Cambridge Companion to the Victorian Novel*, edited by Deirdre David, 77–96. Cambridge: Cambridge University Press.
Churchland, Paul M. 1991. "Folk Psychology and the Explanation of Human Behavior." In *The Future of Folk Psychology: Intentionality and Cognitive Science*, edited by John D. Greenwood, 51–69. Cambridge: Cambridge University Press.
Clark, Andy. 1997. *Being There: Putting Brain, Body, and World Together Again*. Cambridge, MA: MIT Press.
Clark, Andy, and David J. Chalmers. 1998. "The Extended Mind." *Analysis* 58 (1): 7–19.
Clark, Timothy. 2015. *Ecocriticism on the Edge: The Anthropocene as a Threshold Concept*. London: Bloomsbury.
Clarke, Arthur C. 1972. *The Lost Worlds of 2001: The Ultimate Log of the Ultimate Trip*. New York: Signet.
Clarke, Bruce. 2012. "Gaia Is Not an Organism: Scenes from the Early Scientific Collaboration between Lynn Margulis and James Lovelock." In *Lynn Margulis: The Life and Legacy of a Scientific Rebel*, edited by Dorion Sagan, 32–43. White River Junction, VT: Chelsea Green.
———. 2014. *Neocybernetics and Narrative*. Minneapolis: University of Minnesota Press.
Cohen, Tom, Claire Colebrook, and J. Hillis Miller. 2016. *Twilight of the Anthropocene Idols*. London: Open Humanities.
Cohn, Dorrit. 1978. *Transparent Minds: Narrative Modes for Presenting Consciousness in Fiction*. Princeton, NJ: Princeton University Press.
Connolly, William E. 2017. *Facing the Planetary: Entangled Humanism and the Politics of Swarming*. Durham, NC: Duke University Press.
Cortázar, Julio. 1985. "The Night Face Up." In *Blow-Up and Other Stories*, translated by Paul Blackburn, 66–76. New York: Pantheon.
Crace, Jim. 1999. *Being Dead*. New York: Farrar, Straus & Giroux.
Craps, Stef. 2017. "Climate Change and the Art of Anticipatory Memory." *Parallax* 23 (4): 479–92.
Crist, Eileen. 2013. "On the Poverty of Our Nomenclature." *Environmental Humanities* 3 (1): 129–47.
Croft, William. 2002. *Typology and Universals*. Cambridge: Cambridge University Press.
Crutzen, Paul J., and Eugene F. Stoermer. 2000. "The Anthropocene." *Global Change Newsletter* 41: 17–18.

Currie, Gregory. 2010. *Narratives and Narrators: A Philosophy of Stories.* Oxford: Oxford University Press.

Dahlstrom, Michael F. 2014. "Using Narratives and Storytelling to Communicate Science with Nonexpert Audiences." *Proceedings of the National Academy of Sciences* 111 (4): 13614–20.

Darwin, Charles. 1970. *On the Origin of Species.* New York: W. W. Norton.

Davidse, Kristin, and Sara Geyskens. 1998. "Have You Walked the Dog Yet? The Ergative Causativization of Intransitives." *Word* 49 (2): 155–80.

De Landa, Manuel. 1997. *A Thousand Years of Nonlinear History.* New York: Zone.

Deacon, Terrence W. 2006. "Emergence: The Hole at the Wheel's Hub." In *The Re-Emergence of Emergence: The Emergentist Hypothesis from Science to Religion*, edited by Philip Clayton and Paul Davies, 111–50. Oxford: Oxford University Press.

Delazari, Ivan. 2019. "Contrafactual Counterpoint: Revisiting the Polyphonic Novel Metaphor with Faulkner's *The Wild Palms.*" *CounterText* 5 (3): 371–94.

Deleuze, Gilles, and Félix Guattari. 1987. *A Thousand Plateaus: Capitalism and Schizophrenia.* Translated by Brian Massumi. Minneapolis: University of Minnesota Press.

Dinnen, Zara, and Robyn Warhol, eds. 2018. *The Edinburgh Companion to Contemporary Narrative Theories.* Edinburgh: Edinburgh University Press.

Dissanayake, Ellen. 2011. "Prelinguistic and Preliterate Substrates of Poetic Narrative." *Poetics Today* 32 (1): 55–79.

Doležel, Lubomír. 1998. *Heterocosmica: Fiction and Possible Worlds.* Baltimore, MD: Johns Hopkins University Press.

Easterbrook, Steve. 2015. "Who First Coined the Term 'Greenhouse Effect'?" Blog post, August 18, 2015. http://www.easterbrook.ca/steve/2015/08/who-first-coined-the-term-greenhouse-effect/.

Easterlin, Nancy. 2012. *A Biocultural Approach to Literary Theory and Interpretation.* Baltimore, MD: Johns Hopkins University Press.

Egerton, Frank N. 2013. "History of Ecological Sciences, Part 47: Ernst Haeckel's Ecology." *Bulletin of the Ecological Society of America* 94 (3): 222–44.

Eliade, Mircea. 2005. *The Myth of the Eternal Return.* Translated by Willard Trask. Princeton, NJ: Princeton University Press.

Esrock, Ellen J. 2004. "Embodying Literature." *Journal of Consciousness Studies* 11 (5–6): 79–89.

Evans, Vyvyan, and Melanie Green. 2006. *Cognitive Linguistics: An Introduction.* Edinburgh: Edinburgh University Press.

Fauconnier, Gilles, and Mark Turner. 2002. *The Way We Think: Conceptual Blending and the Mind's Hidden Complexities.* New York: Basic Books.

Fludernik, Monika. 1996. *Towards a "Natural" Narratology.* London: Routledge.

———. 2005. "Time in Narrative." In *Routledge Encyclopedia of Narrative Theory*, edited by David Herman, Manfred Jahn, and Marie-Laure Ryan, 608–12. London: Routledge.

Forster, E. M. 1955. *Aspects of the Novel.* San Diego: Harcourt.

Frammartino, Michelangelo. 2010. *Le quattro volte.* Cinecittà Luce.
Frank, Joseph. 1945. "Spatial Form in Modern Literature: An Essay in Three Parts." *Sewanee Review* 53 (4): 643–53.
Friedman, Thomas L. 2007. "The People We Have Been Waiting For." *New York Times*, December 2, 2007. https://www.nytimes.com/2007/12/02/opinion/02friedman.html.
Galchen, Rivka. 2008. *Atmospheric Disturbances.* New York: Farrar, Straus & Giroux.
Gallese, Vittorio, and Michele Guerra. 2012. "Embodying Movies: Embodied Simulation and Film Studies." *Cinema: Journal of Philosophy and the Moving Image* 3: 183–210.
Garrard, Greg. 2012. "Worlds Without Us: Some Types of Disanthropy." *SubStance* 41 (1): 40–60.
———. 2013. "Solar: Apocalypse Not." In *Ian McEwan: Contemporary Critical Perspectives*, edited by Sebastian Groes, 123–36. London: Continuum.
Ghosh, Amitav. 2004. *The Hungry Tide.* New York: HarperCollins.
———. 2016. *The Great Derangement: Climate Change and the Unthinkable.* Chicago: University of Chicago Press.
Gibbs, Raymond W. 2005. *Embodiment and Cognitive Science.* Cambridge: Cambridge University Press.
Gibson, James J. 1986. *The Ecological Approach to Visual Perception.* New York: Psychology Press.
Gilbert, Daniel T. 1991. "How Mental Systems Believe." *American Psychologist* 46 (2): 107–19.
Glenberg, Arthur M., and Michael P. Kaschak. 2002. "Grounding Language in Action." *Psychonomic Bulletin & Review* 9 (3): 558–65.
Goatly, Andrew. 1996. "Green Grammar and Grammatical Metaphor, or Language and the Myth of Power, or Metaphors We Die By." *Journal of Pragmatics* 25 (4): 537–60.
———. 2001. "A Response to Schleppegrell: What Makes a Grammar Green?" In *The Ecolinguistics Reader: Language, Ecology and Environment*, edited by Alwin Fill and Peter Mühlhäusler, 229–31. London: Continuum.
———. 2011. *The Language of Metaphors.* 2nd ed. New York: Routledge.
Gould, Stephen Jay. 1987. *Time's Arrow, Time's Cycle: Myth and Metaphor in the Discovery of Geological Time.* Cambridge, MA: Harvard University Press.
Grady, Joseph E. 2007. "Metaphor." In *The Oxford Handbook of Cognitive Linguistics*, edited by Dirk Geeraerts and Hubert Cuyckens, 188–213. Oxford: Oxford University Press.
Green, Melanie C., and Timothy C. Brock. 2000. "The Role of Transportation in the Persuasiveness of Public Narratives." *Journal of Personality and Social Psychology* 79 (5): 701–21.
Greimas, Algirdas Julien. 1966. *Structural Semantics: An Attempt at a Method.* Lincoln: University of Nebraska Press.
———. 1976. *On Meaning: Selected Writings in Semiotic Theory.* Translated by Paul J. Perron and Frank H. Collins. Minneapolis: University of Minnesota Press.

Grishakova, Marina, and Maria Poulaki, eds. 2019. *Narrative Complexity: Cognition, Embodiment, Evolution.* Lincoln: University of Nebraska Press.

Groff, Lauren. 2018. "At the Round Earth's Imagined Corners." In *Florida,* 15–43. New York: Penguin.

Grusin, Richard. 2015a. "Introduction." In *The Nonhuman Turn,* edited by Richard Grusin, vii–xxix. Minneapolis: University of Minnesota Press.

———, ed. 2015b. *The Nonhuman Turn.* Minneapolis: University of Minnesota Press.

Hampe, Beate, and Joseph E. Grady. 2005. *From Perception to Meaning: Image Schemas in Cognitive Linguistics.* Berlin: De Gruyter.

Hane, Carl E., Robert B. Wilhelmson, and Tzvi Gal-Chen. 1981. "Retrieval of Thermodynamic Variables within Deep Convective Clouds: Experiments in Three Dimensions." *Monthly Weather Review* 109 (3): 564–76.

Haraway, Donna. 2016. *Staying with the Trouble: Making Kin in the Chthulucene.* Durham, NC: Duke University Press.

———, Noboru Ishikawa, Scott F. Gilbert, Kenneth Olwig, Anna L. Tsing, and Nils Bubandt. 2016. "Anthropologists Are Talking—About the Anthropocene." *Ethnos* 81 (3): 535–64.

Harding, Jennifer Riddle. 2017. *Similes, Puns, and Counterfactuals in Literary Narrative.* New York: Routledge.

Hayles, N. Katherine. 1990. *Chaos Bound: Orderly Disorder in Contemporary Literature and Science.* Ithaca, NY: Cornell University Press.

———. 2017. *Unthought: The Power of the Cognitive Nonconscious.* Chicago: University of Chicago Press.

Head, Leslie. 2016. *Hope and Grief in the Anthropocene: Re-Conceptualising Human-Nature Relations.* Abingdon: Routledge.

Hegglund, Jon. 2019. "A Home for the Anthropocene: Planetary Time and Domestic Space in Richard McGuire's *Here.*" *Literary Geographies* 5 (2): 185–99.

———. 2020. "Unnatural Narratology and Weird Realism in Jeff VanderMeer's *Annihilation.*" In *Environment and Narrative: New Directions in Econarratology,* edited by Erin James and Eric Morel, 27–44. Columbus: Ohio State University Press.

Heider, F., and M. Simmel. 1944. "An Experimental Study of Apparent Behavior." *American Journal of Psychology* 57: 243–59.

Heise, Ursula K. 2008. *Sense of Place and Sense of Planet: The Environmental Imagination of the Global.* Oxford: Oxford University Press.

Herman, David. 1997. "Scripts, Sequences, and Stories: Elements of a Postclassical Narratology." *PMLA* 112 (5): 1046–59.

———. 2002. *Story Logic: Problems and Possibilities of Narrative.* Lincoln: University of Nebraska Press.

———. 2003. "Stories as a Tool for Thinking." In *Narrative Theory and the Cognitive Sciences,* 163–92. Stanford, CA: CSLI.

———. 2009. *Basic Elements of Narrative.* Chichester: Wiley-Blackwell.

———. 2013. *Storytelling and the Sciences of Mind.* Cambridge, MA: MIT Press.

———. 2014. "Narratology beyond the Human." *DIEGESIS* 3 (2): https://www.diegesis.uni-wuppertal.de/index.php/diegesis/article/view/165 (accessed July 6, 2020).
———. 2018. *Narratology beyond the Human: Storytelling and Animal Life*. Oxford: Oxford University Press.
Herman, Luc, and Bart Vervaeck. 2009. "Capturing Capgras: *The Echo Maker* by Richard Powers." *Style* 43 (3): 407–28.
———. 2017. "A Theory of Narrative in Culture." *Poetics Today* 38 (4): 605–34.
Hilborn, Robert C. 2004. "Sea Gulls, Butterflies, and Grasshoppers: A Brief History of the Butterfly Effect in Nonlinear Dynamics." *American Journal of Physics* 72 (4): 425–27.
Hofstadter, Douglas R. 1999. *Gödel, Escher, Bach: An Eternal Golden Braid*. New York: Basic Books.
Hogan, Patrick Colm. 2003. *The Mind and Its Stories: Narrative Universals and Human Emotion*. Cambridge: Cambridge University Press.
———. 2011. *Affective Narratology: The Emotional Structure of Stories*. Lincoln: University of Nebraska Press.
Horn, Laurence R. 1989. *A Natural History of Negation*. Stanford, CA: CSLI.
Houser, Heather. 2014. *Ecosickness in Contemporary U.S. Fiction: Environment and Affect*. New York: Columbia University Press.
Hutcheon, Linda. 1994. *Irony's Edge: The Theory and Politics of Irony*. London: Routledge.
Hutto, Daniel D., ed. 2007. *Narrative and Understanding Persons*. Cambridge: Cambridge University Press.
———. 2008. *Folk Psychological Narratives: The Sociocultural Basis of Understanding Reasons*. Cambridge, MA: MIT Press.
———. 2012. "Exposing the Background: Deep and Local." In *Knowing without Thinking: Mind, Action, Cognition, and the Phenomenon of the Background*, edited by Zdravko Radman, 37–56. Basingstoke: Palgrave.
Hutto, Daniel D., and Erik Myin. 2012. *Radicalizing Enactivism: Basic Minds without Content*. Cambridge, MA: MIT Press.
Hutto, Daniel D., Anco Peeters, and Miguel Segundo-Ortin. 2017. "Cognitive Ontology in Flux: The Possibility of Protean Brains." *Philosophical Explorations* 20 (2): 209–23.
Ingold, Tim. 2007. *Lines: A Brief History*. London: Routledge.
Ionescu, Andrei. 2017. "Narrative Strategies of Representing the Environmental Crisis in Ian McEwan's *Solar*." In *Crisis, Risks and New Regionalisms in Europe: Emergency Diasporas and Borderlands*, edited by Cecile Sandten, Claudia Gualtieri, and Roberto Pedretti, 287–304. Trier: WVT.
Iovino, Serenella. 2014. "Storie dell'altro mondo: Calvino post-umano." *MLN* 129 (1): 118–38.
Iovino, Serenella, and Serpil Oppermann. 2012. "Theorizing Material Ecocriticism: A Diptych." *Interdisciplinary Studies in Literature and Environment* 19 (3): 448–75.

———. 2014a. "Introduction: Stories Come to Matter." In *Material Ecocriticism*, edited by Serenella Iovino and Serpil Oppermann, 1–20. Bloomington: Indiana University Press.
———, eds. 2014b. *Material Ecocriticism*. Bloomington: Indiana University Press.
IPCC. 2014. *Climate Change 2014: Mitigation of Climate Change*. Cambridge: Cambridge University Press.
James, Erin. 2015. *The Storyworld Accord: Econarratology and Postcolonial Narratives*. Lincoln: University of Nebraska Press.
James, Erin, and Eric Morel. 2018. "Ecocriticism and Narrative Theory: An Introduction." *English Studies* 99 (4): 355–65.
James, Erin, and Eric Morel, eds. 2020. *Environment and Narrative: New Directions in Econarratology*. Columbus: Ohio State University Press.
Jamieson, Dale. 2014. *Reason in a Dark Time: Why the Struggle Against Climate Change Failed—and What It Means for Our Future*. Oxford: Oxford University Press.
Johnson, Mark. 1987. *The Body in the Mind*. Chicago: University of Chicago Press.
Kafka, Franz. 2005. "The Cares of a Family Man." In *The Complete Short Stories*, edited by Nahum N. Glatzer, translated by Willa Muir and Edwin Muir, 427–29. London: Vintage.
Kanizsa, Gaetano. 1955. "Margini quasi-percettivi in campi con stimolazione omogenea." *Rivista di psicologia* 49 (1): 7–30.
Keen, Suzanne. 2007. *Empathy and the Novel*. Oxford: Oxford University Press.
Kersten, Jens. 2013. "The Enjoyment of Complexity: A New Political Anthropology for the Anthropocene?" *RCC Perspectives* 3: 39–56.
Kidd, David Comer, and Emanuele Castano. 2013. "Reading Literary Fiction Improves Theory of Mind." *Science* 342 (6156): 377–80.
Kimmel, Michael. 2009. "Analyzing Image Schemas in Literature." *Cognitive Semiotics* 5: 159–88.
Kingsolver, Barbara. 2012. *Flight Behavior*. New York: Harper Perennial.
Klecker, Cornelia. 2013. "Mind-Tricking Narratives: Between Classical and Art-Cinema Narration." *Poetics Today* 34 (1–2): 119–46.
Kohlmann, Benjamin. 2014. "What Is It Like to Be a Rat? Early Cold War Glimpses of the Post-Human." *Textual Practice* 28 (4): 655–75.
Kohn, Eduardo. 2013. *How Forests Think: Toward an Anthropology Beyond the Human*. Berkeley: University of California Press.
Koller, Veronika, Andrew Hardie, Paul Rayson, and Elena Semino. 2008. "Using a Semantic Annotation Tool for the Analysis of Metaphor in Discourse." *Metaphorik.de* 15: 141–60.
Kövecses, Zoltán. 2010. *Metaphor: A Practical Introduction*. Oxford: Oxford University Press.
Kubrick, Stanley. 1968. *2001: A Space Odyssey*. Metro-Goldwyn-Mayer.
Kübler-Ross, Elisabeth. 1969. *On Death and Dying*. New York: Macmillan.
Kukkonen, Karin. 2013. "Form as a Pattern of Thinking: Cognitive Poetics and New Formalism." In *New Formalisms and Literary Theory*, edited by Verena Theile and Linda Tredennick, 159–76. London: Palgrave Macmillan.

Kukkonen, Karin, and Marco Caracciolo. 2014. "Introduction: What Is the 'Second Generation'?" *Style* 48 (3): 261–74.

Kuzmičová, Anežka. 2012. "Presence in the Reading of Literary Narrative: A Case for Motor Enactment." *Semiotica* 2012 (189): 23–48.

Lakoff, George. 1999. *Philosophy in the Flesh: The Embodied Mind and Its Challenge to Western Thought*. New York: Basic Books.

———. 1987. *Women, Fire, and Dangerous Things: What Our Categories Reveal about the Mind*. Chicago: University of Chicago Press.

Lakoff, George, and Mark Johnson. 1980. *Metaphors We Live By*. Chicago: University of Chicago Press.

Lambert, Shannon. Forthcoming. "'Mycorrhizal Multiplicities': Mapping Collective Agency in Powers' *The Overstory*." In *Nonhuman Agency in the Twenty-First-Century Novel*, edited by Bettina Burger, Yvonne Liebermann, and Judith Rahn. Basingstoke: Palgrave Macmillan.

Landy, Joshua. 2012. *How to Do Things with Fictions*. New York: Oxford University Press.

Latour, Bruno. 2005. *Reassembling the Social: An Introduction to Actor-Network-Theory*. Oxford: Oxford University Press.

———. 2014. "Agency at the Time of the Anthropocene." *New Literary History* 45 (1): 1–18.

———. 2017. *Facing Gaia: Eight Lectures on the New Climatic Regime*. Cambridge: Polity.

Le Guin, Ursula K. 1983. "Vaster than Empires and More Slow." In *Science Fiction: A Historical Anthology*, edited by Eric S. Rabkin, 494–525. New York: Oxford University Press.

Leech, Geoffrey N., and Mick Short. 1981. *Style in Fiction: A Linguistic Introduction to English Fictional Prose*. London: Longman.

Lethem, Jonathan. 1998. *As She Climbed across the Table*. New York: Vintage.

Leung, Angela K.-y., Suntae Kim, Evan Polman, Lay See Ong, Lin Qiu, Jack A. Goncalo, and Jeffrey Sanchez-Burks. 2012. "Embodied Metaphors and Creative 'Acts.'" *Psychological Science* 23 (5): 502–9.

Levine, Caroline. 2015. *Forms: Whole, Rhythm, Hierarchy, Network*. Princeton, NJ: Princeton University Press.

Levinson, Marjorie. 2007. "What Is New Formalism?" *PMLA* 122 (2): 558–69.

Leys, Ruth. 2011. "The Turn to Affect: A Critique." *Critical Inquiry* 37 (3): 434–72.

Lovejoy, Arthur O. 2001. *The Great Chain of Being: A Study of the History of an Idea*. Cambridge, MA: Harvard University Press.

Lovelock, James. 2000a. *Gaia: A New Look at Life on Earth*. Oxford: Oxford University Press.

———. 2000b. *Homage to Gaia: The Life of an Independent Scientist*. Oxford: Oxford University Press.

———. 2007. *The Revenge of Gaia: Why the Earth Is Fighting Back and How We Can Still Save Humanity*. London: Penguin.

Lovelock, James, and Lynn Margulis. 1974. "Atmospheric Homeostasis by and for the Biosphere: The Gaia Hypothesis." *Tellus* 26 (1–2): 2–10.

Luhmann, Niklas. 1996. *Social Systems*. Translated by John Jr. Bednarz and Dirk Baecker. Stanford, CA: Stanford University Press.

Lutz, Sonja L. 2007. "The Road." Amazon customer review, May 13, 2007. http://www.amazon.com/review/RL547GVFFFXI6.

Malafouris, Lambros. 2013. *How Things Shape the Mind: A Theory of Material Engagement*. Cambridge, MA: MIT Press.

Malina, Debra. 2002. *Breaking the Frame: Metalepsis and the Construction of the Subject*. Columbus: Ohio State University Press.

Malm, Andreas. 2018. *The Progress of This Storm: Nature and Society in a Warming World*. London: Verso.

Mandel, Emily St. John. 2014. *Station Eleven*. New York: Vintage.

Mar, Raymond A., and Keith Oatley. 2008. "The Function of Fiction Is the Abstraction and Simulation of Social Experience." *Perspectives on Psychological Science* 3 (3): 173–92.

———, Keith Oatley, Jacob Hirsh, and Jordan B. Peterson. 2006. "Bookworms Versus Nerds: Exposure to Fiction Versus Non-Fiction, Divergent Associations with Social Ability, and the Simulation of Fictional Social Worlds." *Journal of Research in Personality* 40 (5): 694–712.

Martens, Gunther, and Benjamin Biebuyck. 2013. "Channelling Figurativity Through Narrative: The Paranarrative in Fiction and Non-Fiction." *Language and Literature* 22 (3): 249–62.

Massumi, Brian. 2002. *Parables for the Virtual: Movement, Affect, Sensation*. Durham, NC: Duke University Press.

Maturana, Humberto, and Francisco J. Varela. 1980. *Autopoiesis and Cognition: The Realization of the Living*. Boston: Reidel.

Maxwell, Nicholas. 2000. "The Mind-Body Problem and Explanatory Dualism." *Philosophy* 75: 57–60.

McCarthy, Cormac. 2006. *The Road*. New York: Knopf.

McEwan, Ian. 2010. *Solar*. New York: Knopf.

McGeer, Victoria. 2007. "The Regulative Dimension of Folk Psychology." In *Folk Psychology Re-Assessed*, edited by Daniel D. Hutto and Matthew M. Ratcliffe, 137–56. Dordrecht: Springer.

McGurl, Mark. 2011. "The New Cultural Geology." *Twentieth-Century Literature* 57 (3–4): 380–90.

———. 2012. "The Posthuman Comedy." *Critical Inquiry* 38 (3): 533–553.

McHale, Brian. 1987. *Postmodernist Fiction*. London: Routledge.

———. 2018. "Speculative Fiction, or, Literal Narratology." In *The Edinburgh Companion to Contemporary Narrative Theories*, edited by Zara Dinnen and Robyn Warhol, 317–31. Edinburgh: Edinburgh University Press.

McLaughlin, Robert L. 2004. "Post-Postmodern Discontent: Contemporary Fiction and the Social World." *Symploke* 12 (1): 53–68.

Menary, Richard, ed. 2010. *The Extended Mind*. Cambridge, MA: MIT Press.

Merola, Nicole M. 2014. "Materializing a Geotraumatic and Melancholy Anthropocene: Jeanette Winterson's *The Stone Gods*." *Minnesota Review* 83 (1): 122–32.

Miall, David S., and Don Kuiken. 1994. "Foregrounding, Defamiliarization, and Affect: Response to Literary Stories." *Poetics* 22 (5): 389–407.
Michael, Israel, Jennifer Riddle Harding, and Vera Tobin. 2005. "On Simile." In *Language, Culture, and Mind*, edited by Suzanne Kemmer and Michel Achard, 123–35. Stanford, CA: CSLI.
Moore, Jason W. 2017. "The Capitalocene, Part I: On the Nature and Origins of Our Ecological Crisis." *Journal of Peasant Studies* 44 (3): 594–630.
Morton, Timothy. 2010. *The Ecological Thought*. Cambridge, MA: Harvard University Press.
———. 2013. *Realist Magic: Objects, Ontology, Causality*. Ann Arbor, MI: Open Humanities.
———. 2016. *Dark Ecology: For a Logic of Future Coexistence*. New York: Columbia University Press.
———. 2017. *Humankind*. London: Verso.
Nerlich, Brigitte, and Rusi Jaspal. 2012. "Metaphors We Die By? Geoengineering, Metaphors, and the Argument from Catastrophe." *Metaphor and Symbol* 27 (2): 131–47.
Nersessian, Nancy. 1992. "How Do Scientists Think? Capturing the Dynamics of Conceptual Change in Science." In *Cognitive Models of Science*, edited by Ronald Giere, 3–45. Minneapolis: University of Minnesota Press.
Nixon, Rob. 2011. *Slow Violence and the Environmentalism of the Poor*. Cambridge, MA: Harvard University Press.
Noë, Alva. 2004. *Action in Perception*. Cambridge, MA: MIT Press.
Old, Chris, and Keith Haines. 2006. "North Atlantic Subtropical Mode Waters and Ocean Memory in HadCM3." *Journal of Climate* 19 (7): 1126–48.
Oppermann, Serpil. 2014. "From Ecological Postmodernism to Material Ecocriticism: Creative Materiality and Narrative Agency." In *Material Ecocriticism*, edited by Serenella Iovino and Serpil Oppermann, 21–36. Bloomington: Indiana University Press.
Ortony, Andrew, ed. 1979. *Metaphor and Thought*. Cambridge: Cambridge University Press.
Ozeki, Ruth. 2013. *A Tale for the Time Being*. New York: Penguin.
Palmer, Alan. 2004. *Fictional Minds*. Lincoln: University of Nebraska Press.
Papadaki, Evangelia. 2010. "Feminist Perspectives on Objectification." In *The Stanford Encyclopedia of Philosophy*, edited by Edward N. Zalta. Accessed July 6, 2020. https://plato.stanford.edu/entries/feminism-objectification.
Pendell, Dale. 2010. *The Great Bay: Chronicles of the Collapse*. Berkeley, CA: North Atlantic.
Pier, John. 2017. "Complexity: A Paradigm for Narrative?" In *Emerging Vectors of Narratology*, edited by Per Krogh Hansen, John Pier, Philippe Roussin, and Wolf Schmid, 534–65. Berlin: De Gruyter.
Pimentel, Luz Aurora. 1990. *Metaphoric Narration: The Paranarrative Dimension of* À la recherche du temps perdu. Toronto: University of Toronto Press.

Pollio, Howard R., Tracy B. Henley, and Craig J. Thompson. 1997. *The Phenomenology of Everyday Life: Empirical Investigations of Human Experience.* Cambridge: Cambridge University Press.

Popova, Yanna. 2015. *Stories, Meaning, and Experience.* New York: Routledge.

Potter, Emily. 2009. "Climate Change and the Problem of Representation." *Australian Humanities Review* 46: 67–78.

Poulaki, Maria. 2014. "Network Films and Complex Causality." *Screen* 55 (3): 379–95.

Powers, Richard. 2006. *The Echo Maker.* New York: Farrar, Straus & Giroux.

———. 2018. *The Overstory.* New York: W. W. Norton.

Prince, Gerald. 1988. "The Disnarrated." *Style* 22 (1): 1–8.

Propp, Vladimir. 1968. *Morphology of the Folktale.* Translated by Lawrence Scott. Austin: University of Texas Press.

Pulvermüller, Friedemann. 2005. "Brain Mechanisms Linking Language and Action." *Nature Reviews Neuroscience* 6 (7): 576–82.

Ramsey, William M. 2007. *Representation Reconsidered.* Cambridge: Cambridge University Press.

Reagan, Andrew J., Lewis Mitchell, Dilan Kiley, Christopher M. Danforth, and Peter Sheridan Dodds. 2016. "The Emotional Arcs of Stories Are Dominated by Six Basic Shapes." *EPJ Data Science* 5 (31): https://epjdatascience.springeropen.com/articles/10.1140/epjds/s13688-016-0093-1 (accessed July 6, 2020).

RealClimate. 2008. "Butterflies, Tornadoes and Climate Modelling." RealClimate, April 23, 2008. http://www.realclimate.org/index.php/archives/2008/04/butterflies-tornadoes-and-climate-modelling/.

Richards, I. A. 1936. *The Philosophy of Rhetoric.* Oxford: Oxford University Press.

Richardson, Brian. 2001. "Denarration in Fiction: Erasing the Story in Beckett and Others." *Narrative* 9 (2): 168–75.

Rigby, Kate. 2011. "Gernot Böhme's Ecological Aesthetics of Atmosphere." In *Ecocritical Theory: New European Approaches*, edited by Axel Goodbody and Kate Rigby, 139–52. Charlottesville: University of Virginia Press.

———. 2013. "Confronting Catastrophe: Ecocriticism in a Warming World." In *The Cambridge Companion to Literature and the Environment*, edited by Louise Westling, 212–25. Cambridge: Cambridge University Press.

———. 2015. *Dancing with Disaster: Environmental Histories, Narratives, and Ethics.* Charlottesville: University of Virginia Press.

Rose, Deborah Bird. 2011. *Wild Dog Dreaming: Love and Extinction.* Charlottesville: University of Virginia Press.

Roth, Marco. 2009. "The Rise of the Neuronovel." *n+1*. Accessed July 6, 2020. https://nplusonemag.com/issue-8/essays/the-rise-of-the-neuronovel/.

Ruddiman, William F., and Jonathan S. Thomson. 2001. "The Case for Human Causes of Increased Atmospheric CH_4 Over the Last 5000 Years." *Quaternary Science Reviews* 20 (18): 1769–77.

Ryan, Marie-Laure. 1991. *Possible Worlds, Artificial Intelligence, and Narrative Theory.* Bloomington: Indiana University Press.

———. 2001. *Narrative as Virtual Reality: Immersion and Interactivity in Literature and Electronic Media*. Baltimore, MD: Johns Hopkins University Press.

———. 2006. "From Parallel Universes to Possible Worlds: Ontological Pluralism in Physics, Narratology, and Narrative." *Poetics Today* 27 (4): 633–74.

Ryan, Marie-Laure, and Jan-Noël Thon, eds. 2014. *Storyworlds across Media: Toward a Media-Conscious Narratology*. Lincoln: University of Nebraska Press.

Sartre, Jean-Paul. 1948. *The Psychology of Imagination*. New York: Philosophical Library.

Scalise Sugiyama, Michelle. 2001. "Food, Foragers, and Folklore: The Role of Narrative in Human Subsistence." *Evolution and Human Behavior* 22 (4): 221–40.

Scarry, Elaine. 2001. *Dreaming by the Book*. Princeton, NJ: Princeton University Press.

Schechtman, Marya. 2007. "Stories, Lives, and Basic Survival: A Refinement and Defense of the Narrative View." In *Narrative and Understanding Persons*, edited by Daniel D. Hutto, 155–78. Cambridge: Cambridge University Press.

Schiermeier, Quirin. 2018. "Droughts, Heatwaves and Floods: How to Tell When Climate Change Is to Blame." *Nature*, July 30, 2018. http://www.nature.com/articles/d41586-018-05849-9.

Schmitt, Arnaud. 2014. "Knots, Story Lines, and Hermeneutical Lines: A Case Study." *Storyworlds* 6 (2): 75–91.

Schneider, Ralf, and Marcus Hartner, eds. 2012. *Blending and the Study of Narrative: Approaches and Applications*. Berlin: De Gruyter.

Schooler, Jonathan W., and Tonya Y. Engstler-Schooler. 1990. "Verbal Overshadowing of Visual Memories: Some Things Are Better Left Unsaid." *Cognitive Psychology* 22 (1): 36–71.

Semino, Elena. 2008. *Metaphor in Discourse*. Cambridge: Cambridge University Press.

Semino, Elena, and Kate Swindlehurst. 1996. "Metaphor and Mind Style in Ken Kesey's *One Flew Over the Cuckoo's Nest*." *Style* 30 (1): 143–66.

Seymour, Nicole. 2018. *Bad Environmentalism: Irony and Irreverence in the Ecological Age*. Minneapolis: University of Minnesota Press.

Shaviro, Steven. 2015. *Discognition*. London: Repeater.

Short, Mick. 1996. *Exploring the Language of Poems, Plays and Prose*. London: Longman.

Showalter, Elaine. 1992. "Introduction." In *Mrs. Dalloway*, by Virginia Woolf, xi–xliix. London: Penguin.

Shryock, Andrew, and Daniel Lord Smail, eds. 2011. *Deep History: The Architecture of Past and Present*. Berkeley: University of California Press.

Skinnemoen, Jorunn. 2009. "Metaphors in Climate Change Discourse." MA thesis, University of Oslo.

Slingerland, Edward. 2008. "Who's Afraid of Reductionism? The Study of Religion in the Age of Cognitive Science." *Journal of the American Academy of Religion* 76 (2): 375–411.

Smith, Bruce D., and Melinda A. Zeder. 2013. "The Onset of the Anthropocene." *Anthropocene* 4: 8–13.

Snyder, Katherine V. 2011. "'Time to Go': The Post-Apocalyptic and the Post-Traumatic in Margaret Atwood's *Oryx and Crake*." *Studies in the Novel* 43 (4): 470–89.

Steen, Gerard. 2008. "The Paradox of Metaphor: Why We Need a Three-Dimensional Model of Metaphor." *Metaphor and Symbol* 23 (4): 213–41.
Steffen, Will, Wendy Broadgate, Lisa Deutsch, Owen Gaffney, and Cornelia Ludwig. 2015. "The Trajectory of the Anthropocene: The Great Acceleration." *Anthropocene Review* 2 (1): 81–98.
Szerszynski, Bronislaw. 2007. "The Post-Ecologist Condition: Irony as Symptom and Cure." *Environmental Politics* 16 (2): 337–55.
Tan, Ed S. 1996. *Emotion and the Structure of Narrative Film: Film as an Emotion Machine.* Mahwah, NJ: Lawrence Erlbaum.
Thompson, Evan. 2007. "Look Again: Phenomenology and Mental Imagery." *Phenomenology and the Cognitive Sciences* 6: 137–70.
Trexler, Adam. 2015. *Anthropocene Fictions: The Novel in a Time of Climate Change.* Charlottesville: University of Virginia Press.
Tsing, Anna Lowenhaupt. 2015. *The Mushroom at the End of the World: On the Possibility of Life in Capitalist Ruins.* Princeton, NJ: Princeton University Press.
Turner, Mark. 1996. *The Literary Mind: The Origins of Thought and Language.* New York: Oxford University Press.
Uexküll, Jakob von. 1957. "A Stroll through the Worlds of Animals and Men: A Picture Book of Invisible Worlds." In *Instinctive Behavior: The Development of a Modern Concept*, edited by Claire H. Schiller, 5–80. New York: International Press.
Ulstein, Gry. 2017. "Brave New Weird: Anthropocene Monsters in Jeff VanderMeer's 'The Southern Reach.'" *Concentric* 43 (1): 71–96.
Van de Velde, Sebastiaan, Benjamin J. W. Mills, Filip J. R. Meysman, Timothy M. Lenton, and Simon W. Poulton. 2018. "Early Palaeozoic Ocean Anoxia and Global Warming Driven by the Evolution of Shallow Burrowing." *Nature Communications* 9 (1): https://www.nature.com/articles/s41467-018-04973-4 (accessed July 6, 2020).
VanderMeer, Jeff. 2014a. *The Southern Reach Trilogy 1: Annihilation.* New York: Farrar, Straus & Giroux.
———. 2014b. *The Southern Reach Trilogy 2: Authority.* New York: Farrar, Straus & Giroux.
———. 2014c. *The Southern Reach Trilogy 3: Acceptance.* New York: Farrar, Straus & Giroux.
———. 2017. *Borne.* New York: Farrar, Straus & Giroux.
Varela, Francisco J., Evan Thompson, and Eleanor Rosch. 1991. *The Embodied Mind: Cognitive Science and Human Experience.* Cambridge, MA: MIT Press.
Velleman, J. David. 2003. "Narrative Explanation." *Philosophical Review* 112 (1): 1–25.
Vermeulen, Pieter. 2015. "Don DeLillo's *Point Omega*, the Anthropocene, and the Scales of Literature." *Studia Neophilologica* 87: 68–81.
———. 2020. *Literature and the Anthropocene.* New York: Routledge.
Vico, Giambattista. 1999. *New Science.* Translated by David Marsh. London: Penguin.
Vonnegut, Kurt. 2011. *Galápagos.* New York: RosettaBooks.
Walsh, Richard. 2017. "Beyond Fictional Worlds: Narrative and Spatial Cognition." In *Emerging Vectors of Narratology*, edited by Per Krogh Hansen, John Pier, Philippe Roussin, and Wolf Schmid, 461–78. Berlin: De Gruyter.

———. 2018. "Narrative Theory for Complexity Scientists." In *Narrating Complexity*, edited by Richard Walsh and Susan Stepney, 11–26. New York: Springer.
Walsh, Richard, and Susan Stepney, eds. 2018. *Narrating Complexity*. New York: Springer.
Watt, Ian. 1957. *The Rise of the Novel*. Berkeley: University of California Press.
Weik von Mossner, Alexa. 2014. "Science Fiction and the Risks of the Anthropocene: Anticipated Transformations in Dale Pendell's *The Great Bay*." *Environmental Humanities* 5 (1): 203–16.
———. 2017. *Affective Ecologies: Empathy, Emotion, and Environmental Narrative*. Columbus: Ohio State University Press.
West, Geoffrey. 2017. *Scale: The Universal Laws of Growth, Innovation, Sustainability, and the Pace of Life in Organisms, Cities, Economies, and Companies*. London: Penguin.
Whitehead, Colson. 2011. *Zone One*. New York: Doubleday.
Winterson, Jeanette. 2009. *The Stone Gods*. Boston: Houghton Mifflin Harcourt.
Wohlleben, Peter. 2017. *The Hidden Life of Trees: What They Feel, How They Communicate*. Translated by Jane Billinghurst. London: William Collins.
Wojciehowski, Hannah Chapelle, and Vittorio Gallese. 2011. "How Stories Make Us Feel: Toward an Embodied Narratology." *California Italian Studies* 2 (1): https://escholarship.org/uc/item/3jg726c2 (accessed July 6, 2020).
Wolfe, Cary. 2010. *What Is Posthumanism?* Minneapolis: University of Minnesota Press.
Woods, Derek. 2014. "Scale Critique for the Anthropocene." *Minnesota Review* 83: 133–42.
Woodward, Amanda L., Ann T. Phillips, and Elizabeth S. Spelke. 1993. "Infants' Expectations About the Motion of Animate Versus Inanimate Objects." In *Proceedings of the Fifteenth Annual Meeting of the Cognitive Science Society*, 1087–91. Hillsdale, NJ: Lawrence Erlbaum.
Woolf, Virginia. 2011. *The Waves*. Edited by Michael Herbert and Susan Sellers. Cambridge: Cambridge University Press.
Yamamoto, Mutsumi. 1999. *Animacy and Reference: A Cognitive Approach to Corpus Linguistics*. Amsterdam: John Benjamins.
Zeki, Semir, and Jonathan Stutters. 2012. "A Brain-Derived Metric for Preferred Kinetic Stimuli." *Open Biology* 2 (2): https://pubmed.ncbi.nlm.nih.gov/22645660/ (accessed July 6, 2020).
Zemanek, Evi. 2012. "A Dirty Hero's Fight for Clean Energy: Satire, Allegory, and Risk Narrative in Ian McEwan's *Solar*." *Ecozon@* 3 (1): 51–60.
Zunshine, Lisa. 2006. *Why We Read Fiction: Theory of Mind and the Novel*. Columbus: Ohio State University Press.
Zurru, Elisabetta. 2017. "The Agency of the Hungry Tide: An Ecostylistic Analysis." In *The Stylistics of Landscapes, the Landscapes of Stylistics*, edited by John Douthwaite, Daniela Francesca Virdis, and Elisabetta Zurru, 191–231. Philadelphia: John Benjamins.

Index

The page references in italics represent figures and tables in the text.

Abbott, Porter, 111
Abram, David, *The Spell of the Sensuous*, 2, 4, 7–8, 11, 187n1, 188n13
actor-network theory, 101, 193n4
aesthetics: of literary form, 3; modernist, 193n9; politics and, 7
agency: causation and, 112; human, 17, 22, 160–61; human and nonhuman, 120, 141, 163–65; intentionality and, 18, 112; narrative, 37, 98; and nonhuman instigation, 17, 104–5
Alber, Jan, 72
allegory, 43
analogy: between the human and the nonhuman, 176; multiscalar use of, 43; and nonhuman realities, 43; structural, 175; visual, 44, 175
animacy scale, 145–46, 149, 151, 158
Anthropocene, 3, 9–10, 32, 37, 115–36; agency of humanity in, 98; climate change and, 141, 161, 189n31; complexity of, 10, 27–48, 177, 179; discussions on, 117–18, 181; distinctive temporality of living in, 54; facing up the realities of, 133–34; literature of, 199n18; narrative and, 179; perception and, 131–36; standard account of, 93; temporality of, 177. *See also* human-nonhuman mesh
anthropocentrism: and analogical practices, 176; anthropomorphic interpretations and, 160; capacity of narrative to move beyond, 177; critique of, 149–50, 157–58; and narrative practices, 179; resistance to, 112, 157; of story, 22
anthropomorphism, 97–99, 109, 166–68; and audience involvement, 198n2; cultivation of, 160; and metaphor, 159–60; of the nonhuman, 151, 157; personification and, 194n12; pitfalls of, 164; strategic, 160
Appadurai, Arjun, 160
Arpaia, Bruno, *Qualcosa, là fuori*, 25, 118, 131–36
art: and cave painting, 70; experience of, 195n11; landscape, 41; science and, 121
Askin, Ridvan, 126
Atwood, Margaret: objectification and irony in, 147–50; *Oryx and Crake*, 26, 141–54, 157
Austen, Jane, 29

Bacigalupi, Paolo, *The Windup Girl*, 143
Ballard, J. G., *The Drowned World*, 79
Balzac, Honoré de, 29
Banfield, Ann, 106
Baranger, Michel, 27, 29, 33, 190n5
Barnard, Rita, 37
Barthes, Roland, 4
Bellone, Enrico, 132

Bennett, Jane, *Vibrant Matter*, 17–18, 97–98, 100, 116–17, 120, 135, 160
Berger, James, *After the End*, 77
Bernaerts, Lars, 98, 195n9, 196n15
Besser, Stephen, 175–76
Biebuyck, Benjamin, 141, 156–57
Bixler, Andrea, 110–11
Blanchot, Maurice, *The Writing of the Disaster*, 77
Bordwell, David, 39, 41
Boroditsky, Lera, 57, 60
Bracke, Astrid, 19
Bradbury, Ray, 23; "A Sound of Thunder," 51–53, 57, 59, 64
Brooks, Peter, *Reading for the Plot*, 56
Browning, Elizabeth Barrett, 7
Bruner, Jerome, 90
butterfly effect, 52, 55, 64, 72; and climate change, 54; and narrative form, 59, 70
Byatt, A. S., *Ragnarök*, 24

Calvino, Italo, *Cosmicomics*, 160
Cameron, James, *Avatar* (film), 175, 199n16
capitalism: as an abstract entity, 101; and climate change, 32; global, 3; rise of, 32, 93; as a sociopolitical structure, 98–99; system of, 10–11
Carroll, Lewis, *The Hunting of the Snark*, 164
Castano, Emanuele, 47
causation: and agency, 112; of catastrophe, 82; complex, 77, 82; culture and concepts of, 60; direct, 104–5; mental, 56; narrative time and, 53; nonlinear, 77, 82; psychological, 34, 57; time and, 63, 74
Chakrabarty, Dipesh, 10, 32, 99
Chalmers, David, 117, 120
chaos theory, 51
characters: consciousness of human, 113; and intentionality, 177; narrative evocation of mind of, 118–19; and nonhuman actants, 112; promotion of places to, 109–10; psychology of, 110, 130; reconceptualization of, 117; somatic experience of, 156; structuralist approach to, 111, 193n2; subjectivity of, 100
Chiang, Ted, "Story of Your Life," 55, 59–66
cinema. *See* film
Clark, Andy, 117, 120–21; theory of extended cognition of, 190n6
Clark, Timothy, *Ecocriticism on the Edge*, 20
Clarke, Bruce, 170, 198n9, 199n16
climate change, 8–10, 47, 71, 161, 169; abstraction in, 8–9; and Anthropocene, 141, 161, 189n31; anthropogenic, 133, 139, 155–57; capitalism as main driver of, 32; challenges raised by, 20, 179; and contemporary novels, 79; and desertification, 131; disastrous effects of, 135; discourse on, 142; and ecosystemic variations, 45; embodiment of, 156; gradual devastation of, 78; "greenhouse effect" and, 140; heat wave and, 54; issues of, 131; more-than-human scale of, 143; nonhuman realities of, 157; present-day anxieties about, 142; and satire, 153–56; science of, 8, 12, 132, 140, 191n2; species capable of causing, 31. *See also* global warming; science
cognition: anthropocentric, 146; centrality of vision in, 2; "e-approaches" to, 121–22, 134, 195n9; embodied, 45, 117, 191n12, 195n4, 195n11, 198n12; enactive, 195n9; and evolution, 74; influence of language on, 60; linear thinking in, 75; narrative and levels of, 22. *See also* mind
cognitive archeology, 160
cognitive linguistics, 57, 72, 190n11, 196n3
cognitive literary theory, 74; new formalism and, 189n26
cognitive metaphor theory, 139–40, 142, 158, 196n2. *See also* metaphor
cognitive science, 122
colonialism, 10
comic books, 24, 33, 47, 79; science fiction, 84
complex systems theory, 18, 24, 26–27, 140, 170, 189n2; loops in, 29–33;

nonlinearity in, 52; self-organization in, 29–30, 51. *See also* morphodynamics; nonlinearity
Connolly, William, 174, 191n3
Conrad, Joseph, *Heart of Darkness*, 28, 190n4
consciousness: embodied, 134–35; evocation of, 37, 118, 136; hard problem of, 198n14; heightened, 134; of time, 63–66
Cortázar, Julio, 23; "Continuity of Parks," 32–33; "The Night Face Up," 55, 59–66
Crace, Jim, *Being Dead*, 25, 100, 106–7
Crist, Eileen, 98, 188n10
critical theory, 6
Crockford, Susannah, 181
Crutzen, Paul, 9
cultural studies, 6, 9
culture: biology and, 198n14; complexity of human, 32; language and, 121, 191n12; mind and, 121; nature and, 53; non-Western, 61; and perception of physical world, 64; symbolic ecosystem of, 31; and technology, 132

Dahlstrom, Michael, 20–21
Danforth, Christopher, 6
Darwin, Charles, 14, 110; *On the Origin of Species*, 13, 169
Deacon, Terrence, 24, 27, 30–32, 188n20, 198n14
death, 56, 65–66
Defoe, Daniel, *Robinson Crusoe*, 143
De Landa, Manuel, *A Thousand Years of Nonlinear History*, 54, 75
Deleuze, Gilles, 36
discontinuous sampling, 55. *See also* nonlinearity
Dissanayake, Ellen, 4, 187n3
Dodds, Peter Sheridan, 6
Doležel, Lubomír, 78
Donne, John, 143; "The Son Rising," 151–52
dualism, 102–4, 123–24, 194n15; critique of, 122, 132–34; culturally stratified forms of, 120; overcoming thinking that reflects, 118–21, 141, 176, 181, 193n3; in separation of mind and world, 135

Easterlin, Nancy, 18; *A Biocultural Approach to Literary Theory and Interpretation*, 119
ecocriticism, 19–21, 77, 119, 161, 188n23, 192n4; and "cultural representations," 23; fundamental premises of, 20; material, 17, 97, 120, 160; scale in, 190n16; studies in, 189n25
ecolinguistics, 18; contemporary work in, 25; "green grammar" in the field of, 100, 112
ecological ethics, 179. *See also* ecology
ecological philosophy, 2, 188n9. *See also* ecology
ecology: crisis of, 2, 9, 20, 93, 133, 140, 154–57, 162–63, 179; fragile relations of, 1–2; importance of plants to, 73; science of, 14. *See also* ecological ethics; ecological philosophy
econarratology, 111, 189n31
ecoterrorism, 40, 73
Eliade, Mircea, 153, 191n13
emergence, 29–31, 198n14; amplification of, 30; technical definition of, 190n5; typology of, 32
emotion: and assumption, 160; and belief change, 20; changing valence of, 59; and fiction, 47; of infants, 5; language and, 6, 140; of narrator, 166; negative, 6; positive, 6; prototypes of, 5; stylistic foregrounding and, 20
England, 182
environmentalist movement, 8, 40, 169
Epic of Gilgamesh, 92
evolution, 45, 110–11; cognition and, 74; and geological processes, 119; and human brain, 115–16
extended mind hypothesis, 117, 120

Fauconnier, Gilles, 162
fiction: Anthropocene, 10, 141–43, 158, 195n6; climate change, 192n16; contemporary, 23–24, 47, 118, 181, 189n32;

fiction (*continued*)
  disanthropic, 106; dystopian, 142–43; ecological, 3; and emotion, 47; and film, 18, 37–38, 159; and folk psychology, 198n13; formal complexity of, 20; formative, 21; imagery of, 82; postapocalyptic, 15, 25, 71, 77–94, 108, 192n3; postmodernist, 24, 190n8; psychological impact of reading, 47; realist, 23–24; serious, 189n30; zombie, 88–94. *See also* novel, the; science fiction
film, 24, 33, 47, 79, 161; animation, 159, 166, 175; and embodied cognition, 191n19; experiment in, 166–67; fiction and, 18, 37–38; and human absence, 106–7; narrative complexity in, 190n4; network narratives in, 41–42, 190n14. *See also* film theory
film theory, 39. *See also* film
Florida, 1–2
Fludernik, Monika, *Towards a "Natural" Narratology*, 22, 67, 97, 194n10
form: abstraction of, 11–16, 175; affective, 20–21; analogical, 14; cognitive, 20, 189n26; complexity of, 180; conceptual, 19–20; devices of, 19; ideological, 19; imagistic, 14, 19; invisibility of, 12; literary, 19; natural, 11; spatial, 188n18. *See also* narrative form
formalism, 13. *See also* new formalism
Forster, E. M., 33–34, 55–56
Frammartino, Michelangelo, *Le quattro volte* (*The Four Times*, film), 34–36, 35, 73
Fransoo, Ruben, 26, 141
Friedman, Thomas, 54
Frost, Robert, 1

Gaia hypothesis, 26, 168–70, 173, 198n10
Galchen, Rivka, *Atmospheric Disturbances*, 16, 25, 118, 126–30, 133, 135–36, 161, 196n15
Garrard, Greg, 106, 155
geology: nonhuman reality of, 153, 157; physical complexity of, 32

geometry: of human characters in more-than-human world, 1; of human-nonhuman relations, 3; imagery of, 3; sensory, 3
Ghosh, Amitav: *The Great Derangement*, 22–23; *The Hungry Tide*, 109
Gilbert, Daniel, 81
Giltsch, Adolf, 14
globalization, 45, 47, 98
Global South, 9
global warming, 2–3, 71, 107, 140–41; effects of, 45, 131, 140. *See also* climate change
Goatly, Andrew, 100; "Green Grammar and Grammatical Metaphor," 102–6, 109, 111–12, 140–41, 193n6
Golding, William, *The Lord of the Flies*, 169
Gould, Stephen Jay, 60
Greimas, Algirdas Julien, 4, 25, 99–103, 111–12, 149
Groff, Lauren, 1–2; "At the Round Earth's Imagined Corners," 1, 3, 7
Grusin, Richard, 16, 119
Guattari, Félix, 36

Haeckel, Ernst: *Generelle Morphologie der Organismen* (*General Morphology of Organisms*), 14; *Kunstformen der Natur* (*Art Forms in Nature*), 14, 15
Haraway, Donna, 10, 174
Hayles, Katherine, 43; *Unthought*, 176, 194n2
Heider, Fritz, 159, 161, 166–67
Heise, Ursula, 8; *Sense of Place and Sense of Planet*, 168–69
Henley, Tracy, 181
Herman, David, 18, 22, 77, 92, 192n1, 193n7; *Narratology beyond the Human*, 43, 140
Herman, Luc, 98, 125
Hilborn, Robert, 51
Hirsh, Jacob, 47
historiography, 67. *See also* history
history: agent of, 99; biological, 11; change in course of, 53; cultural, 11; divine intervention in human, 92; evolutionary, 3, 30, 36, 45, 53, 105,

120, 132, 170, 176, 181, 185; geological, 2, 9, 23, 181–84; and global warming, 32; human, 70; intellectual, 27; of material object, 38; and narrativity, 67; of nonhuman world, 64; nonlinear conception of, 54, 72; philosophy of, 153; prescientific conception of, 71; of science, 132; of technological progress, 44; temporality and, 60. *See also* historiography

Hofstadter, Douglas, *Gödel, Escher, Bach*, 53, 66, 153, 190n7

Hogan, Patrick Colm, 5–6, 187nn4–5

Horn, Laurence, *A Natural History of Negation*, 81

human cognition. *See* cognition

human-nonhuman mesh, 7–11, 15–25, 31–33, 54, 73–75, 98, 103, 121–22, 175–76, 193n12; abstract notion of, 42; Anthropocenic, 157; and catastrophe, 82, 93; as complex system, 27–48; dynamic instability of, 177; imagination of, 181; interactions of, 189n25; as loop, 63, 66; materiality of, 24; metaphor and, 112–13, 143–44, 177; multiscalarity and, 140–41, 157; in narrative, 111, 118, 159; nonlinearity of, 176; reciprocity of, 107–9; trickling down of, 136. *See also* Anthropocene; interdependency

Hutto, Daniel, 55, 122, 189n28, 195n3

imagination: cultivation of, 163, 181; of evolutionary history, 185; of form, 2, 186; heuristic value of, 176; isomorphic, 175–77; and multiscalarity, 45; phenomenology of, 81; postapocalyptic, 79; of reader, 82–87; rethinking of, 158; unprecedented challenges for, 179

Iñárritu, Alejandro González, *Babel* (film), 38–39, 84

industrialization, 3, 9, 93; globalization and, 16; large-scale, 31, 98; and the novel, 22, 24

industrial revolution. *See* industrialization

intentionality, 24, 38, 47, 93; and agency, 18, 112, 169; character and, 177; direct, 93; goals and, 62, 177; and inanimate world, 63; language of, 169; and nonhuman realities, 112; of region, 109–10; unlikely outcomes that break with, 110

interdependency, 27, 29; of complex systems, 33, 37–42, 51; human-nonhuman, 100, 113, 117, 141; of humans with humans, 42; of humans with plants, 42; postapocalyptic fiction and, 77. *See also* human-nonhuman mesh; intersubjectivity

Intergovernmental Panel on Climate Change (IPCC), 54, 75

intersubjectivity, 40, 42; embodied, 166–68; and social cognition, 48; social knowledge and, 22; tensions of, 173. *See also* interdependency; subjectivity

Ionescu, Andrei, 26, 141

Iovino, Serenella, 17, 97, 120, 160

irony, 26, 142–43; and environmentalism, 197n13; as a form of perspective-taking, 197n12; objectification and, 147–50; satire and, 154

James, Erin, *The Storyworld Accord*, 18, 111

Jamieson, Dale, 8

Japan, 108

Johnson, Mark, 57, 102, 128, 139

Kafka, Franz, 24; "Cares of a Family Man," 97–98; *The Castle*, 78; *The Metamorphosis*, 164

Kanizsa, Gaetano, 16, 80

Kanizsa triangle, 80–83, *80*, 88, 91

Kersten, Jens, 28, 47

Kidd, David Comer, 47

Kiley, Dilan, 6

Kimmel, Michel, 59

Kingsolver, Barbara, *Flight Behavior*, 45–47, 143

Klecker, Cornelia, 62

knowledge: and narrative, 101; neuroscientific, 133; in a nonhuman being, 65; scientific, 8, 16, 20, 23, 127, 130–35; social, 22. *See also* science

Kohn, Eduardo, *How Forests Think*, 12–13, 188n20
Kubrick, Stanley, 191n18; *2001: A Space Odyssey* (film), 43–46, 44
Kuiken, Don, 20
Kuzmičová, Anežka, 87–88

Lakoff, George, 57, 102, 128, 139
Landy, Joshua, *How to Do Things with Fiction*, 21
language: abstract form and, 1, 19; affective, 6; of aliens, 63; as a complex semiotic system, 31; computational, 172; conceptual abilities and the processing of, 117; and culture, 121, 191n12; diversification of, 69; and dualism, 7, 25, 102–4, 193n6; and emotion, 6, 140; figurative, 107; hierarchical structures of thinking and, 180; influence on cognition of, 60; of intentionality, 169; metaphorical, 43, 45, 139–46, 155, 157–58, 161–62, 169, 173; negation in, 80–83; of postmodernist fiction, 24; power of literary, 106, 140; and representation, 122; stylistic form of, 134; syntactic organization of natural, 100–102; of systems theory, 170; tense system of, 65; and transitivity, 102–4. *See also* metaphor
Latour, Bruno, 101, 111, 160, 193n4, 198n11; "Agency at the Time of the Anthropocene," 99; *Facing Gaia*, 169–70
Le Guin, Ursula K., 23; "Vaster than Empires and More Slow," 26, 163, 168–76
Lethem, Jonathan, *As She Climbed across the Table*, 26, 163–67, *167*, 176–77, 184
Levine, Caroline, *Forms*, 6–7, 13
Lévi-Strauss, Claude, 4
linearity, 20–21; breakdown of, 89; disruption of, 73, 78; elimination of, 190n10; of embodied interaction, 75; and humor, 143; metaphorical mappings that eschew, 176; and nonlinearity, 73, 176, 190n10; as psychological bias, 75, 191n8; and reality, 72
literary language. *See* language

literary studies, 4, 6, 19, 28, 77; cognitive, 18, 55, 82; ideology in, 6; large-scale shifts in the practice of, 187n6
looping temporality, 26, 55, 60–66. *See also* nonlinearity; time
Lorenz, Edward Norton, 51–52, 54, 191n2
Lovelock, James, 26, 168–70, 173–74
Luhmann, Niklas, 27

Malafouris, Lambros, *How Things Shape the Mind*, 160
Mandel, Emily St. John, *Station Eleven*, 25
Mar, Raymond, 47, 55
Margulis, Lynn, 169–70
Martens, Gunther, 141, 156–57
Marvell, Andrew, "To His Coy Mistress," 171
materiality: account of, 97; efficacy of, 17; embodied, 125; of human-nonhuman mesh, 24; nonhuman, 16, 37, 106; subjectivity and, 98, 121; of world, 117
McCarthy, Cormac, *The Road*, 25, 79–80, 85–88, 90, 133, 143, 193n8
McEwan, Ian, *Solar*, 26, 141–43, 146–57, 162
McGuire, Richard, *Here* (comic strip), 35–37, *36*, 41–42, 73, 190n10, 190n12
McHale, Brian, 192n14; *Postmodernist Fiction*, 32–33
media: discourse in, 21, 158; the institution of, 48; narrative repertoire in, 180. *See also* media studies; science communication
media studies, 28. *See also* media
memory: as cognitive function, 144; evolutionary, 31; ocean, 109, 194n11
Merilees, Philip, 51
Merleau-Ponty, Maurice, 7–8
mesh. *See* human-nonhuman mesh
metaphor, 1, 18, 26, 43–46, 105, 128, 139–50, 159–77; abstract, 183; anthropomorphic, 18, 26, 162; bidirectionality of, 162–64, 176; "blending theory" model of, 162; conceptual, 102; conventional, 144; creative, 112, 140, 144, 158–59, 162, 173–74, 177, 198n12;

and human body, 157; and human-nonhuman mesh, 112–13, 143–44, 177; and imagery, 2; language rich in, 43, 45, 139–46, 155, 157–58, 161–62, 169, 173; main types across three novels of, *147, 148;* material, 130; and multiscalarity of complex systems, 157; and narrative, 197n7; narrative form and, 141; nonlinear play of, 174; organismic, 26; overview of the codes used in the analysis of, *145;* overview of the usage of, 146–47, 152–53; personifying, 165; "perspective-changing" function of, 140; phenomenological use of, 197n14; polyphonic nature of, 173; problem with, 170; and simile, 196n17, 197n10; spatial, 164; trouble with, 173; value of, 26; visual, 139, 141; workings of, 26, 139. *See also* cognitive metaphor theory; language

meteorology, 32, 161

Miall, David, 20

mind: cognitive models of, 25; and culture, 121; dualistic view of, 133, 135; "e-approaches" to, 117, 119, 195n9; evolution of, 31; imagery of, 80–83, 86–88; intrinsic attunement to nonhuman patterns of, 117; materialist approach to, 118; and matter, 126; metaphysical autonomy of, 135; sciences of, 117–18, 120, 122; and world, 129, 135. *See also* cognition

Mitchell, Lewis, 6

"model storm," *129,* 130

modernity, 10

Moore, Jason, 10

Morocco, 38

morphodynamics, 30. *See also* complex systems theory

Morton, Timothy, 3, 8, 11, 32, 54, 190n7, 198n5; *The Ecological Thought,* 27, 199n3; *Humankind,* 164

multiscalarity, 27, 29, 181; and analogical mappings, 46; of complex systems, 33, 43–48, 51, 157; formal nature of the problem of, 174; and human-nonhuman mesh, 140–41, 157, 176; narrative, 158–62; work of, 168

mythology: non-Western, 24; premodern, 24

Naples, 17

NARMESH, 181

narrative form, 3, 11, 14, 23, 186, 187n7; abstraction of, 3, 12, 21; and affect, 5–6, 177; anthropocentrism of, 23, 111–12; chain-like, 167–68, *167;* complexity and, 28, 33, 176–77, 179; covert dualism in, 22, 111; definition of, 4–7; engagement of audiences with, 58; experimentation in, 22; fragmented, 91; and human-nonhuman interdependency, 117; image schemata and, 58–59; linear, 58–59, 70, 91–93, 191n8; and metaphor, 141; and narrative strategies, 99; nonlinear, 15, 20, 74, 79; pervasiveness of, 23; and scientific models, 194n11; significance of, 7; structuralist account of, 25; teleological, 67, 70–71. *See also* form; narrative impact; narrative theory; network narrative

narrative impact, 19–23, 25, 179, 190n3; of catastrophe, 91–94, 107; conceptualization of, 23; and linearity of form, 75. *See also* narrative form

narrative theory, 3, 16–19, 28, 55, 58, 67, 80, 101, 196n20; cognitive psychology and, 22; early, 4; narrative and, 98; persuasion in, 20–21; postclassical, 18, 187n2; recent work in, 27–28, 118; structuralist, 18; "tellability" in, 191n6. *See also* narrative form

narratology. *See* narrative theory

natural resources, 11, 143, 153, 156

natural world: appreciation of, 116; encounters with, 2, 119; and evocation of consciousness, 118; exploitation of, 2; forms of, 8; human agency and, 105; patterns of, 1; visual forms in, 14. *See also* nonhuman

Nature Communications, 31

nature writing, 19

negation: in language, 80–83, 88; in space, 85–88; strategies of, 90, 93
neoliberalism, 10
Nersessian, Nancy, 13, 16, 188n15
network narrative, 39–41, 190n14; "complex causality" of, 41. *See also* narrative form
neuronovel, 25, 118, 135, 195n6; critical reading of, 195n7. *See also* novel, the
new formalism, 6–7, 13; and cognitive literary theory, 189n26. *See also* formalism
New York City, 89
New York Times, 54
Noë, Alva, 122
Nolan, Christopher, *Memento* (film), 28, 190n4
nominalization, 104, 110–13
nonhuman, the: anthropomorphic readings of, 160; ethics of transactions with, 179–80; history of nonhuman world, 64; instigation and, 17, 104–5, 166, 177; knowledge in nonhuman beings, 65; nonhuman actants, 97–113, 117, 177; personification of nonhuman spaces, 109; reality and, 1, 11–12, 16, 33, 82, 92, 99, 103, 111, 122, 133; rethinking imagination of, 158; subjectivity and, 103, 112, 116–19, 157, 163. *See also* human-nonhuman mesh; natural world
nonlinearity, 25, 27, 80, 180; of catastrophe, 88–94; in complex systems, 29, 33–37, 52; epistemological value of, 54–55; of the human-nonhuman mesh, 176; and the Kanizsa triangle, 81; linearity and, 73, 176, 190n10; as a matter of degree, 190n10; narrative, 55, 60, 74, 84, 177; spatial models of, 72–74, 74; of temporality, 77–94. *See also* complex systems theory; looping temporality
novel, the: climate crisis and, 26, 40, 66–67, 142; contemporary, 19, 143, 189n30; industrialization and, 22, 189n29; irony in, 142; narrative and,
22–23, 179; network narratives in, 39–41; polyphony in, 199n15; temporal structure of, 90, 142. *See also* fiction; neuronovel

Oatley, Keith, 47, 55
Oppermann, Serpil, 17, 97, 120
Oxford English Dictionary, 27
Ozeki, Ruth, *A Tale for the Time Being*, 39, 100, 108–9

Pendell, Dale, *The Great Bay*, 25, 55, 60, 66–75, 168
perception, 81–82, 132; embodied, 133; embodied intersubjectivity and, 166–67; intensification of, 134; phenomenology of, 135
Perrault, Charles, 56
Peterson, Jordan P., 47
phenomenology, 7–8; of perception, 135. *See also* philosophy
philosophy: of body, 7–8; enactivist, 132, 195n3; of history, 153; and metaphysical separation between human and nonhuman realities, 111; of mind, 55, 135, 190n6, 196n12; and nonhuman turn, 116, 119, 121–22; poststructuralist, 6, 134; psychology and, 90; science and, 104. *See also* ecological philosophy; phenomenology
Pier, John, 34
poetry: of Browning, 7; of Frost, 1
politics: and aesthetics, 7; decision-making in, 10; power in, 7
Pollio, Howard, 181
posthumanism, 145; early, 192n3
Potter, Emily, 121–22
Poulaki, Maria, 41
Powers, Richard: *The Echo Maker*, 25, 100, 104–5, 118, 123–26, 135, 143; *The Overstory*, 39–43, 68, 73, 190n15
Propp, Vladimir, 4, 99
psycholinguistics, 125, 196n14
psychology: cognitive, 22, 125; developmental, 74; ecological, 195n5; of environmental activism, 40; evolutionary,

119; of fictional characters, 110, 130; folk, 159, 161, 189n28, 191n4, 198n1, 198n13; and narratives, 55, 136, 159; of negation, 81; phenomenological, 181; and philosophy, 90; scientific, 134, 161; social, 20

Reagan, Andrew, 6
RealClimate (website), 54
realism, 23; conventions of, 24; displacement of, 71; psychological, 62
reality: abstract, 161; astronomical, 168; complex systems at multiple levels of, 30; deterministic understanding of, 72; dream and, 61–62, 73; experiential, 167; human, 1, 11–12, 82, 111, 122, 150, 162; and human brain, 131; linear understanding of, 72; material, 20, 23; more-than-human, 25, 41, 45, 130, 141, 161, 174, 185; narrative as virtual, 191n5; nonhuman, 1, 11–12, 16, 33, 82, 92, 99, 103, 111, 122, 133, 141, 150–57, 162; physical, 176; preapocalyptic, 71; scientific representation of, 135, 195n7; two temporal planes of fictional, 80; unstable, 103
religion, 35; cognitive account of, 194n15; and environmental crisis, 181
representation: and affect, 130, 139; concept of, 121; as conceptual activity, 134; critique of, 118–19, 129; cultural, 20, 23; direct, 86; language and, 122; reconceptualization of, 122; scientific, 129–30, 135; strictures of, 121
Richardson, Brian, 80, 192n5
Romero, George, *Night of the Living Dead* (film), 88
Rosch, Eleanor, 117, 120, 122, 132
Rose, Deborah Bird, *Wild Dog Dreaming*, 179
Roth, Marco, 118, 130, 135
Ryan, Marie-Laure, *Possible Worlds, Artificial Intelligence, and Narrative Theory*, 56, 59

"Sapir-Whorf" hypothesis, 60, 193n6. *See also* language

Sartre, Jean-Paul, *The Psychology of Imagination*, 82
satire: of climate change skepticism, 127; on limitations of scientific institutions, 143, 153–57
Saussure, Ferdinand de, 4
Scalise Sugiyama, Michelle, 55
Scarry, Elaine, 83
Schmitt, Arnaud, 37, 39, 68
science: and affect, 133; and art, 121; claims to objectivity of, 23; of climate change, 8, 12, 132, 140, 191n2; complexity, 27, 188n20, 189n1; of complex systems, 72; conceptual form of, 16; critique of, 154–55, 195n7; deranged, 142; dualistic biases of, 8; and environmental crisis, 11; and experience, 133; history of, 132; large-scale processes modeled by, 157; and myth, 72; and philosophy, 104; reductionism of thinking in, 47; rejection of, 12; visual representations in, 13–14. *See also* climate change; knowledge; science communication
science communication, 28, 155; media discourse and, 158. *See also* media; science
science fiction, 52, 63, 143, 168–75. *See also* fiction
Semino, Elena, 153–54, 196n2
Shelley, Mary: *Frankenstein*, 150; *The Last Man*, 78
Shiel, M. P., *The Purple Cloud*, 78–79
Simmel, Marianne, 159, 161, 166–67
social psychology. *See* psychology
space: embodied intersubjectivity and, 168; and geometry, 1, 166–68; negative, 85–88; physical interactions with, 57; universe and, 146
Stanley Robinson, Kim, *Forty Signs of Rain*, 143
Steen, Gerard, 46, 140
St. John Mandel, Emily, *Station Eleven*, 39, 79–80, 83–85, 90
structuralism, 4, 6, 18, 25, 111; models of, 100–101, 111; narratology of, 99;

structuralism (*continued*)
   precedents in, 100–102; theory of actants of, 100–103; theory of character of, 111, 193n2
Stutters, Jonathan, 115–17, 133
subjectivity: affect, emotion, and, 195n11; anthropocentric understanding of, 194n2; autonomy and, 148–49; breakdown of, 135; of character, 100; and culture, 147, 149; disruption of, 105; hierarchical and teleological thinking and, 180; and identity, 101; and materiality, 98, 121; and the natural world, 1–2, 135; and nonhuman, 103, 112, 116–19, 157, 163; projection of anthropomorphic, 194n10. *See also* intersubjectivity
supervenience, 30
Sweden, 182
Swindlehurst, Kate, 153–54

technology, 108; of artificial intelligence, 145; culture and, 132; history of progress in, 44
teleology, 66; narrative, 67, 70
television, 79
Thompson, Craig, 181
Thompson, Evan, 81, 117, 120, 122, 132
time: anomalies of, 192n14; and causation, 63, 74; consciousness of, 60, 63–66; culture and concepts of, 60; cyclical, 191n13; deep, 181, 184–85; geological, 70; linear progression in, 58; lived experience of, 134; teleological explanation of, 66. *See also* looping temporality
transitivity, 102–4
Trexler, Adam, 10, 192n4, 195n6

Tsing, Anna, 10; *The Mushroom at the End of the World*, 16–17
Turner, Mark, 74, 162

Vandermeer, Jeff, 24; *Annihilation*, 189n31; *Borne*, 164; "Southern Reach" trilogy, 25, 100, 109
Varela, Francisco, 117, 120, 122, 132
Velleman, David, 4–6
Vermeulen, Pieter, 19, 78, 189n30, 192n2, 192n7, 199n18
Vervaeck, Bart, 98, 125
Vico, Giambattista, 153
video games, 79
Villeneuve, Denis, *Arrival* (film), 63
Vonnegut, Kurt, 23; *Galápagos*, 25, 100, 110–11

Walsh, Richard, 58, 189n2
Weik von Mossner, Alexa, 18, 67
Wells, H. G., "The Star," 78
West, Geoffrey, 176
Westerford, Patricia, 40
Whitehead, Colson, *Zone One*, 25, 79–80, 88–94, 107–8, 143
Winterson, Jeanette, *The Stone Gods*, 26, 141–43, 146–54, 157
Woods, Derek, 161
Woolf, Virginia: *Mrs. Dalloway*, 90; *To the Lighthouse*, 90, 106; *The Waves*, 106
World Wildlife Fund, 139
Wright, Alexis, *The Swan Book*, 24

Yamamoto, Mutsumi, 146

Zeki, Semir, 115–17, 133
Zurru, Elisabetta, 109

Recent books in the series
UNDER THE SIGN OF NATURE: EXPLORATIONS IN ECOCRITICISM

Marco Caracciolo • *Narrating the Mesh: Form and Story in the Anthropocene*

Tom Nurmi • *Magnificent Decay: Melville and Ecology*

Elizabeth Callaway • *Eden's Endemics: Narratives of Biodiversity on Earth and Beyond*

Alicia Carroll • *New Woman Ecologies: From Arts and Crafts to the Great War and Beyond*

Emily McGiffin • *Of Land, Bones, and Money: Toward a South African Ecopoetics*

Elizabeth Hope Chang • *Novel Cultivations: Plants in British Literature of the Global Nineteenth Century*

Christopher Abram • *Evergreen Ash: Ecology and Catastrophe in Old Norse Myth and Literature*

Serenella Iovino, Enrico Cesaretti, and Elena Past, editors • *Italy and the Environmental Humanities: Landscapes, Natures, Ecologies*

Julia E. Daniel • *Building Natures: Modern American Poetry, Landscape Architecture, and City Planning*

Lynn Keller • *Recomposing Ecopoetics: North American Poetry of the Self-Conscious Anthropocene*

Michael P. Branch and Clinton Mohs, editors • *"The Best Read Naturalist": Nature Writings of Ralph Waldo Emerson*

Jesse Oak Taylor • *The Sky of Our Manufacture: The London Fog in British Fiction from Dickens to Woolf*

Eric Gidal • *Ossianic Unconformities: Bardic Poetry in the Industrial Age*

Adam Trexler • *Anthropocene Fictions: The Novel in a Time of Climate Change*

Kate Rigby • *Dancing with Disaster: Environmental Histories, Narratives, and Ethics for Perilous Times*

www.ingramcontent.com/pod-product-compliance
Lightning Source LLC
Chambersburg PA
CBHW021754171125
35560CB00014B/796